DATE DUE
JUL 26 2013
DISCARD

ABDEL BARI ATWAN is Editor-in-Chief at the London-based newspaper, *Al Quds al-Arabi*, which he has edited for the last twenty years. Atwan interviewed Osama bin Laden in the late 1990s and has cultivated uniquely well-placed sources from within the various branches of Al Qaeda over the last fifteen years. His other works include *The Secret History of al-Qa'ida* and *A Country of Words: A Palestinian Journey from the Refugee Camp to the Front Page* (both published by Saqi Books).

www.abdelbariatwan.com

'Abdel Bari Atwan has long been one of the sharpest commentators about Al Qaeda and the Middle East in general. Now he turns those sharp analytical skills to what the future holds for Al Qaeda and its affiliated groups in the Middle East as some of the early promise of the Arab Spring begins to sour. His prognosis is dismaying: In countries from Syria and Libya to Yemen, Al Qaeda and its allies are poised for a comeback. Atwan's sobering assessment deserves a wide audience.'

—Peter Bergen, author of *Manhunt: The Ten-Year Search for Osama bin Laden—from 9/11 to Abbottabad*

After bin Laden

Al Qaeda, the Next Generation

ABDEL BARI ATWAN

THE NEW PRESS

NEW YORK
LONDON

First published in Great Britain by Saqi Books, London, 2012
Published in the United States by The New Press, New York, 2013
Distributed by Perseus Distribution

ISBN 978-1-59558-899-9 (hc.)
ISBN 978-1-59558-900-2 (e-book)

Library of Congress Cataloging-in-Publication Data

Atwan, Abdel Bari.
After bin Laden : Al Qaeda, the next generation / Abdel Bari Atwan.
pages cm
Includes bibliographical references and index.
ISBN 978-1-59558-899-9 (hc. : alk. paper) 1. Qaida (Organization) 2. Terrorism—Religious aspects—Islam. 3. Terrorism—Islamic countries. 4. Terrorism—Africa, North. I. Title.
HV6432.5.Q2A887 2013
363.325—dc23 2012039732

The New Press publishes books that promote and enrich public discussion and understanding of the issues vital to our democracy and to a more equitable world. These books are made possible by the enthusiasm of our readers; the support of a committed group of donors, large and small; the collaboration of our many partners in the independent media and the not-for-profit sector; booksellers, who often hand-sell New Press books; librarians; and above all by our authors.

www.thenewpress.com

Printed in the United States of America

2 4 6 8 10 9 7 5 3 1

Contents

Abbreviations

AFRICOM	US Africa Command
AIS	Islamic Salvation Army (Algeria)
AMISON	African Union Mission in Somalia
AQAM	Al Qaeda and Associated Movements
AQAP	Al Qaeda in the Arabian Peninsula
AQIM	Al Qaeda in the Islamic Maghreb
AQSP	Al Qaeda in the Sinai Peninsula
AQY	Al Qaeda in Yemen
ARS	Alliance for the Re-Liberation of Somalia
DDoS	Distributed Denial of Service
DRS	Directorate of Intelligence and Security (Algeria)
EIJ	Egyptian Islamic Jihad
EIJM	Eritrean Islamic Jihad Movement
ETIM	East Turkistan Islamic Movement
FATA	Federally Administered Tribal Areas (Pakistan)
FCR	Frontier Crimes Regulation (Pakistan)
FIS	Front Islamique du Salut/Islamic Salvation Front (Algeria)
FJP	Freedom and Justice Party (Egypt)
FLN	Front de Libération National (Algeria)
FSA	Free Syria Army
FSF	Facilities Security Force (Saudi Arabia)
GIA	Groupe Islamique Armé/Armed Islamic Group (Algeria)
GID	General Intelligence Department (Jordan)
GICM	Moroccan Islamic Combatant Group
GSPC	Salafist Group for Preaching and Combat (Algeria)
HN	Haqqani Network
HuM	Harkat ul-Mujaheddin (Pakistan)
ICU	Islamic Courts Union
IEC	Islamic Emirate of the Caucasus
IED	Improvised Explosive Device
IFT	Islamic Front in Tunisia
IMG	International Monitoring Group (UN)
IMU	International Movement of Uzbekistan
ISAF	International Security Assistance Force

ISI	Inter-Services Intelligence (Pakistan)
ISOI	Islamic State of Iraq
JeM	Jaish-e-Mohammad
JI	Jamaa al-Islamiya
LCC	Local Coordination Committees (Syria)
LeT	Lashkar-e-Taiba
LIFG	Libyan Islamic Fighting Group
LIMC	Libyan Islamic Movement for Change
LNA	Libyan National Army
MDJC	Movement for Democracy and Justice in Chad
MEI	Movement for an Islamic State (Algeria)
MFO	Multinational Force and Observers
MIA	Islamic Armed Movement (Algeria)
MICG	Moroccan Islamic Combatant Group
MMA	Muttahida Majlis-e-Ama
MSC	Mujahideen Shura Council (Iraq)
MSP	Movement for a Peaceful Society (Algeria)
NCC	National Coordination Body for Democratic Change (Syria)
NFSL	National Front for the Salvation of Libya
NMLA	National Movement for the Liberation of Azawad
NRO	National Reconciliation Ordinance
NTC	National Transitional Council (Libya)
NWFP	North-West Frontier Province (Pakistan)
OSAFA	Office for Supervising the Affairs of Foreign Agencies
PJD	Justice and Development Party (Morocco)
SCAF	Supreme Council of the Armed Forces (Egypt)
SSIS	State Security Investigation Service (Egypt)
SNC	Syrian National Council
SNM	Somali National Movement
SOFA	Status of Forces Agreement (Iraq)
SSP	Sipah-e-Sahaba (Pakistan)
TFG	Transitional Federal Government (Somalia)
TIP	Turkistan Islamic Party
TMC	Tripoli Military Council
TTP	Tehrek-e-Taliban (Pakistani Taliban)

Preface

I take no pride in the fact that many of the developments I predicted in this book have since become grim reality. Indeed, regional chaos in the Middle East and North Africa is even more widespread than I anticipated and has increased the opportunities and operating space available to extremist groups, most notably those affiliated with Al Qaeda.

When I finished the present edition in summer 2012, it was clear that the ongoing security vacuum caused by civil war in Syria would act as a magnet for international *jihadis.* Now there are thousands of foreign extremists from many countries (including Britain) fighting alongside the semi-official Free Syria Army (FSA) and recruitment is flourishing, with daily reports of government atrocities a potent rallying call.

Large numbers of Islamist fighters from Libya are of particular concern—battle-hardened, they bring with them highly sophisticated weapons looted from Gaddafi's arsenals, including shoulder-launched SAM missiles (MANPADs), which can bring down aircraft. Only a quarter of Gadaffi's 20,000 MANPADs have been retrieved, despite concerted efforts by the US to buy them back from Al Qaeda–linked extremists, who are mostly based in Benghazi.

It has emerged that US Ambassador to Libya Christopher Stevens was in Benghazi on weapons-related business when he and three colleagues were murdered on 11 September 2012 by Al Qaeda affiliate Ansar al-Shari'a, which has close links to Al Qaeda in Iraq. This was a devastating blow to the States, which had not lost an ambassador under such circumstances since 1979 when Adolph Dubs was killed in Kabul.

Days later, a Libyan ship carrying the largest-ever (400 tons) consignment of weapons bound for Syrian rebel brigades docked in Turkey.

Unlike other Arab revolutions, the Syrian conflict is essentially sectarian, pitting the Alawite/Shi'i regime against Sunni rebels. As a result, Al Qaeda–style Salafi-*jihadis* embedded in the opposition have been able to radicalize indigenous fighters. The ostensibly secular FSA invited radical preacher Adnan al-Arour—infamous for his anti-Shi'i rhetoric—to address the first meeting of its Joint Command in autumn 2012.

In a replay of the Afghan *mujahideen* war against the Soviet invaders during the 1980s, the West finds itself in the same trenches as the *jihadis* in Syria.

Currently, Russia, China, Iran and Hizbullah back the Assad regime, while the West and the Gulf states are aligned with the Sunni rebels. The potential for regional—and even global—escalation is obvious. No wonder the West hesitates to intervene militarily and the 'Friends of Syria' are in disarray, having failed to convene since July 2012.

The role of Pakistan in the Afghan experience is now being played by Turkey, whose border with Syria is the main transit point for funding, arms and fighters—just as Peshawar was through the 1980s.

Illustrative of how the *jihadi* element has become an acceptable (if unwelcome) part of the Syrian uprising, the man charged with receiving *jihadi* recruits in Istanbul before sending them to fight in Syria is a key aide to former Lebanese prime minister Saad Hariri, who is the secular leader of Lebanon's March 14 bloc and one of America's key regional allies. The men who played the same role in 1980s Afghanistan were Abdullah Azam and his aide at that time: Osama bin Laden. Their office was known as 'Al Qaeda' (the base), which is how America's nemesis got its name.

Al Qaeda thrives on chaos, and its affiliates will be looking to expand their reach to an unprecedented level if a peaceful solution to the Syrian crisis is not brokered in the near future. Syria has become an epicentre of instability, and related sectarian fighting has already spilled over its borders into Lebanon and Jordan. Turkey has beefed up its military presence along its 900 km border with Syria following several transborder skirmishes.

In the absence of a negotiated peace in Syria, the US may intervene militarily at the same time as it launches an attack on Iran—despite reelected President Obama's comments that 'a decade of war is over'. Nevertheless, given that Syria has no politically united opposition, such a move would likely worsen rather than improve the security situation on the ground. The Iraq experience shows that regime change by force fans the flames of extremism and does not always bring about the desired result—Iraq is now under de facto Iranian control.

Initially, the Arab Revolutions may have looked set to improve the security situation for Israel by dismantling large, hostile powers such as Libya and Syria. In the event, the opposite outcome appears likely.

Regional instability has allowed Israel's real enemies, Al Qaeda–linked extremist groups, to gain footholds in strategically vital areas such as Sinai, Jordan and the Gaza strip. The future of the Israeli-occupied Golan Heights in Syria, which supplies Israel with one third of its water, also depends on the outcome of the current battle for power in Damascus.

Developments in Egypt may suggest an emerging regional trend which sees the Islamists participating politically on not just the local, but also the world stage. Who would have imagined that President Mohammed Morsi, the Moslem Brotherhood's second choice for the role, would have turned out to be a political heavyweight and a major force in international diplomacy? Western engagement with the Islamist Muslim Brotherhood would have been unthinkable prior to the Arab revolutions.

While the Islamist parties fared surprisingly badly in the Libyan post-revolutionary elections, continuing chaos and the failures of the country's fledgling government have benefited the extremists. Ansar al-Shari'a is only one of several armed jihadist groups, and hundreds of independent, warring, armed militias of all persuasions are still in de facto control of much of the country. The government has no effective army or security or police force.

Libyan fighters and weapons also helped Al Qaeda in the Islamic Maghreb (AQIM) and its allies to exploit a security vacuum caused by a military coup in Mali in March 2012. AQIM is now in total control of three regions in northern Mali that have become what CNN recently described as a 'quasi Al Qaeda state'. *Jihadi* recruits from other countries are migrating to the region, which increasingly resembles Afghanistan during Osama bin Laden's heyday, with military training camps and entire towns operating under the most extremist interpretation of Shari'a law.

The African Union (AU) is expected to deploy an international force in an attempt to recapture northern Mali but, interestingly, has also called for talks with AQIM in order to 'find a political solution to the crisis'. In this book, I discuss the potential for political engagement with Al Qaeda as a serious means of eliminating its threat, but, prior to the latest AU proposal, no government or supranational body had countenanced such a move.

AQIM has now become the network's strongest branch and, because of its proximity to Europe, presents the most realistic threat to the West. Nevertheless, the West is unlikely to intervene in yet another theatre, although the US is actively engaged in training government forces in several African countries.

Since I wrote this book, Kenyan and AU troops have had some success in routing Al Qaeda–linked al-Shabaab from its stronghold in Somalia's Kismayo. However, I would urge caution in claiming victory here. As I discuss in the book, part of the *jihadi* strategy is *hijra* (flight or migration), which involves a displacement of fighters for a temporary period, usually to another battleground (in this case, quite possibly to northern Mali), only to return when the circumstances are more favourable.

While al-Shabaab may have temporarily melted away to its remaining strongholds in the interior, Somalis have long blamed the chaos and instability that has plagued them for more than twenty years on 'foreigners' and outside interference—an analysis the Islamists share. If the new president Hassan Sheikh Mohammad is unable to function without hefty international support, the country is still effectively ungovernable, and elements of the population may once again look to al-Shabaab to provide some semblance of (albeit extremist) law and order.

US drone campaigns in Yemen and Pakistan have also succeeded in sending the *jihadis* underground, but, again, this is not a long-term solution, and the unacceptably high incidence of civilian casualties has been shown to act as a recruitment driver for radical groups.

Iraq and Afghanistan, where violence continues unabated, remain a gloomy template for the failures of the 'War on Terror', demonstrating that military invasion serves no purpose other than to further destabilize the target country at enormous expense and for dubious motives.

A distinct historical pattern is emerging whereby a military intervention in a Moslem country by a superpower (or its proxy) inevitably results in the emergence of a powerful *jihadi* movement. The first was the Afghan *mujaheddin,* which was quickly followed by the Shi'i Hizbullah, founded in response to the 1982 Israeli invasion of southern Lebanon during the civil war.

And this brings me to my final point, which concerns the ongoing escalation of tensions with Iran. Political Islam and *jihadi* ideology are not exclusively Sunni. Iran-backed Shi'i sleeper cells already exist in many countries: in 2012 alone, they attacked in Bulgaria (where a suicide bomber killed eight Israeli tourists on a coach) and Delhi (where an Israeli diplomat's car was blown up).

If the current trajectory towards chaos and anarchy in the Middle East continues—and especially if there is war with Iran—we may see a network of Shi'i extremism emerging, a parallel Shi'i version of Al Qaeda.

But that is the subject for another book.

London
29 October 2012

Introduction: After bin Laden

Our jihad . . . cannot be stopped, disrupted, or delayed by the death or capture of one individual, no matter who he is or how elevated his status . . .
Abu Yahya al-Libi, June 2011

They're still a real threat, there's still Al Qaeda out there. And we've gotta continue to put pressure on them wherever they're at.
Leon Panetta, US Defense Secretary, 26 January 2012

Osama bin Laden is dead, but the movement he co-founded more than two decades ago is stronger and more widespread than ever, with a presence across much of the Middle East, parts of Africa and Asia and even in Europe and North America. Pursued by the world's most formidable intelligence organisations and an army of bounty hunters, Osama bin Laden was effectively a fugitive and in deep hiding from November 2001 onwards. Whilst he continued to make some strategic and operational decisions, he had already become a figurehead rather than an active commander long before his assassination in Abbottabad in May 2011. For his followers, Osama bin Laden's 'martyrdom' enhances his legend and has immortalised him as an icon, a role model and a rallying point for *jihad*.

Before 9/11, Al Qaeda was a relatively small, centralised and hierarchical group, based in Afghanistan; it was almost destroyed when the US pounded its hideouts with massive bombs in retaliation for the 'raids on New York and Washington'. Had Osama bin Laden been killed then, the organisation would almost certainly have perished with him. The 2003 invasion of Iraq by Coalition forces breathed new life into the organisation when thousands of young men answered the call to *jihad* there.

Meanwhile Al Qaeda itself gradually transformed into an ideology—Islamist first and foremost but also political—which did not depend upon a centralised leadership. Now a system of regional emirs, local consultative councils and deputies has produced a horizontal organisational paradigm which is much harder to target and destroy.

Over the years, the senior leadership—and in particular the new emir of Al Qaeda 'central', Ayman al-Zawahiri—has doggedly cultivated a complex network of franchises (such as Al Qaeda in the Arabian Peninsula and Al Qaeda in the Islamic Maghreb), allies (the Taliban, for example), affiliated groups (such as Nigeria's Boko Haram), sleeper cells of home-grown terrorists (like the men who carried out the London bombings) and so-called lone-wolf attackers (most recently, Mohammed Mehra who murdered seven in Toulouse in March 2012).

In addition, Al Qaeda has spent years embedding itself in other causes and insurgencies: in Afghanistan, in Iraq, in Somalia and, most recently, in northern Mali where separatist Tuaregs, supported by fighters from local Al Qaeda offshoots, have declared the independent state of Azawad. Having been initially caught on the back foot, Al Qaeda–linked groups have also been able to exploit the regional insecurity caused by the so-called Arab Spring to expand their operation room, particularly in Libya and Syria.

A source close to the ideologue told me that al-Zawahiri has long sought to encourage 'every Muslim land to have its own version of Al Qaeda'. International, and favouring horizontal command structures that anticipate the regular loss of leaders, ensuring each has ready, trained deputies in place, Al Qaeda no longer resembles the original group. Indeed Al Qaeda 'central' has become less relevant, more akin to an advisory and consultation group, and al-Zawahiri's role is one of exhortation and commentary rather than military overlord.

American drones are the biggest danger Al Qaeda faces and have killed several key Al Qaeda figures, including al-Zawahiri's deputy Attiyah Abdel Rahman (in August 2011); the 'Sheikh of the Internet', Anwar al-Awlaki (in September 2011); and the deputy leader of Al Qaeda in the Arabian Peninsula (AQAP), Fahd al-Quso (in May 2012). In addition, the West has made headway by coordinating intelligence efforts with several countries, most notably Saudi Arabia. In May 2012, a three-way CIA, MI6, Saudi 'sting' resulted in a double agent successfully infiltrating AQAP and walking away with a newly developed 'underwear bomb' which he handed over to forensic specialists for analysis.[1]

However, the Al Qaeda network is like a mature tree whose branches are easily seen but which is supported by an invisible, and increasingly complex, underground root system. The problem for those prosecuting the 'war on terror' is that cutting off a branch (even big branches like bin Laden, Rahman, Awlaki and al-Quso) does little to weaken the roots which are nurtured by a fertile mix of grievances and aspirations.

The network has been involved in some notable military achievements. The Iraqi insurgency claimed that it had routed the world's greatest superpower when the US withdrew the last of its troops in December 2011, and Al Qaeda's closest allies, the Taliban, are likely to return to power in Afghanistan after more than a decade of relentless struggle.

In 2010 US President Barack Obama described Al Qaeda as 'constantly evolving and adapting'[2]—characteristics that have enabled Al Qaeda–linked *jihadi* groups to resist vastly superior national and international forces in possession of the very latest weapons and technology.

The significant change in the nature and organisation of the group has been recognised by the Western intelligence community who now refer to the ideologically linked *jihadi* network as 'Al Qaeda and Associated Movements' (AQAM)—a practice I will adopt for the purposes of this book.

In his eulogy for Osama bin Laden in June 2011, Ayman al-Zawahiri detailed 'the Sheikh's' legacy—which he packaged as 'disasters for America'. The first was the 9/11 'raids on New York and Washington'; the second, 'America's defeat in Iraq at the hands of the *mujahideen*'; the third, 'Afghanistan, where NATO troops are mired in the mud of defeat and bleeding from a constant onslaught'; the fourth, 'the fall of America's corrupt agents' in Tunisia, Egypt, Libya and Yemen and the 'imminent collapse of her slave in Syria'.

Whilst Al Qaeda cannot reasonably claim to have provoked the Arab Spring revolutions, it is true that the organisation has always identified its two main targets as the 'far' and 'near' enemies—the former being America and her allies, the latter the region's 'apostate' dictators and tyrannical regimes.

It is tempting to process Al Qaeda pronouncements on recent events as opportunism; the truth is quite the opposite—the leadership has pursued a clear strategy for more than a decade. This was eventually condensed into a short document entitled 'Al Qaeda's Strategy to 2020' which I received (by e-mail) from Al Qaeda in 2005 and published in *al-Quds al-Arabi.* It is remarkable, in retrospect, to compare the document's seven posited 'stages' towards re-establishing the Islamic Caliphate with actual events on the ground over the past ten years.

The first stage—and Osama bin Laden told me this when I met him in 1996—was to 'Provoke the ponderous American elephant into invading Muslim lands where it would be easier for the *mujahideen* to fight them'. This, of course, has been under way since October 2001 when US troops occupied Afghanistan in retaliation for 9/11, and then invaded Iraq in 2003.

Stage 2: 'The Muslim nation (the *umma*) wakes from its slumbers and is enraged at the sight of a new generation of "crusaders" intent on occupying large parts of the Middle East and stealing its valuable resources. The *umma* arms itself and organizes widespread *jihad*.' The seeds of the hatred towards America that Al Qaeda was banking on were planted when the first bombs dropped on Baghdad in 2003. When the Iraqi insurgency began, thousands of recruits from all over the Muslim world flocked to join the fight, and continue to offer themselves to the growing list of *jihadi* causes. Western economic, diplomatic and military targets have been subject to attack in every country where AQAM has a presence.

Stage 3: 'The confrontation between the *mujahideen* and NATO expands throughout the region, engaging the West in a long-term war of attrition. A *jihad* Triangle of Horror is created in Iraq, Syria and Jordan.' The *jihadis* claim they have already won the war of attrition in Iraq and NATO have fared no better in Afghanistan: with the conflict in its eleventh year, the Taliban are back in control of more than two-thirds of the country.

Attacks inside Iraq have continued long after the departure of NATO troops, suggesting that Al Qaeda maintains a strong presence there; in May 2012 UN Secretary-General Ban Ki Moon declared that Al Qaeda had managed to establish a stronghold in the heart of the Syrian revolution. Also in 2012, an AQAM group in Jordan, led by Abu Mohammad al-Tahawi, renounced a previous commitment to nonviolence.

Stage 4: 'Al Qaeda becomes a global network, a set of guiding principles, an ideology, transcending national boundaries and making affiliation or enfranchisement exceptionally easy.' This process has already begun, as outlined above and as we will see in more detail in the course of this book.

Stage 5: 'The US, fighting on many fronts to maintain its oil supplies from the Middle East and to guarantee the security of Israel, is stretched beyond its limits and capabilities. The US military budget is crashed into bankruptcy and economic meltdown ensues.' Al Qaeda leader Ayman al-Zawahiri has long insisted that the war on America is economic as well as military, frequently citing *The Rise and Fall of the Great Powers* by Yale historian Paul Kennedy. Kennedy's thesis posits three major causes for the downfall of empires, based on historical observations: one, the spiralling costs associated with an expanding military presence around the world; two, the costs of ensuring security at home; three, powerful competition in trade and commerce. All of these can be said to apply to America today and it is a striking coincidence that the amount of the 2011 US deficit ($1.3 trillion) exactly equates with the amount spent, to the end of 2011, on the wars in Iraq and Afghanistan together with 'enhanced security'.[3]

Stage 6: 'The overthrow of the hated Arab dictators and the establishment of an Islamic Caliphate throughout the Middle East.' We will be examining the Arab Spring in the next chapter but the strong participation of the Islamists, both among the rebel forces in Libya and in the post-revolutionary landscape regionally, was as unanticipated as the revolutionary events themselves. It is not inconceivable that the Islamist parties will prevail in elections across the region, setting a new political default system with unknown consequences. The Taliban already refer to the whole of Afghanistan as an 'Islamic Emirate' and several smaller emirates have been established across the Middle East in areas where the *jihadis* hold sway—in southern Yemen, for example, or the Sahel.

The final stage: 'The ultimate clash of civilizations and a mighty, apocalyptic battle between the "Crusaders" and the "Believers" which is won by the latter who then establish a global caliphate.' However far-fetched this may seem, this is what Al Qaeda, its allies and its affiliates believe, and this is what they are fighting for.

AQAM seemingly has the resources to maintain a relentless onslaught and we will be looking at the main theatres of conflict in more detail in the course of this book. The following is a snapshot of the range of current AQAM activity.

The group that causes the West most concern is in Yemen, where Al Qaeda in the Arabian Peninsula (AQAP) controls large swathes of the south and centre of the country, threatening to take control of the strategic port of Aden. On the other side of the Gulf of Aden, al-Shabaab (which formally joined Al Qaeda in February 2012) is also in control of significant parts of the country.

The withdrawal of US troops from Iraq has seen the Al Qaeda–led insurgent umbrella, the Islamic State of Iraq (ISOI), step up attacks on government and domestic security targets as well as escalating sectarian tensions in the country. The Taliban, in collaboration with Al Qaeda and the Haqqani network, appear to have gained the upper hand against NATO forces in Afghanistan. The Pakistani Taliban (TTP) is increasingly powerful on the other side of the border and often collaborates with its Afghan counterpart.

Al Qaeda in the Islamic Maghreb (AQIM) controls much of the Sahel and is actively involved with Boko Haram and the Tuareg insurgency in Mali. The Islamic Emirate of the Caucasus (IEC) continues to target the Russian homeland, with three major attacks on its transport system between November 2009 and January 2011 in which nearly 200 people were killed. AQAM groups in Indonesia, Thailand and China remain active as do affiliates in Uzbekistan and other ex-Soviet Muslim states.

Attacks of the magnitude of 9/11, the March 2004 Madrid bombings or the July 2005 suicide attacks on London transport have been prevented by increased security and greater vigilance. However, AQAM remains an active threat in Europe and the US homeland. In March 2012, 'lone wolf' operative Mohammed Mehra killed three soldiers, three Jewish children and a rabbi in Toulouse. On 5 November 2009, another 'lone wolf', Major Nidal Malik Hasan, opened fire on colleagues at Fort Hood military base in Texas, killing thirteen and wounding thirty.

A report by the US Congressional Research Service published in November 2011 warned of a significant increase in 'lone wolf' *jihadi* attacks, and said that individuals had been arrested in connection with thirty-two actual, planned or failed attacks on US soil in just seventeen months from May 2009 until October 2010.

In addition to realised attacks, there were several thwarted attempts to commit atrocities in the West. On Christmas Day 2009, 23-year-old Umar Farouq Abdulmutullab tried to set off a bomb hidden in his underpants on board a flight bound for Detroit. In April 2012, the CIA foiled an identical plot involving a more sophisticated version of the underpants bomb—one that had no metal parts and would have passed unnoticed through airport security allowing the suicide bomber to board a US-bound flight of his choosing.[4] Both bombs are believed to be the work of AQAP's Ibrahim Hassan al-Asiri, Al Qaeda's infamously ingenious 'master bomb-maker'.

In September 2010, Al Qaeda in the Arabian Peninsula (AQAP) claimed responsibility for the explosion on board a UPS cargo plane in Dubai—which downed the plane and killed two—saying it was a 'test run'. Two months later explosives hidden in printer ink cartridges were sent from Yemen to be shipped by UPS planes; one package, addressed to a Chicago synagogue, was discovered in Dubai while the other was defused in Britain with just seventeen minutes left to go before it detonated. Forensic experts believe that these attacks were also designed by Ibrahim Hassan al-Asiri and that he remains the single most potent threat to the US.

In June 2007 a doctor, Bilal Abdullah (who was born in Britain of Iraqi descent), and a PhD student, Kafeel Ahmed (an Indian Muslim), drove a burning jeep loaded with propane canisters into Glasgow airport; fortunately they were prevented by police and members of the public from detonating the gas. The same men had left a bomb, which did not explode, outside a London nightclub the day before. In May 2010 a car bomb failed to detonate in New York's Times Square, where it had been left by 30-year-old Pakistan-born Faisal Shahzad who had obtained US citizenship just one year earlier. Shahzad told investigators that he had been trained for his mission in Pakistan. In December 2010, the residents of Stockholm experienced their first suicide bombing which thankfully only killed its perpetrator, Taimour Abdel Waheb al-Abdali, an Iraqi-Swede.[5]

The Life and Death of Osama bin Laden

Osama bin Laden joined the ranks of 'martyrs' on 2 May 2011. This—as he told me fifteen years before his death—was a long-cherished ambition and one that is shared by many *jihadis*. It is still not clear what happened on the night of 2 May 2011 when two specially adapted Black Hawk helicopters landed in Osama bin Laden's Abbottabad compound, but the man was tried, judged and executed without ever having set foot in the International Criminal Court which the international community upholds as the preferred judicial apparatus to deal with war crimes. In May 2012, Amnesty International published a report which criticised the assassination as 'illegal and extrajudicial'.[6]

I met Osama bin Laden briefly on several occasions and in November 1996 was invited to interview him in his mountain hideout in a series of caves in the Tora Bora mountains of Afghanistan. I spent the best part of three days there in his company. I found him to be a humble, quietly spoken individual who had a gently mocking sense of humour.

I am probably the only journalist who can claim to have slept in the same cave as Osama bin Laden. It was a terrifying experience because our mattresses were perched on planks slung over cases of hand grenades while above our heads dozens of machine guns and rifles hung from the roof. I feared that any—or all—of them could go off at any moment and hardly dared move, lying rigidly, wide awake. Osama bin Laden, however, slept like a baby all night long with his Kalashnikov by his side.

We went for a long walk through the mountains one afternoon and he talked about his life in *jihad* and his desire to die a martyr. He loved poetry and recited verses at length; he also wrote many poems himself. I would never have imagined that this man would be behind one of the most devastating terrorist attacks in history just five years on, although plans for 9/11 were already under way, as I later learnt.

Following my trip to Tora Bora his close colleagues, like Abu Hafs al-Masri, would contact me with news and information every so often; when the 1998 'Declaration of the Global Islamic Front for *jihad* against the Crusaders and Jews' was drawn up, my paper *al-Quds al-Arabi* was the first to receive the faxed announcement.

Osama bin Laden was born in Riyadh, Saudi Arabia, on 10 March 1957. He was the forty-third of fifty-three siblings, the twenty-first of twenty-nine brothers. His father, Mohammad Awad bin Laden, originally came from Hadramut in Yemen and, having started out as a labourer on Saudi building sites, created a construction empire which became the biggest in the Arab world. He was a close adviser to the ruling al-Saud family, lending them a fortune in the mid-1960s when the national treasury ran out of liquid cash. He was rewarded with lucrative contracts, including extensive works at Mecca and Medina, Saudi Arabia's two most sacred places.

Osama's mother, Aliyah Ghanem, was a renowned beauty who came from a Sunni family in the Alawite-dominated region of Latakia in north-eastern Syria. Aliyah Ghanem was Mohammad bin Laden's fourth wife and Osama was very attached to her. Osama married his cousin, Najwa Ghanem, when he was 17. He studied economics and business administration at King Abdul-Aziz University in Jeddah where he attended lectures by renowned radical Islamic scholars such as Mohammed Qutb and Dr Abdullah Azzam, who would have a lasting influence on him.

In 1982, Osama joined the Afghan *jihad*. In 1988 he established an office to record the names of the *mujahideen* and inform the families of those who were killed. The name of this register was 'Al Qaeda' ('the base' or 'foundation'), and that is how the organisation got its name. Most Islamist sources say that the embryonic Al Qaeda network was established at this point.

Bin Laden preferred to live an austere lifestyle which he expected his wives and children to share. He was bitterly disappointed when two of his sons, Abdullah and Omar, decided to return to Saudi Arabia and a life of luxury. Bin Laden married five times in all, having divorced his second wife, Khadijah Sharif (Um Ali), in the 1990s after she begged him to allow her to leave their life of hardship in Sudan.

His third wife, Khairiah Sabar, who holds a doctorate in child psychology and is from a well-known Saudi family, joined the ménage in 1985—by all accounts she was chosen by Najwa and is seven or eight years bin Laden's senior. She had one son, Hamza, who made headline news round the world in 2008 when, aged just 16, he appeared in a video inciting other youths to join the *jihad*. Khairiah was living in her own apartment in the Abbottabad compound when the US SEALs raided in the middle of the night.

Bin Laden's fourth wife is the sister of one of his closest comrades in the Afghan *jihad*. From another well-known Saudi family, Siham al-Sharif was married to bin Laden in 1987. She is well educated and a teacher of Arabic. She had four children, including Khalid (who was killed with Osama in the raid) and was also taken into custody in Abbottabad.

Najwa, Khadijah and Siham had been by the Al Qaeda leader's side in Sudan through the 1990s and at Tarnak farm in Kandahar, where he would live until 2001. When 17-year-old Amal al-Sadah arrived from Yemen to become bin Laden's fifth bride in 2000, the other three wives were reportedly upset and this may be one of the factors that contributed to Najwa's decision to leave just before 9/11. Bin Laden had not met Amal before their wedding and said that he had been told she was much older, that her youth was as much a shock to him as to them, but that he couldn't now send her back as to do so would dishonour her. This failed to mollify the older women.

Interviewed by the Pakistani investigators following her arrest in Abbottabad, Amal has provided several key pieces of information, filling in some 'gaps' in the bin Laden narrative. When the Taliban were ousted by the US in November 2001, it is now known that Osama fled alone to Kunar, a remote province in northern Afghanistan. He had worked out a meticulous plan for the safety of his remaining wives and many children and warned them he would not be able to make contact for a long time.

Khairiah went to Iran, along with several other members of the extended family, including her own son Hamza and bin Laden's third son, Saad. Khairiah was kept under house arrest until 2010. Amal and Siham went first to Karachi, Pakistan's largest sea port, where they spent several months before Amal was smuggled back into Yemen in 2002. She was interviewed in Sanaa by both *al-Majallah* and *The Times* of London and was briefly held in custody after a mysterious gun battle at her father's house.[7]

Amal reported that she was reunited with bin Laden in 2003 in a remote part of Pakistan's Swat district before moving to a safe house in Haripur later the same year where she gave birth to a daughter, Aasia. A boy, Ibrahim, followed in 2004. Bin Laden drew up the plans for the compound in Abbottabad which was built in the middle of a large parcel of agricultural land he paid for and which was bought in the name of one of his Pakistani comrades. The family moved in in early summer 2005 and Amal had two more children, Zainab, who was born in 2006, and Hussein, 2008. It is believed that Osama bin Laden had sired a total of thirteen sons and fifteen daughters by the end of his life. Siham also moved to Abbottabad at some point, with Khalid and three other children, and Khairiah arrived in 2010, accompanied by Hamza.

Amal was sleeping in the same room as Osama when the SEALs arrived under cover of darkness, broke down the door and shot him dead. Amal threw herself between bin Laden and the gunmen, sustaining a serious leg injury. Her brother reports that she still walks with a limp. Hamza escaped during the raid but the three wives and a total of eleven children and grandchildren were taken into custody by Pakistani police. The SEALs had cuffed their hands behind their backs (even the smallest four-year-old) before bundling the corpses of bin Laden and Khalid into the remaining helicopter (one had crashed when trying to land) and taking off.

The US claims it buried Osama bin Laden at sea, something that is totally unacceptable in the rigid form of Islam he espoused and will breed resentment and anger for years to come. Presumably this was so that there could be no shrine or place of pilgrimage for followers of the Al Qaeda leader. In April 2012 all three widows and a total of eleven children and grandchildren were deported to Saudi Arabia.

In my first book on the subject, *The Secret History of al-Qa'ida*, published in 2006, I noted that, alive or dead, Osama bin Laden 'will remain one of the key historical figures of our times'. The Al Qaeda leader played a leading role in reviving the concept of the *umma* (global community of Muslims) and demonstrated, in the most dramatic way, that it was possible to attack the 'far' enemy—America—and greatly damage the morale of her troops and civilians as well as her economy.

America thrives on the simplistic 'good guys/bad guys' paradigm and shifted the focus of national enmity onto Osama bin Laden after 9/11. In the Abbottabad shoot-out bin Laden was the one who 'bit the dust' but no realistic commentator has yet suggested that the death of Osama bin Laden, however it is spun, will mark the end of 'the war on terror'. The USSR's ultimate implosion had nothing to do with America's sustained campaign against communism, or the wars it fought to defeat it (in Vietnam for example). Saddam Hussein's execution did not vindicate America's invasion of Iraq but saw the insurgency enter a much bloodier phase.

Historical precedents suggest that, far from extinguishing a militant Islamist movement, eliminating its leader can have the opposite effect. When the Egyptian Muslim Brotherhood's theologian Said Qutb was hanged in 1966, Islamism enjoyed a region-wide renaissance—both Osama bin Laden and his deputy, Ayman al-Zawahiri, revered Qutb and subscribed to his radical ideology. The Israelis assassinated Hamas leader Sheikh Yassin in 2004, hoping his death would lead to a decline in the movement's fortunes, but by 2006 Hamas was sufficiently popular to win the majority of seats in Palestinian parliamentary elections.

A spokesman for the Islamic State of Iraq, Abu Mohammad al-Adnani, described Osama bin Laden thus: 'he became a Glory for our *umma*, the religious Muslim leader of his age; the most blessed to have walked on earth in our time.' Osama bin Laden himself expressed this wish: 'that my blood would become a beacon that arouses the zeal and determination of my followers'. The mythical aura of invincibility that surrounded Osama bin Laden during the ten years it took the US to track him down will now be replaced by the glow of martyrdom and a treasury of legends.

I was not surprised that Osama bin Laden was tracked down in Pakistan. The Pakistani Inter-Services Intelligence (ISI) have a long history of supporting *jihadi* movements, many of them established to further the Pakistani government's own geo-political agenda (in Kashmir, for example). A whole year before the raid on bin Laden's compound, US Secretary of State Hillary Clinton stated clearly in an interview with CBS that, 'Somewhere in this [Pakistani] government are people who know where Osama bin Laden and the [sic] Al Qaeda is.'[8]

Al Qaeda has had a significant presence in Pakistan for at least a decade—thousands of fighters fled to what has become known as the Emirate of Waziristan in late 2001 as American planes bombarded their Tora Bora headquarters in retaliation for 9/11.

Subsequently, many travelled further afield inside Pakistan and several high-profile Al Qaeda leaders have been captured in the country's teeming cities: Abu Zubayda, allegedly head of operations, was captured in Faisalabad in March 2002; Khalid Sheikh Mohammad was found in Rawalpindi in March 2003; Abu Musab al-Suri, a key strategist and propagandist who was implicated in the Madrid bombings, was caught in Quetta in November 2005; and Amir al-Huq, the coordinator of Osama bin Laden's security team, was arrested in Lahore in 2008. As we have seen, two of Osama bin Laden's wives found refuge in Karachi in 2001, and Amal al-Sadah told investigators that she had also lived with her husband in Peshawar and Haripur.[9]

The fugitive Al Qaeda leaders enjoyed the protection of long-standing friends and allies in the Haqqani network which, allegedly, operates under the aegis of the Pakistani Army and ISI. Leaked diplomatic cables reveal that by 2008 the Haqqani leadership had moved from north Waziristan to two locations, one near Rawalpindi and one near Peshawar (both within easy driving distance of Abbottabad).[10] Abbottabad is home to the Pakistani equivalent of Sandhurst and has a strong ISI presence. It is all but inconceivable that the security establishment did not know who was living in the conspicuously large compound.

In the months following bin Laden's death, the regional government sacked seventeen doctors and fifteen female health workers who had (probably unwittingly) participated in the elaborate CIA 'sting' which eventually confirmed bin Laden's presence in the Abbottabad compound. The team called at every house in the area offering children free vaccinations. The project's leading medic, a surgeon called Dr Shakeel Afridi, was a CIA agent who identified bin Laden by DNA samples collected from the compound. In May 2012, Afridi was sentenced to thirty-three years in jail for 'conspiring against the state'.[11]

Locals referred to the bin Laden compound as Waziristan Haveli (*haveli* meaning mansion), presumably in reference to the connection of both its inhabitants and their visitors to the Islamic Emirate of Waziristan. It is reasonable to assume that many Haqqani and Al Qaeda personnel relocated from Waziristan to escape increasingly accurate US drone strikes on their bases there. This assumption is further endorsed by the fact that a secret meeting of 300 *jihadis* took place in Rawalpindi (not more than 100 km from Abbottabad) in early June 2008, as reported by Associated Press and Express India.

Ensconced in Abbottabad, Osama bin Laden tried to resume his role as an active, hands-on leader. In early June 2008 he issued instructions for planned attacks on US interests that would culminate in something 'greater than 9/11'; reliable sources affirmed that he had managed to personally contact Al Qaeda–affiliated groups in several countries, instructing them to cease all negotiations with government agencies and move onto the offensive.[12] One result was the 17 September 2008 attack on the US Embassy in Sanaa, Yemen, in which sixteen people lost their lives. It may well be that the 26 November 2008 massacres in Mumbai were also the bitter fruit of Osama bin Laden's incitement.

Furthermore we know that he was visited in Abbottabad in the months leading up to his assassination by leaders of Al Qaeda–linked groups—for example, Umar Patek, the leader of Indonesian Jemaa Islamiya, who was arrested there in January 2011 (a fact that Pakistani authorities did not disclose until March 2011).[13]

Taliban leader, Mullah Omar, is presumed to be based in the Pakistani city of Quetta—from where his 'Quetta *shura*' directs and coordinates attacks inside Afghanistan and elsewhere. Pakistan was one of only three countries in the world to recognise the legitimacy of the Taliban's former rule in Afghanistan and there is no reason to think that Mullah Omar, in semi-exile, would not enjoy the protection and support of (at least an element within) the Pakistani security services. Since the two organisations are so close, it is logical that that protection would extend to Al Qaeda leaders.

Osama bin Laden's one-time chief bodyguard Nasser al-Bahri described the relationship between the Taliban and Al Qaeda in unequivocal terms in 2010: 'The Taliban and Al Qaeda have become a single entity, but the American media seeks to obscure this inconvenient truth.'[14] Papers found in the Abbottabad compound include regular communications between bin Laden and al-Zawahiri with the Taliban in which the leaders discuss joint actions and plans.[15]

Regarding cooperation between Pakistan's military and security establishments and Al Qaeda, al-Bahri makes the extraordinary claim that there was 'an agreement between Al Qaeda and the Islamabad army' whereby bin Laden could send recruits for professional training. According to al-Bahri, forty young *jihadis* spent between six months and a year with the Pakistani Army and four received top-level commando training which they imparted to others on their return. The ISI also apparently sent instructors to the training camps and provided Al Qaeda with 'modern equipment and information'; al-Bahri adds that the ISI convinced the Taliban to ask Osama bin Laden to hand over control of the Al Qaeda training camps to them in 1999—'in this way Islamabad could exert even more influence, via the Taliban'. When Pakistan tested its nuclear weapons in 1998, al-Bahri recalls, 'Al Qaeda sent messages of congratulation to the Pakistani president as well as to the head of the ISI.'[16]

Operationally, too, AQAM has expanded its reach inside Pakistan, largely through its alliance with the Pakistani Taliban (TTP) and Lashkar-e-Taiba (LeT). In May 2011, in revenge for the security forces 'allowing' the assassination of Osama bin Laden, Al Qaeda fighters mounted a spectacular attack on Pakistani Navy base Mehran in Karachi. A group of fifteen men armed with machine guns and rocket-propelled grenade launchers (RPGs) stormed the base and killed at least four Navy personnel. They also destroyed two Lockheed aircraft (worth $36 million each) and a helicopter, all of which had been given to Pakistan by the US as part of the 'war on terror'.[17]

Other attacks avenging the death of the Al Qaeda leader demonstrated the undiminished capacity the Taliban and AQAM possess on both sides of the border: eighty-nine Pakistani recruits and officers were killed when twin suicide bombers struck a paramilitary academy in the North-Western Frontier town of Charsadda on 14 May 2011;[18] in Afghanistan a Chinook helicopter carrying members of the same SEAL team that killed bin Laden was shot down in the Tangi valley in August 2011, killing all thirty-two men on board—the worst loss of US military personnel in a single incident in the whole war.[19]

A New Leadership

After some delay, Osama bin Laden's deputy, the sexagenarian Dr Ayman al-Zawahiri, was appointed Al Qaeda's new emir in June 2011. According to reliable sources, al-Zawahiri had been in charge of strategy and forward planning for many years prior to bin Laden's death.

Ayman al-Zawahiri is a hard-liner who follows the *Takfir* ideology whereby those who do not follow the narrow Salafist interpretation of Sharia are considered 'apostates'. Al-Zawahiri was the main driver behind expanding the AQAM network, encouraging the formation of new organisations and persuading existing groups to come under the Al Qaeda umbrella—his most recent success in this respect saw Somalia's al-Shabaab officially announce that it had joined Al Qaeda, pledging allegiance to al-Zawahiri in February 2012.

Al-Zawahiri was the leader of Egyptian Islamic Jihad (EIJ) when it formally merged with Al Qaeda in 1998. He was greatly irritated and frustrated by the debilitating in-fighting that went on among Egypt's *jihadi* groups in the 1990s. Despite al-Zawahiri's exhortations to maintain unity, squabbling and breakaway splinter groups continue to destabilise AQAM.

On a personal level, al-Zawahiri lacks the 'charm' of bin Laden; most people who have spent time with him describe him as overbearing and uncompromising. Al-Bahri writes, 'Bin Laden always tried to convince us whereas al-Zawahiri sought to impose his ideas. Bin Laden listened to us, al-Zawahiri didn't let us speak . . . the Sheikh [bin Laden] tried to change al-Zawahiri's character but did not succeed.'[20] It is unlikely that al-Zawahiri will draw new recruits to the organisation simply on the basis of personal charisma, as Osama bin Laden and, latterly, Anwar al-Awlaki undoubtedly did. His personal failings may also undermine his authority over the wider AQAM network in time, especially if he does not make his mark by overseeing 'spectacular' attacks on Western targets or Israel.

Al-Zawahiri described Osama bin Laden as 'the man who said "no" to America'[21] and the latter's focus was always on the 'far enemy'. Analysts have observed that 70 percent of bin Laden's speeches and messages concerned America, Israel or the West. Al-Zawahiri, on the other hand, has historically concerned himself more with regional struggles. Even before the Arab Spring only 15 percent of al-Zawahiri's utterances were directed at the West. Al-Zawahiri's focus is likely to be on harming Western interests locally, by attacking economic, diplomatic and military targets and by exploiting the opportunities offered by the Arab Spring. Al-Zawahiri has also made it clear that Israel remains a key issue, saluting the 'heroes' who regularly blow up the gas pipeline from Egypt to Israel and asserting that post-revolutionary Egypt must focus on liberating 'our people in Palestine'.[22] Al-Zawahiri is a highly intelligent man and has modified his tone of late; some of his most recent video and audio postings suggest he does not wish to alienate the 'man on the Arab street' with vitriolic outpourings.

In November 2011, for example, al-Zawahiri declared that he would like the Coptic Christians to live in peace alongside the Muslims in Egypt.[23] It is possible, as we will consider in more depth in the next chapter, that Al Qaeda intends to develop a political wing in order to participate more effectively in the post-revolutionary landscape.

Meanwhile the Afghan Taliban's 'emir of the faithful', Mullah Omar, is emerging as the supreme spiritual leader of the wider *jihadi* movement. During his eulogy for Osama bin Laden, al-Zawahiri affirmed that all those who are fighting *jihad* are under the command of Mullah Omar; he renewed Al Qaeda's *bayat* (oath of allegiance) to him, 'We promise to listen to him and obey him in good times and in bad and in the course of *jihad* for the sake of Allah and establishing Sharia and uplifting the oppressed.'[24]

In November 2011 TTP leader Hakimullah Mehsud also urged 'all *jihadis* to rise above their differences and unite under the banner of the emir of the believers, Mullah Omar'.[25] The shadowy Ilyas Kashmiri, a top Al Qaeda military commander and leader of the 313 Brigade, opined in a rare 2009 interview that Osama bin Laden and Mullah Omar were the chosen leaders of the *umma*.[26] In August 2011 Abu Mohammad al-Adnani, the spokesman for the Islamic State of Iraq, referred to 'The high, honourable, mountain-like and mighty leader; the zealous, as generous as the oceans, Mullah Mohammad Omar' and said that the Taliban were 'our protectors'.[27] Deputy AQAP leader Said al-Shihri pledged his organisation's allegiance to Mullah Omar in a January 2012 posting on *jihadi* forums.

Since the death of Osama bin Laden, several wealthy Gulf donors have preferred to send funds to the Taliban rather than the diminished Al Qaeda 'central' group, according to sources in Pakistan. It is increasingly likely that the Taliban will return to, or at least share, power in the near future. Given the close ties and loyalties between a widening spectrum of AQAM groups and the Taliban, this could have serious security and political implications both for the region and for the West.

Al Qaeda's Second Generation

Like many of the first generation of Al Qaeda leaders, Ayman al-Zawahiri (who was born in 1951) has spent the best part of his adult life in *jihad*. His first wife, Azza Nweir, and three children (one of them a daughter with Down's syndrome) were killed in a US air strike on the family's Afghan home in December 2001—an event which is said to have 'sharpened his hatred' of America. (Al-Zawahiri subsequently married the widow of Tariq Anwar, an operations chief in Al Qaeda who had been killed in an earlier US air raid.)

Most long-standing AQAM members have brought up families and their children form a second generation which has never known anything other than a fugitive lifestyle fraught with danger, receiving their education in military training camps and with no other prospect in life but *jihad*.

Nasser al-Bahri has provided some fascinating information about the lives of Osama bin Laden's children—all of whom stayed with him into adulthood with the exception of Abdullah, the eldest, and Omar. How were these children brought up? According to al-Bahri, bin Laden was not 'harsh' with them. The children were given 'tasks, religious instruction, prayers and military training' and were forbidden to play computer games. All bin Laden's sons are good horsemen like their father, al-Bahri reports, and they were allowed to mix freely with the other *jihadis*' children, playing football and swimming in the river which flowed past the Kandahar compound inhabited by the Al Qaeda leadership from 1996 to 2001. When they were older they were encouraged to spend their free time cultivating pieces of land provided for them and some, like Saad, established businesses.

The second son, Abdelrahmane, was as tall as his father (6 feet 5 inches) and was often used as a decoy by bin Laden's bodyguards when the leader had to travel; as a reward, he was the only son permitted to ride his father's favourite thoroughbred horse, Adham.

According to al-Bahri, bin Laden's favourite sons were Mohammad and Saad and they were constantly at his side. Mohammad was the one who resembled bin Laden the most in character, while Saad 'always had a smile on his lips and was the most mischievous; he loved to give his unsuspecting companions hedgehog to eat'.[28]

In the aftermath of 9/11, Mohammad and Othman stayed by

their father's side. Saad bin Laden went to Iran, while Hamza and Khalid, who were still young children, were found a safe haven with their mothers in Pakistan. By the mid-2000s however, the sons had regrouped in Waziristan. A letter dated April 2011 by bin Laden which was seized in the Abbottabad compound suggests that Saad had been killed while Mohammad and Othman were still alive.[29] Khalid was killed with Osama bin Laden in May 2011 in Abbottabad.

Osama bin Laden's daughters were married within the *jihadi* community in Kandahar.[30] Marriages within AQAM are frequently strategic, designed to cement alliances between leaders, organisations, tribes or factions and to ensure the continuation of *jihad*. Saad bin Laden married a Yemeni girl in order to develop tribal links—bin Laden had long harboured notions of relocating Al Qaeda to Yemen. Mohammad bin Laden married Khadija, the daughter of Abu Hafs al-Masri, aka Mohammad Atef, the infamous Al Qaeda military planner and bin Laden's right-hand man until his death in November 2001. Hadi al-Ordoni, a Jordanian member of Al Qaeda's military committee, married one of al-Zawahiri's daughters.[31] AQIM's southern emir Mokhta Belmokhtar married within the indigenous Tuareg tribes of the Sahara desert, thus assuring himself and his organisation of their loyalty.

AQAM members come from a wide range of nationalities, tribes, class and educational backgrounds—something which is unusual in the Arab world where such differences often prevent social contact, let alone marriage. This 'open door' policy, coupled with shared ongoing grievances against Israel and the West, may explain why there is no apparent shortage of new recruits after more than two decades and despite the death of bin Laden. The new generation of AQAM is tougher, more ruthless and even more extremist than their predecessors who, in turn, lament a widespread lack of what they consider to be 'real Islamic scholarship' among these hot-headed young men.

As well as youths from the Arab countries, Africa and Pakistan, disaffected second- and third-generation Muslims from Western countries continue to make the long journey to 'the fields of *jihad*' in significant numbers; men from this group are also responsible for attacks at home—Mohammed Mehra who shot seven dead in Toulouse in March 2012, for example, was the son of Algerian immigrants; the men who perpetrated the 2005 London transport bombings were second-generation British

Pakistanis, as was their handler, Birmingham-born Rachid Rauf, who was killed by a drone in Pakistan in 2008.

The past few years have witnessed another new phenomenon: Caucasian converts from non-Muslim backgrounds in Western countries. Some commentators claim these constitute up to 20 percent of the organisation's membership.[32]

Why the 'War on Terror' Has Failed

Despite the more than a trillion dollars which have been spent on the 'war on terror', Al Qaeda is not only still here, but is expanding its reach and influence. In my opinion, there are several reasons for the 'success' of this historically unprecedented network, or ideological movement.

We have already considered the horizontal leadership structure and system of deputisation which ensure that, whilst undeniably damaging, the deaths of individual leaders can be absorbed by the movement. We have seen, too, that the sheer number of enfranchised groups and individuals, and the network of alliances, collaboration and loyalties, make the movement's infrastructure, the 'roots', impossible to target.

AQAM groups, as well as individual fighters, are able to survive by virtue of extreme mobility, both within a country and internationally. An effective military device, this strategy also has a deeply religious connotation, that of *hijra*—best translated as 'migration' or 'flight'—which derives from the *hijra* of the Prophet Muhammad and his companions from Mecca to Medina in AD 638 to evade an assassination attempt. This was seen as such a significant moment in the history of Islam that the year in which it occurred was designated the first year of the Islamic calendar by the Caliph Umar.

Once engaged in conflict, *mujahideen* battalions will abandon a fight if it becomes apparent that they cannot imminently prevail, migrating to a new one or going into hiding. Often, the original battle is resumed when the enemy is off guard or complacent. The strategy is successful because, on departure, the fighters leave behind them a logistical infrastructure, ready for a possible return. This is how it works: in 2006, America's twin policies of the so-called Awakening and a military 'surge' in Iraq made Al Qaeda's position in that country untenable and thousands of *jihadis* migrated to Afghanistan where the Taliban had regained control over much of the country; here Al Qaeda already had allies, training camps, safe houses and secure communication channels. By 2009, the bulk of Al Qaeda fighters had again migrated, and this time, because the AQAM network had expanded, the choice was wider: some returned to Iraq where they launched several devastating attacks within Baghdad's Green Zone; some went to the Pakistani side of the border where the Taliban leadership was ensconced and from where attacks inside Afghanistan were launched; others went to Yemen to join the newly fledged Al Qaeda in the Arabian Peninsula (AQAP), while still others travelled to Somalia where al-Shabaab was gathering pace.

At the end of 2011 Al Qaeda fighters announced a return to Afghanistan with a hallmark sectarian massacre of Shi'i Muslims celebrating *Ashura*.[33] April 2012 saw the worst violence in the history of the present conflict as Al Qaeda, Haqqani and Taliban fighters joined forces to simultaneously lay siege to the Afghan parliament, NATO headquarters and the US, British, German and Russian Embassies in Kabul as well as other targets in Logar, Paktia and Jalalabad.

In recent years, groups such as AQIM have developed mobile training camps involving small numbers of recruits (often not more than five) who never stay in one location for more than a few hours, sleeping in caves and other naturally occurring shelters at night.

In October 2009, Yemen-based AQAP's online journal, *Sada al-Malahim*, carried an article by its leader, Nasir al-Wahaishi, with the title 'War is Deception'. Al-Wahaishi identified unpredictability, the surprise element, as one of Al Qaeda's greatest and most successful weapons and I believe he is correct. Al Qaeda pioneered the widespread use of suicide bombing—the most deadly 'surprise'—among *jihadi* groups from the late 1990s onwards and have deployed increasingly sophisticated and cunning Improvised Explosive Devices (IEDs) since they were first appraised of the techniques to manufacture them by Saddam Hussein's Republican Guard during the Iraqi insurgency.

The phrase 'War is Deception' became something of a slogan and was taken up by other AQAM leaders. Mustafa Abu al-Yazid, Al Qaeda's leader in Afghanistan, used it to hail the 31 December 2009 attack at Fort Chapman in Kosht by a triple agent, Jordanian Humam Khalil Abu-Mulal al-Balawi, for example. This incredibly complicated 'sting' operation resulted in the deaths of seven top CIA agents. Similar deceptions involving *jihadis* posing as policemen or soldiers before turning on their erstwhile 'comrades', as well as the infiltration of security services, are now quite commonplace, particularly in Afghanistan and Iraq, jeopardising the effective transfer of security from NATO to indigenous governments.

The most serious attack on US soil since 9/11 took place on 5 November 2009 at one of the largest US military bases in the world, Fort Hood in Texas. A high-ranking military figure and psychiatrist, Major Nidal Malik Hasan was meant to be assessing a group of officers and men due to depart for a tour of duty in Afghanistan when he opened fire on them with a semi-automatic weapon, killing thirteen and wounding thirty. Hassan's parents came from Palestine and it transpired that he had been in regular e-mail contact with the late Anwar al-Awlaki, AQAP's American-born cleric, who commended the attack and called Hassan a '*jihadi* hero'. The American establishment sought to downplay the incident, with Barack Obama describing it as 'an incidence of workplace violence' when Hassan's trial began in November 2011.[34]

The element of surprise is also present in the type and calibre of person recruited for suicide missions. Humam Khalil Abu-Mulal al-Balawi, the CIA bomber, was a quietly spoken doctor; London university-educated 23-year-old Umar Farouq Abdulmutullab (the failed Detroit bomber) was the polite son of a wealthy Nigerian banker. The failed attempt to explode a jeep laden with propane gas canisters inside Glasgow International Airport on 30 June 2007 was carried out by an Indian engineering PhD student, Kafeel Ahmad, and a doctor of Iraqi descent, Bilal Abdullah, who was working in an NHS hospital.

AQAM groups continue to find ever more cunning ways of concealing explosives. In August 2009, AQAP's notorious master bomb-maker, Ibrahim Hassan al-Asiri, sent his own brother to assassinate Saudi Prince Nayaf with explosives hidden in his rectum—Prince Nayaf survived the blast, Abdullah, clearly, did not; bombs in underpants and ink cartridges, as we have seen, provided at least four near misses. In September 2011, a Taliban suicide bomber assassinated former Afghan Prime Minister Burhanuddin Rabbani with a bomb hidden in his turban.

In both Iraq and Afghanistan, deadly IEDs have been cunningly concealed under rocks, dug into the road, hidden in potholes, hidden in rubbish, taped to bicycles, and stuffed inside human cadavers, dead animals and, on one occasion at least, inside living sheep which were then herded towards a US foot patrol.[35]

Observers of AQAM groups have noted a greatly increased intelligence capacity in recent years—the Fort Chapman attack, for example, was the result of months of surveillance and collaboration between three major AQAM groups (the Pakistani Taliban, the Afghan Taliban and Al Qaeda 'central') and was described by intelligence journal *Stratfor* as 'worthy of a state actor'. This operation is described in more detail in the chapter on Afghanistan.

Meanwhile the use of spies, double agents, imposters and infiltrators is a particular problem in Afghanistan where so-called Green on Blue attacks—whereby an Afghan soldier or policeman turns fire on his Western 'comrades'—claimed twenty-two NATO soldiers' lives in the first four months of 2012.

AQAM attacks can also achieve a high body count by their sheer ruthlessness and tenacity. During the final days of November 2008, gunmen from Lashkar-e-Taiba (LeT) set a gruesome precedent when they laid siege simultaneously to ten different locations across Mumbai for three days, shooting and hurling hand grenades in an indiscriminate massacre which left at least 173 dead, with 308 wounded. Anwar al-Awlaki and other leaders praised the attack and urged others to emulate it. Several 'Mumbai-style' attacks were thwarted in the UK and Europe in 2010,[36] but in Afghanistan and Pakistan they have become part of the Taliban repertoire. In November 2011, at least 150 were killed in simultaneous attacks lasting more than twenty hours in two different locations in northern Nigeria when large groups of Boko Haram *jihadis*, who say they were trained in Somalia, went on the rampage.[37]

The Causes Remain

The West is increasingly keen to engage the Taliban in diplomacy—something the *mujahideen* interpret as NATO's concession of defeat. To date the results have been disastrous: in September 2011 the main negotiator, ex-Afghan President Burhanuddin Rabbani, was assassinated by the Al Qaeda–affiliated Haqqani Network. The message was clear: AQAM and the Taliban do not intend to give up their fight against America and her allies until their grievances are addressed.

In his 'Eighth Message to the Egyptian People' in December 2011, Dr Ayman al-Zawahiri gave a concise reminder of what these are: 'Crusader Westerners have killed hundreds of thousands of our sons, brothers, women and elders, occupied our lands, stolen our resources, aided their agents [i.e. tyrannical regimes] in suppressing us and implanted Israel in our midst as their advance force, guarding their interests and threatening our existence and future with her nuclear bombs.'[38]

In June 2011 President Obama announced the start of the withdrawal of NATO troops from Afghanistan by the end of 2011. When August 2011 turned out to be the bloodiest month yet for US troops (sixty-six died in a series of bombings and ambushes) that decision was reversed and now the administration says US troops will stay until at least 2014. The US has escalated drone attacks against insurgency targets in Yemen, Somalia and Pakistan, often with unintended consequences. In November 2011 a drone accidentally killed twenty-four Pakistani soldiers, resulting in a serious breakdown in diplomatic relations already strained after the apparent collusion between the ISI and Osama bin Laden.

In Pakistan alone, drones have killed over 4,000 civilians.[39] There is plenty of anecdotal evidence that civilian deaths increase recruitment to, and re-energise, insurgencies. A US think tank, the National Bureau of Economic Research, produced a paper on the subject in 2010 and concluded, 'We find strong evidence that local exposure to civilian casualties caused by international forces leads to increased insurgent violence over the long-run, what we term the "revenge" effect.'[40]

Losses are heavy on both sides of the 'war on terror'. NATO casualties in Afghanistan now total nearly 3,000 and 2011 saw the biggest loss of life among Coalition troops in the ten-year history of the conflict.[41] Civilian deaths in Afghanistan were also at their highest in 2011 with nearly 1,500 killed in the first six months alone.[42] In Iraq, more than 4,800 Coalition soldiers had been killed by the end of 2011 and estimates put civilian casualties at well over 100,000.

It is an indication of just how militarily significant the Taliban and AQAM have become that the casualty statistics cited above are more suggestive of international conflict than terrorism. During the 'troubles' in Northern Ireland which lasted the best part of thirty years, 3,600 military and civilian deaths were attributable to IRA and loyalist attacks. ETA, the Basque separatist movement, has killed 800. The Abu Nidal group and its associates were responsible for 900 deaths in terror attacks. The Japanese Aum Shinrikyo, which used a weapon of mass destruction (sarin nerve gas) in the Tokyo underground, injured 6,000 but only twelve people actually died.

Conclusion

The deaths of bin Laden and other key leaders, such as Anwar al-Awlaki, have not destroyed Al Qaeda as some commentators have suggested. Instead, the organisation has expanded its reach by cementing new alliances and exploiting the opportunities regional turmoil affords. It has also fundamentally changed in nature, becoming an ideology and a network of associated local movements with a shared global agenda.

The new Al Qaeda is harder for security services to track down and destroy—drones can target the leadership, but not a mind-set. In response to the increasingly sophisticated instruments of war deployed against them, the *jihadis* are turning to cunning and deceit, developing their own intelligence capabilities, migrating and hiding in difficult terrain and in cities, in Muslim lands and the West . . . in short, becoming what Al Qaeda cleric Abu Saad al-Amili describes as 'soldiers of a new type that the enemy has not met before and cannot find.'[43]

AQAM is an unprecedented phenomenon: a terror network with the clout—and many of the resources—of a state actor. It has battalions and weapons, it has the apparatus of government and its own judicial system, it has funding and fiscal policies. In territorial terms it has yet to dominate an entire country, although two-thirds of Afghanistan is Taliban-controlled and AQAP have taken over much of southern and central Yemen in the course of the Arab Spring.

As we have seen, apart from Yemen and Afghanistan, AQAM is a notable force in Pakistan, Somalia, Iraq and Libya; it is expanding in Syria, Jordan, Gaza, the Maghreb, Indonesia, Chechnya and Uzbekistan. It is seeping further eastwards into the Muslim former Soviet republics and China where the Uyghur Islamists in Xinjiang region have been active since 2009.

AQAM is also expanding southwards. Western security analysts are greatly concerned by the 'Africanisation' of AQIM. Whereas before it presented an immediate threat to mainland Europe it has now started reaching down into Africa where like-minded groups in Chad, Niger and Mauritania are now under the AQIM umbrella. The powerful al-Shabaab in Somalia is overtly affiliated to Al Qaeda and AQIM has issued several statements in support of terror acts carried out by Nigeria's Boko Haram. In 2012 a new group calling itself 'Al Qaeda in the Lands Beyond the Sahel' announced its arrival in northern Nigeria by murdering two Western hostages in March 2012. The perceived 'war against Islam' continues to recruit for AQAM among an enlarged and diversified catchment which now includes a significant proportion of Western converts.

The Arab Spring revolutions, which we will consider in detail in the next chapter, threatened to eclipse the appeal of the *jihadi* movement by offering an alternative conduit for resistance. Instead they have, to date, provided new opportunities for AQAM—particularly in Libya, Syria and Egypt. The dominance of Islamist parties at the ballot box in several countries suggests that the path of conservative Islam is still the preferred choice for the majority—a frustrating outcome both for the young secularists who fought so bravely on the streets to secure the freedom to vote and for the West which now fears a regional takeover by armed Islamists.

In the following chapters we will consider the nature and activities of AQAM post–bin Laden and show how the Al Qaeda project and the dream of a global caliphate remain undiminished; the roots of the movement have grown deep and complex over the decades, fuelled by anger and resentment whose causes have not diminished. The new generation of *jihadis* is in place; its members benefit from all the know-how and experience of their predecessors to which they bring an even more radical approach, greater ruthlessness, opportunism, cunning and an increasingly sophisticated arsenal of weapons and technology.

1

The Arab Spring and Al Qaeda

Oh how great are these days we are living. Praise Allah who has lengthened our life to witness these great events and momentous happenings and to view with our own eyes the fall of the Arab tyrants—those slaves of America—and the collapse of their regimes.
Ayman al-Zawahiri, 14 October 2011

The series of successive revolutions across the Arab world, which began in Tunisia in January 2011, took everybody by surprise—from the ousted dictators and their Western backers to Al Qaeda, which had long sought their downfall. Preconceptions and political narratives about 'the Middle East' were shattered; only now are the pieces coming back together to form a new reality through the prism of the Arab Spring. The purpose of this chapter is to consider the nature and role of Al Qaeda in the emerging political landscape.

The youthful protestors' demands for freedom and Western-style democracy—the antithesis of the Islamist agenda—initially suggested that extremist *jihadi* groups were facing redundancy, that peaceful protest could achieve what decades of violence had not, that the *jihadis'* demands for Sharia rule were outdated and unwelcome.

When the first round of free elections brought unanticipated success for Islamist parties in Tunisia, Egypt and Morocco, however, another interpretation was called for. The largely secular and middle-class leaders of the uprisings were outnumbered at the ballot box by poor, conservative Muslim voters opting for an Islamic state.

Many of the protestors' concerns and demands dovetail with those of conservative Muslims and radical Islamists alike, and they are essentially political demands: the call for an end to corruption, elitism, the plundering of national wealth for the benefit of the few, societal inequalities, the absence of a free and fair judiciary and so on. The question now is whether a new kind of political system will emerge from the Arab Spring: a form of democratic government which can incorporate the disparate elements of Arab societies and meet their needs.

There are already signs that the democratic process has been tampered with to side-line the Islamists, however. In Egypt, ten presidential candidates, including three prominent Islamist hard-liners, were 'disqualified'[1] in April 2012 by the ruling military junta, the Supreme Council of the Armed Forces (SCAF). In June 2012 SCAF went even further and dissolved the Islamist-dominated parliament. Days later SCAF announced new constitutional rules limiting the powers of head of state and boosting those of the military before conceding, after several days delay, that the Muslim Brotherhood's 'spare candidate', Mohammed Morsi, had won the presidential election.

In Libya, electoral legislation underwent several changes since it was first drafted in January 2012, and the June 2012 ballot for 200 seats in a 'National Conference' saw 120 'constituency seats' for independent candidates and just 80 'list seats' for members of political parties—apparently in an effort to reduce the influence of the Muslim Brotherhood's Justice and Development Party. (At the time of writing, the liberal National Forces Alliance, headed by Gaddafi's former economic advisor, Mahmoud Jabril, had won more than half the party seats.)

In a March 2012 interview, a Pakistani Taliban commander, Wali-ur-Rehman Mehsud, voiced the AQAM interpretation of events: 'America and the West are trying to make their cause "democracy" and impose it on them but the people are becoming more aware . . . the people are selecting religious parties to govern them. Therefore the effort is purely an Islamic movement.'[2]

Writing in April 2011, Osama bin Laden was already celebrating the 'unprecedented opportunities' offered by the Arab Spring and the popularity of Islamist parties; he asserted that 'most of the region will have governments [formed from] the Islamic parties' and asked his correspondent to remind his fellow *jihadis* in Arab Spring countries to be 'patient and deliberate, and warn them against entering into confrontations with the Islamist parties'. He expressed the hope that 'The more time passes . . . the more widespread will be the correct understanding [i.e. the Al Qaeda vision, apparently contained in a book by Muhammad Qutb called *Concepts That Should Be Corrected*] among the coming generations of Islamic groups' and noted, 'A sizeable element within the Muslim Brotherhood and those like them hold the Salafi doctrine . . . so their return to true Islam is only a matter of time, Allah willing.'[3] Nor was Al Qaeda against the principle of the ballot as has been suggested. Ayman al-Zawahiri stated as long ago as 2009 that 'Elections under the umbrella of an Islamic constitution, run by trustworthy hands, are to be welcomed.'[4]

In Libya, the revolution swiftly developed into an armed confrontation. Osama bin Laden had already signalled 'the necessity of sending some qualified brothers to the field of revolution in their countries'[5] and significant numbers of Al Qaeda–linked *jihadis* were among the leaders and fighters who eventually defeated Gaddafi—with help from NATO after UN Security Council Resolution 1973 sanctioned the imposition of a no-fly zone over Libya.

By October 2011, the world's press noted with some astonishment that Al Qaeda and Islamic State of Iraq flags were being flown in several places across Libya. Meanwhile, two distinct elements had emerged within the triumphant National Transitional Council (NTC): the secularists and the Islamists. This schism would come to characterise the post-revolutionary landscape in other countries too.

Rather than losing its relevance, AQAM potentially benefits from the post-revolutionary process in the following ways:

- Confrontation between the Islamists and secularists is inevitable, with polarisation bringing greater extremism in its wake; a weakened central government will produce a power vacuum which AQAM is always quick to inhabit.

- In some countries the interim government or military might block the Islamist parties' participation in elections or, if they succeed at the ballot box, deny their mandate to rule. In such a case, violent extremism gains legitimacy and support: exactly this scenario occurred in Algeria in 1991, leading to a decade of bloody civil war and the deaths of up to 200,000 people.

- If revolution fails to usher in widely anticipated changes for the better, disappointment may produce more extremist ideological tendencies; Niall Ferguson, Professor of History at Harvard University, is one leading academic who has predicted that the Arab Spring will benefit Al Qaeda in this way.[6]

- In Syria, Bahrain and Saudi Arabia, the Arab Spring is likely to re-energise the burgeoning Shi'i–Sunni sectarian conflict which Al Qaeda has been fomenting for years in Iraq and which increases its operational room throughout the region.

- Western security experts have pointed out that both domestic and foreign intelligence agencies were greatly compromised by the uprisings and that this, too, benefits Al Qaeda.[7]

The Arab Spring has yet to run its course but it is my feeling that the upheavals across the region will benefit reactionary elements among the Islamists, in the short term at least. Yes, the revolutions were prompted by economic factors such as unemployment and the unfair distribution of wealth, but other factors to do with self-respect and national pride were, arguably, even more important. I agree with those commentators who explain the Islamists' success at the ballot box in terms of international politics: 'there is a problem of dignity in the Arab world,' Maati Monjoub, a Moroccan political analyst, told AP following his country's November 2011 elections. 'People see the Islamists as a way of getting out of a sense of subjugation and inferiority towards the West.'

The invasions of Iraq and Afghanistan by the US-led Coalition were widely perceived as humiliating and belittling. These feelings, of course, were mirrored on the domestic level where the individual felt her/himself to be disempowered by the state.

Post-revolution opinion polls, conducted by both Western and reputable Arab companies, found that the vast majority of citizens in Tunisia, Egypt and Libya want their new governments to oppose continued US military presence in the region, refuse conditional aid packages and break ties with Israel.[8] The failure of regional leaders to stand up to Israel in the past—particularly during the 2008–9 winter onslaught on Gaza which left 1,400, mostly civilian, Palestinians dead—highlighted the gap between the will of the people and the policy of governments wishing to avoid the ire of the Washington administration. In several countries, including Egypt, Tunisia and Saudi Arabia, pro-Gaza marches and demonstrations were banned.

The region's conservative Muslims (who presently form the majority) do not view 'the West' and its values with admiration or envy. The preferred model is Islam, which provides both a sense of shared regional identity and a framework on which to construct post-revolutionary societies. For Osama bin Laden, the Arab Spring marked the beginning of a 'new era for the whole *umma*' which would see 'the end of American influence in the Islamic world'.[9]

A Political Tsunami

The Arab Spring erupted in January 2011 following the death by self-immolation of a vegetable peddler, Mohamed Bouazizi, the main bread-winner for a widowed mother and six siblings. Bouazizi, who was just 27 years old, staged his deadly protest outside the offices of the municipal authority whose officials had earlier solicited bribes from the impoverished young man and then confiscated his stock and overturned his cart. The revolution that followed toppled 75-year-old Tunisian dictator Zine el Abidinde ben Ali—who had been in power since 1987—in just ten days.

The story of jobless Mohamed Bouazizi gives us a snapshot of the immediate causes for the uprisings. Across the region, youth unemployment is between 25 and 30 percent in countries where social security benefits are virtually non-existent. Even graduates cannot find a position and, in countries rife with corruption, anyone who does have a job will have had to pay a bribe for it. There are millions of Bouazizis across the Arab world. Day after day they get on with their lives, patiently doing whatever it takes to scrape by. Protest and complaint were unthinkable for decades under autocratic regimes kept firmly in place by brutal force and a ruthless security apparatus.

The secret police are swift to identify potential troublemakers who get to taste the regional speciality—torture—before being imprisoned or disappearing. The US favoured the Arab world for its 'extraordinary rendition' programme; an ex-CIA officer described how, 'If you want a serious interrogation, you send a prisoner to Jordan. If you want them to be tortured, you send them to Syria. If you want someone to disappear—never to see them again—you send them to Egypt.'[10]

In the past, anything resembling a march or demonstration would be put down in the most violent manner. We witnessed the knee-jerk reactions of the Tunisian, Egyptian, Bahraini, Yemeni, Algerian, Libyan and Syrian regimes—all used extreme violence on their own people: 30,000 civilians died in the Libyan revolution and at least 20,000 had been killed in Syria at the time of writing (July 2012); 219 were killed in Tunisia when security forces opened fire on protestors; 384 died in Egypt, with 6,467 wounded mostly due to gunshots, firebombs and rocks hurled by paid thugs; in Bahrain seven protestors were shot dead as they slept in Pearl Square and 150 were injured.

Meanwhile the ruling families and a nepotistic, corrupt 'elite' lived lives of ostentatious wealth—wealth that had often been plundered from the nation's natural resources, including oil, and, in some cases, foreign aid. Leaders' families and fellow clansmen monopolised the most lucrative contracts and franchises for which they also received hefty bribes.

The Tunisian ex-President Ben Ali fled with a personal fortune of more than $3 billion whilst it is estimated that Egypt's Mubarak had accumulated some $70 billion. Libya's main financial vehicle, the Libyan Investment Authority, used oil revenues not to provide schools or hospitals for the Libyan people but to invest more than $60 billion around the world—in companies such as the *Financial Times*, Fiat and Juventus football club—and to set up a hedge fund in London.

There are demographic causes too: around 50 percent of the region's population are now under 25, while the average age of the autocratic rulers is over 70 years old. There is also a growing middle class, many of whom have studied abroad and speak European languages. It was mostly this class, together with workers' unions in countries where they are allowed, that organised the protests.

Nor can we underestimate the role played by the Internet in informing and galvanising the Arab street. Fifty-six million Arabs are regular cybernauts and their number is rapidly increasing. Despite efforts by most Middle Eastern regimes to censor and control the Internet, technically savvy young people are able to outwit their oppressors in this respect. Indeed, the elderly dictators seemed oblivious of the independent digital media—the Egyptian regime's first response to the uprising was to send tanks to protect the television centre.

The unprecedented freedom of information available in cyberspace helped fuel resentment. WikiLeaks detailed the *nouveau-riche* excesses of the Tunisian regime, for example, which explained why ben Ali's ex-hairdresser wife was popularly referred to as the *Reine des voyous* (Queen of the Louts); Libyan cyber-surfers unearthed disgraceful incidences of their nation's wealth being squandered abroad by Gaddafi's sons—Muatassim paid Beyoncé and Usher $5 million to entertain guests at his New Year's Eve party on the Caribbean island of St Barts in 2010/11, in grotesque one-upmanship with brother, Saif al-Islam, who had reportedly paid Mariah Carey $1 million to sing four songs the year before. The Saudi Arabian people were dumbfounded by the news, freely available on the Internet, that Prince Saud Abdulaziz bin Nasser al Saud had been convicted of murdering his gay lover/servant in a London hotel in February 2010.

Social networking on Facebook and Twitter, and the sophistication of today's mobile phones, helped protestors organise and gather support with unprecedented rapidity. The ousting of Egyptian President Hosni Mubarak on 11 February took a mere seventeen days. The fire of revolution continued to rage through the Arab world and none seemed safe from contagion. To date fifteen countries have suffered serious unrest.[11] The region's remaining dictators panicked; both ben Ali and Mubarak had used extreme violence against the unarmed protestors and yet they had fallen. New tactics for survival had to be developed and these varied from country to country.

Yemen's protests began on 3 February 2011 and continue unabated despite President Saleh having finally handed the reins of power to his deputy, 66-year-old Field Marshal Abd-Rabouh Mansour Hardi, in February 2012. With more than 2,000 peaceful protestors dead, Yemen is still in a state of chaos. The new president has inherited several challenges to his authority all at once: on top of the Arab Spring protests there is a full-blown secessionist movement in the south of the country, a rebellion in the north by the Shi'i Houthi tribes, an extremely active and dangerous branch of Al Qaeda (Al Qaeda in the Arabian Peninsula—AQAP), and a military and tribal split within the regime.

Yemen is a poor country with no oil to speak of. Whereas its neighbours the wealthy Gulf Cooperation Council (GCC) countries have an average per-capita GDP of over $60,000, in Yemen it is just $2,500. The regime was reluctantly drawn into the 'war on terror' by the offer of $150 million a year in US aid. In fact Al Qaeda has been the Yemeni regime's main source of income since AQAP made its headquarters there in January 2009 under the leadership of Osama bin Laden's former aide, Nasir al-Wahaishi. With so many pressures on an already weak administrative structure, implosion is inevitable. Yemen is on its way to becoming a failed state and AQAP has already exploited the security vacuum to seize vast swathes of the south and centre of the country and declare Islamic emirates there.

When protests began in Bahrain on 14 February, the US was alarmed. Bahrain houses the American Navy's Fifth Fleet and a cooperative regime is crucial to US strategic plans to limit Iranian influence in the Gulf. The other Gulf States feared contagion and anxiously watched from the sidelines as King Hamad bin Isa al-Khalifa attempted to dampen the flames of revolution by giving every family in the kingdom 1,000 dinars (around $2,500).[12] The protests continued unabated. Most of those who set up camp at the Pearl roundabout were Shi'i Muslims—the Shi'i form 70 percent of Bahrain's population but the regime is run by Sunnis. After three nights sleeping in tents and on the ground, the protestors were savagely attacked by security forces under cover of darkness. When demonstrations continued, the King declared a state of emergency and called in help from other Gulf States.

Saudi Arabia, which had every reason to fear contagion, and in addition has a restive Shi'i minority in its oil-rich eastern province, played the Iran card. Claiming that America's regional nemesis was behind events in Bahrain, and was agitating for unrest inside Saudi Arabia itself, ensured that the most brutal crackdown inside its own boundaries would be tolerated by Western backers who also feared for their own oil supplies.[13]

In February 2011 Saudi King Abdullah returned from medical treatment abroad and announced benefits in housing, social services and education in a package worth $129 billion.[14] Even this largesse failed to mollify the kingdom's own dissidents, however, who continued with arrangements in cyberspace for a real-life 'Day of Rage' on 11 March 2011. The protestors were not even able to assemble, so overwhelming was the security presence. A few days later Riyadh sent at least 1,600 troops[15] to Bahrain under the banner of the GCC's 'Peninsula Shield', the UAE added 500 policemen and the protestors in Bahrain were dispersed. The Shi'i minority in the east of Saudi Arabia demonstrated against this violent oppression of their co-religionists and were met with a 'zero tolerance' crackdown.

Next, the founders of Saudi Arabia's first political party, the Islamic Umma Party, were rounded up and imprisoned. The radical name is indicative of another reason why the regime and the US fear a loosening of the security situation inside Saudi Arabia—the 95 percent of young Saudi males who told pollsters that they supported bin Laden in 2001, and the 97 percent who opposed any form of cooperation with the US-led attack on Iraq in 2003, had not gone away.[16] Al Qaeda would be quick to inhabit any security vacuum in the 'Land of the Two Holy Places'.

In July 2011 the Saudis pressed for more material support from Washington, packaging this as a bid to counteract burgeoning Iranian influence in the Gulf. The US obliged with a $90 billion arms deal which included warships, helicopters and missile defence systems.[17] In addition, the Americans initiated a programme to create and train a small private army—the Facilities Security Force (FSF)—designed to 'protect sensitive Saudi oil installations'. The 35,000-strong FSF, largely composed of mercenary soldiers and private security guards, had actually been in the pipeline since 2007 (as WikiLeaks cables revealed), and would be used as much to protect the regime against internal dissent as against potential attack by Iran.[18]

Libya's revolution originated in Benghazi, in the east of the country, which has long been a hotbed of radical Islam. Colonel Muammar Gaddafi responded to the protests with immense brutality and the situation descended almost immediately into armed struggle from which the rebels—a motley crew of *jihadis*, tribesmen, CIA assets and secular liberals—emerged victorious after eight months, with some help from NATO. Gaddafi died a brutal death at the hands of the rebels who captured him as he attempted to flee through the Sahara desert.

15 March 2011 brought the biggest surprise of the Arab Spring when mass protests broke out in Syria, where the same family has ruled with an iron fist since Hafez al-Assad overthrew his erstwhile comrade, President Salah Jadid, in 1970. I am going to focus on Syria at this point because the outcome here threatens to reset the regional balance of power if the current regime (dominated by the Shi'i Alawite sect) is replaced by one governed by the Sunni majority. Russia and China were quick to demonstrate support for President Bashar al-Assad, as was (Shi'i) Iran; the West and the Gulf States, however, aligned themselves with the Sunni rebels. In a great historical irony, the West and the Gulf States find themselves aided by Al Qaeda which is now active in the fight against Assad and continues to destabilise the Shi'i-dominated regime in Baghdad.

Syria has a long history of Islamic militancy. The country's branch of the Muslim Brotherhood was all but annihilated in 1982 when Hafez al-Assad's Alawite-dominated regime slaughtered up to 40,000 Islamists during an uprising in Hama in 1982. A whole generation was too shell-shocked by that experience to offer any further resistance—a phenomenon noted by bin Laden in a letter retrieved from Abbottabad in which he spoke of 'a new light of hope' emerging with the youth 'which had not lived that awful experience of Hama . . . most of the Syrians who joined the *mujahideen* in Afghanistan and Iraq were young,' he added.[19]

Hafez's son, Bashar, who succeeded him on his death in 2000, initially appeared to be a more compromising character. Bashar had studied medicine in London, qualifying as an eye doctor, and his wife, Asma, the daughter of a consultant at a top London hospital, was brought up in Britain. Asma's family are Sunni and the marriage was a political one which proved popular among the Syrian people who longed for sectarian reconciliation and political reform. One of Bashar's first decisions as president was to release 600 political prisoners and the first year of his rule was characterised by a resurgence of political and social debate. The so-called Damascus Spring ended abruptly in August 2001 when Assad ordered the arrest and imprisonment of leading liberal figures who had been calling for free and fair elections.

Though Bashar al-Assad may have been reform-minded at the outset, he was soon under immense pressure from the military and the regime's several intelligence and security services not to weaken the authoritarian apparatus his father had established. Instead, he was persuaded to adopt the Chinese model whereby economic reforms would allow the continuation of the political status quo.

It is said that as many as sixteen intelligence and security units work independently of each other (and largely of central government) in an atmosphere of secrecy and mistrust. With membership of the outlawed Muslim Brotherhood punishable by death and the secret police constantly vigilant for any kind of dissent, Syria's human rights record is among the worst in the Middle East.

In the early 1990s, the US cherished hopes of friendly relations with Syria after al-Assad senior joined forces with the Coalition against Saddam Hussein in 1990 and even attended the Madrid Peace conference, aimed at settling the Palestine–Israeli conflict, in 1991. Assad had hoped to regain the Golan Heights in exchange for his efforts, resuming his anti-Israeli stance when it became clear this was not forthcoming. Bashar's enmity towards Israel, his alliance with Iran, his support for Hizbullah and his occupation of Lebanon saw President Bush label Syria part of the 'Axis of Evil' in 2002. In 2004, Bush imposed sanctions on the regime which, he said, had been facilitating the free flow of Al Qaeda fighters into Iraq. The 2005 assassination of former Lebanese Prime Minister Rafik Hariri, widely believed to have been carried out by Syrian secret agents, confirmed its pariah status which was little improved by Assad's decision to withdraw all Syrian troops from Lebanon a few months later.

The Syrian people were increasingly unhappy with the political and economic domination of the Alawite sect. Assad's cousin, Rami Makhlouf, entirely controlled Syria's business sector and the regime was rife with corruption. Leaked cables show that Washington has been supporting opposition groups outside Syria since 2006, including the Movement for Justice and Development, a pro-democracy group based in London.[20] The Bush administration also offered grants of up to $5 million to 'reformers in Syria' but, according to a 2008 cable, 'no bona fide opposition member will be courageous enough to accept funding,' so terrified were they of reprisals by the regime. Bush's successor, Barack Obama, made efforts to improve relations with Syria, opening an embassy in Damascus in January 2011 after a six-year absence.

On 15 March 2011 there were the first mass protests in Daraa and, despite a sustained and brutal assault on his own people, Assad is still facing determined opposition more than a year later. In the latter part of 2011, armed revolutionary factions started to appear and there were calls in *jihadi* chat-rooms to muster a *mujahideen* army to help the people of Syria depose their tyrannical (and non-Sunni) leader.

In December 2011, two suicide bombers blew up intelligence compounds in Damascus, killing 44 and wounding 160. The nature of the attacks and their targets suggested to me that this was the work of Al Qaeda. In early January 2012, another suicide bomber struck an intelligence target and on 10 February 2012 two suicide bombers targeted security installations in the Syrian commercial capital Aleppo.

On 11 February, confirmation of Al Qaeda's engagement inside Syria came in the form of a videotape from Ayman al-Zawahiri which was posted on major *jihadi* sites, titled 'Onward Lions of Syria'. Al-Zawahiri urged *jihadis* from neighbouring countries such as Iraq, Turkey, Lebanon and Jordan to migrate to Syria to join the fight; he exhorted the Syrian people to 'continue your revolt and anger, do not accept anything but independent, respectful government'. As the regime's violence against the demonstrators escalated, Saudi-financed satellite television stations also began inciting Syrian and foreign Sunnis to launch a *jihad* against the regime.

With Al Qaeda resurgent in Iraq, a large number of battle-hardened and experienced *jihadis* were only hours away from Syria with which it shares a 500 km border. Since the Iran-backed regime in Iraq had expressed its support for Assad, there now existed a sectarian motive for *jihad* in both countries.

Unlike Iraq, where around 35 percent of the population are Sunni, the sectarian map in Syria works in Al Qaeda's favour; Sunni Muslims (including Kurds) are in the majority at 75 percent of the population. Northeastern Syria has been something of an Al Qaeda stronghold since 2003, when fighters passed through on their way to join the insurgency against the occupation of Iraq; with the success of the US 'surge' in 2006, thousands of fighters returned to the area, seeking refuge from NATO attack. Several high-ranking Al Qaeda leaders hail from Syria, including the strategic mastermind Mustafa Setmarian Nasser (Abu Musab al-Suri), currently imprisoned by the Assad regime.

During the 2000s, several home-grown *jihadi* factions emerged in Syria, including Monotheism and Jihad (an AQAM group—the same name was initially given to what would become Al Qaeda in Iraq by Abu Musab al-Zarqawi), Tawhid and Jihad in Syria, and Islamic Jihad. These hard-line groups consider Assad, as a non-Sunni Muslim, to be a heretic—a judgement endorsed by his government's decision to ban women from wearing the *hijab* in universities in 2010.

Iraqi intelligence reported a steady flow of Al Qaeda fighters from the Islamic State of Iraq (ISOI) across the border into Syria from late 2011; the infrastructure which had been established to facilitate the flow of *jihadis* into Iraq via Syria was now in service the other way. There were reports, too, of arms being smuggled from Mosul through the Rabia crossing and into Syria.

Jordanian officials also intercepted several cargos of arms bound for the Syrian *jihad* originating from Saudi Arabia.[21] The Jordanian city of Irbid, near the Syrian border, is another long-standing transit point for migrating fighters. A group of militant *jihadis* in Jordan, led by Abu Mohammad al-Tahawi, renounced their commitment to nonviolence and travelled to help the *mujahideen* in Syria. In July 2012 Israeli news services claimed that up to 5,000 additional international *jihadis* were mustering on the Turkish and Lebanese borders with Syria.[22]

Al Qaeda–linked fighters from Lebanon's refugee camps also found their way to Syria. In late April 2012, a high-profile leader of the Lebanese group Fatah al-Islam, Abdel-Ghani Jawhar, was killed in Qusayr, near the city of Homs which correspondents described as 'crawling with *mujahideen*'. As in Libya, the international *jihadi* community was poised to play a major role in the revolution.

As images of the Assad regime's merciless slaughter of innocent civilians and first-hand reports that his thugs were raping women and targeting, even torturing, children were uploaded on YouTube and subsequently beamed on television screens across the world, Al Qaeda–linked *mujahideen* were swiftly repackaged as heroes to the rescue.

Syria's sectarian instability is a tinderbox with the possibility for regional escalation. The country's demographics are largely a result of colonial intervention in the past. After the First World War, greater Syria was divided between Britain and France and broken up into smaller entities: the British Mandate covered the newly created Trans-Jordan and Palestine while the French were given what is today's Syria and the artificially created Lebanon. Faced with widespread revolt, the French partitioned Syria and fomented disputes between the country's various religious and ethnic groups.

As I have noted, the al-Assad family are from the Alawite sect—a persecuted minority until Hafez seized power in 1970. The Alawite still account for no more than 12 percent of the country's 22 million inhabitants. There are around 2 million Kurds in Syria; other significant minorities are Christians (10 percent) and Druze (3 percent).

The tensions which arise from the anger of the more radical Sunni element at being governed by 'heretics', and the persecution fears of the minorities, are further exacerbated by the involvement of outside powers. Syria's proximity to Israel and its historic ties with Palestine, combined with a strong, well-equipped army, make it a powerful ally and a worrying enemy, which partly explains the West's apparent reluctance to become involved in the present uprising, despite the obvious potential for civil war.

Assad's friends on the world stage include Shi'i Iran, which has been offering the regime material help in suppressing the uprising, ranging from crowd-control equipment to 'cyber-intelligence' equipment which enables the regime to track dissidents online. Russia and China vetoed several UN resolutions condemning the violence in Syria. Syria is highly important to Russia as its sole Arab ally, home to Moscow's only Mediterranean naval base (at Tartus), and a valuable source of revenue with $4 billion annual expenditure on arms.

In November 2011, with a NATO no-fly zone to protect civilians being mooted, Russia supplied Assad with sophisticated S-300 anti-aircraft missiles and sent a warship to Tartus in January 2012.[23] This demonstration of support for the regime coincided with Iranian war games and missile tests in the straits of Hormuz, emphasising the risk of regional escalation which might see Israel in an extremely vulnerable position.

The West would like to see the so-called arc of resistance—between

Iran, Syria, Hizbullah in Lebanon and Hamas—broken, but also fears the ascendance of the Islamists who have a long history of struggle in Syria. The Druze and Christian minorities have sided with the regime during the uprisings. Mindful of the sectarian massacres at Shi'i shrines and Christian churches in Iraq, they prefer the relative safety of a secular regime—however repressive—to one which would allow AQAM to thrive.

Those ranged in opposition against the Assad regime have yet to establish a cohesive identity. There are at least four rival organisations with varying agendas for change. The grassroots Local Coordination Committees (LCC) is based inside Syria; with a website, Facebook and Twitter accounts, the group has been proactive in coordinating demonstrations, issuing statements to the media and collating the statistics of 'martyrs' and injured.[24] The Syrian National Council (SNC), led by Burhan Ghalioun, is based in Istanbul; it contains a significant proportion of Muslim Brotherhood members but has no real mandate to represent the people who are facing tanks and snipers on the streets. The SNC has only been recognised as the voice of the opposition by Tripoli but lacks the influence to gather other groups under its umbrella. The National Coordination Body for Democratic Change (NCC) is Syria-based; it opposes any foreign intervention and many protestors suspect it of collusion with the Assad regime. In December, Burhan Ghalioun was reported to be about to enter national unity talks with the NCC, although this was swiftly denied when protestors reacted angrily.

The Free Syria Army (FSA) is the only group to endorse armed conflict and claims to have 15,000 men; it is made up of defectors from Assad's forces, *jihadis* returning from Iraq and Afghanistan and up to 600 fighters who were dispatched from Libya following the fall of Gaddafi.[25] Abdel Hakim Belhadj—the ex-LIFG leader—is known to have met with the FSA leadership in Turkey at the end of November 2011. In February 2012 an Al Qaeda–style 'martyrs' brigade' of suicide bombers was formed within the FSA.

When the SNC held its inaugural conference in Tunis in December 2011 it did not invite the participation of the FSA. Suggestions that it is backed by the CIA seem plausible, given its insistence that Assad's army is key to establishing an alternative regime. As we have seen in Egypt, any transition plan that involves the army is simply a means of maintaining the status quo with a different face.

If Syria is torn apart by a civil war—which looks increasingly likely—AQAM will most likely take a leading role in the insurgency, as it did in Iraq. If the network is able to establish itself in what Nasser described as 'the heart of the Arab world', it will be perilously close to neighbouring Israel.

In several other countries the authorities have succeeded in hanging on to power either by offering financial rewards for submission (as in Saudi Arabia) or by cracking down heavily on the first flickers of revolt (Algeria, for example). That is not to say that change will not come to these regimes; on the contrary I believe that this revolutionary process will march inexorably through the entire region. For once, the entire Arab world is on the same page of history. Why did the people of so many countries suddenly and simultaneously find the courage to rise up against their brutal oppressors having endured their situation for decades?

Islam, Identity and Revolution

During the Arab Spring protests, the same two chants were heard in every country: 'the People want the regime to fall', and 'from the mountains to the sea, all Arabia shall be free'. There is a deeply rooted sense of commonality among Arabs which historically found political expression in pan-Arabism and Arab nationalism. Both ideologies are largely discredited—the first for its failure to liberate Palestine and the latter for producing the region's most bloody dictators, the Ba'athist Saddam Hussein, Hafez Assad and his son, Bashar. This innate drive for unity, however, now provides political Islam with its historical window of opportunity since its ideology is rooted in the notion of the Muslim *umma*—the community of believers.

The 1916 Sykes–Picot agreement between France and Britain reneged on the promise of a united Arab state and carved up the territory instead, creating artificial new nation-states. Osama bin Laden pointed to this moment in history as the beginning of the humiliation of the Arab peoples, a view widely shared across the region. In the aftermath of the Second World War, the Middle East became central to the Cold War struggle between the US and the USSR, with the superpowers competing for influence in what the US State Department now adjudged to be 'a stupendous source of strategic power and one of the greatest material prizes in world history'.[26]

The catastrophic failure of the combined Arab armies to intervene effectively when the state of Israel was established in 1948—at a time when it would have been relatively easy to prevail—was an enduring source of shame and recrimination which further disunited the Arab nations. Later, American intervention on the side of Israel in the 1967 Six-Day War would result in another humiliating defeat for the Arab armies which was repeated in 1973. A legacy of guilt, frustration and humiliation has placed the necessity of justice for the Palestinians at the centre of Arab political discourse, from Arab nationalism to Al Qaeda's global *jihad* ideology.

During the Cold War period the Arab world found itself increasingly polarised—Egypt and Syria allied with the USSR while America solidified relationships with the oil-rich Gulf countries and Israel. Egypt's Gamal Nasser was the region's most charismatic and persuasive proponent of pan-Arabism through the 1950s and 1960s, but his dream of unity had no real chance of success given the backdrop of warring superpowers. A 'United Arab Republic' (UAR) comprising Syria and Egypt briefly emerged in 1958 but had little hope of expansion beyond other USSR-backed regimes. Both Iraq and Southern Yemen briefly dallied with the idea of becoming part of the UAR but the project was effectively over by 1961.

The Iranian revolution of 1979 alarmed both superpowers. It demonstrated that a great Western-backed regime can fall as a result of a Muslim uprising and led to a revival of political Islam and the idea of *jihad*. Consequently, the US and the USSR fomented hostility between Middle Eastern countries. Arab unity was perceived as a threat to the (albeit different) political and economic agendas of both superpowers; regional instability was to be preferred. When the Iran–Iraq War erupted in 1980 the superpowers poured money and arms into the eight-year conflict that cost the lives of 2 million Iranians and half a million Iraqis—with the US funding both sides.

While the region's governments were at odds with each other, political Islam was gaining ground as a potent social force. The notion of the *umma*, the Muslim nation, as an entity of 1.6 billion people which did not acknowledge national boundaries and shared distinct common causes, provided a new focus for the pan-Arab sentiments that had never really left the Arab street.

During the 1980s, the war in Afghanistan witnessed the birth of a transnational Islamist army, the *mujahideen*, as thousands of Arabs went to defend their Afghan co-religionists in the first great modern '*jihad*'. Whereas the combined national Arab armies had experienced nothing but defeat against Israel and her allies, the *mujahideen* (albeit backed by Washington) engaged the mighty USSR in a ten-year war of attrition . . . and won.

With the implosion of the USSR, America's strategy for regional hegemony was unchallenged and increasingly militarised. The arrival of 100,000 US soldiers on Saudi Arabian soil in 1990 as the first Gulf War got under way was unprecedented, and marked a new era in Middle Eastern history. Until now, the superpowers had fought regional wars by proxy; now there were boots on the ground. For Saudi-born Osama bin Laden (who was then regarded as a national hero for his participation in the Afghan *jihad*), his homeland and America became his sworn enemies and the seeds of 9/11 were sown.

The US invaded Afghanistan in 2001 and Iraq in 2003, building up a massive military presence in the Middle East.[27] The US actively sought the cooperation of the region's regimes—even the most merciless—and was implicated in military coups that produced a willing partner. Few of the region's leaders were ultimately able to resist the expert courtship of the West's ambassadors. Even Colonel Gaddafi was rehabilitated into the international community shortly before his fall. These 'friendly' governments were kept in power with training (military, security, intelligence), and through generous aid agreements and arms deals.

For the people of the Middle East, the monolithic paradigm of the regional tyrant backed by the world's only superpower had long seemed unshakeable. The challenge came not from national governments or armies but the Islamist *mujahideen* in Afghanistan, in Palestine, in Iraq. When the US invaded Afghanistan and Iraq they gave the Muslim world a new rallying cry and thousands of young men flocked to the new battlefields of *jihad* where the Taliban and Al Qaeda were leading the insurgencies. Now a new equation replaced the Cold War stand-off; an ideologically motivated polarisation which saw Islam pitted against the *kufr* (non-believers), revisiting the medieval crusades which lasted more than a century.

At home too, the greatest challenges to the regime and the most strident demands for reform often came from armed Islamist groups. In Egypt, al-Gama'a al-Islamiyya and Egyptian Islamic Jihad assassinated President Anwar Sadat in 1981, infuriated by his rapprochement with Israel. Over time the Islamists organised themselves politically and formed transnational, pan-Arab networks. The Muslim Brotherhood, for example, established branches throughout the Arab world.

For at least a generation, the Islamists have been able to achieve what pan-Arabism failed to deliver. The transnational *mujahideen* and globalised AQAM groups have catered for a collective identity (the Muslim *umma*) and provided a rallying point (Islam and *jihad*). They have also been the most visible and effective opposition to regional tyrants and the hegemonic impulses of the world's remaining superpower alike.

In an interview for this book, Saudi political commentator Saad al-Faqhi observed: 'The common factor that has made these revolutions spread like wild fire is the Islamic identity. Though it may not be expressed clearly it is there in the Arab subconscious.' This is not to say that the brave people who took to the streets during the Arab Spring did so out of any kind of religious impulse—many are liberals and secularists—only that the ground had been prepared (perhaps even subconsciously) and a process of empowerment had begun.

Another significant factor in the shift from dissent to revolution which has been somewhat overlooked in most analyses of the Arab Spring is the catastrophic economic collapse of the West which began in 2008 and was predicted by Al Qaeda as long ago as 2005. Suddenly the power behind the regional thrones was not, after all, indomitable.

Led by their desire for freedom, for the fall of the regime and the right to choose their own leaders, the protestors believed that victory can be earned through persistence, patience, bravery and a willingness to die a 'martyr' for one's cause. These qualities broke down the 'fear barrier' and are all key tenets of *jihadi* ideology.

The West's Response to the Arab Spring

The Arab Spring presented the West with a new series of moral and political dilemmas. The protection of democracy and freedom had been the banner under which they fought the 'war on terror'; now those key principles were threatening the tenure of their principal allies in the region. The strategic, economic and diplomatic implications were immense. Years spent establishing and backing sympathetic regimes had ensured the steady flow of oil, lucrative business contracts for Western firms, the assurance of a non-aggressive stance towards Israel and a regional balance of power.

Since the leaders of Arab countries had long ruled without a democratic mandate from their people, the decisions they made and the policies they followed had little to do with the inclinations of the men and women who were taking to the streets to topple them. A transfer of power to civilian governments could prove disastrous for Western projects across the region.

Self-interest initially prevailed over the human rights and aspirations of the Arab masses. France offered to send riot police to Tunisia to quell the protests and backed Tunisian dictator ben Ali until he fled in January 2011.[28] The US initially backed both ben Ali and Egypt's President Mubarak; at the end of January 2011, Vice President Joe Biden told a press conference that Mubarak should not step down and said he had been 'An ally of ours in a number of things. I would not refer to him as a dictator.'[29]

The Obama administration was slow to realise that the tide of popular uprising was too strong to be stopped, at which point it started to look for allies among the opposition; in the case of Egypt this meant the military which formed the interim governing body, the Supreme Council of the Armed Forces (SCAF) and which, at the time of writing, appears to have little intention of relinquishing its grip on power and is accused of being just as oppressive as the Mubarak regime.

The West's allies among the Gulf States moved to create an immunity to revolution among the region's monarchs, encouraging Morocco and Jordan to differentiate themselves from the republics and providing them with generous funding. The toppling of a king remains something of a psychological barrier to the Arab Spring impetus.

In December 2011, a year into the Arab Spring, President Obama approved a $53 million arms deal to Bahrain as the regime attacked protestors still trying to make their voices heard.[30] As we have noted above, the US Navy's Fifth Fleet is based in Bahrain, courtesy of the current regime which has also been protected by Saudi troops. Since the protestors are mostly the majority Shi'i, the unwelcome prospect of an Iran-friendly new regime in such a strategically important location saw pragmatism prevail over ethics for US policy-makers in this instance.

The arms industry is important to both the American and British economies, especially in a recession. In December 2011, in what the *Washington Post* described as 'an economic windfall', the Obama administration congratulated itself on having brokered a $30 billion deal with Saudi Arabia (possibly the most repressive regime on the planet) for fighter jets and weaponry.

Britain's Prime Minister, David Cameron, had no qualms about leading a January 2011 arms trade delegation to the Middle East with the revolutions in Tunisia and Egypt in full swing and as the fighting in Libya began. Libya had been one of Britain's 'priority' arms sales market countries and the UK had the largest pavilion at the Libyan arms trade fair, LibDex, in November 2010. According to the Campaign Against the Arms Trade (CAAT), in February 2011 Britain provided tear gas and crowd-control ammunition to the regimes of Bahrain and Libya. The closeness of Britain to the Gaddafi regime was engineered by Tony Blair who became a 'close, personal friend of the family' according to Saif al-Islam Gaddafi and was an adviser to the multi-billion dollar Libyan Investment Authority.

The West had failed to keep up with the speed of events in Tunisia and Egypt. The future governance of the latter is of particular concern to the West because Egypt has long been instrumental in assuring the security of Israel, having had a peace treaty with that country since 1979.

By the time the first protests occurred in Libya, a policy of what Tony Blair (wearing his 'Middle East peace envoy' hat) called 'controlled changes' had been developed. Tailored to protect Western interests, this policy could endorse both military intervention—in the case of Libya—and non-intervention—in the case of Bahrain and Saudi Arabia. As Tony Blair remarked in the context of the Arab Spring, 'inaction is also a decision'.[31]

Bizarrely, French philosopher Bernard-Henri Levy had a central role in convincing President Sarkozy to commit to the NATO military intervention (via UN Security Council Resolution 1973) that would prove instrumental in unseating Gaddafi. Why was this native of Paris so eager to affect the course of history in Libya? In his book *La guerre sans l'aimer*, Zionist Levy describes how he was convinced that the Libyan rebels would form an Israel-friendly government, and was dispatched by a 'contact' in the NTC to convey a message to that effect to Israeli premier Benjamin Netanyahu. On 2 June 2011, having consulted with French foreign minister Alain Joppé, Netanyahu offered this endorsement of the rebels: 'the State of Israel hopes that when a new government will arise in Libya, it will advance peace and security for all peoples of the entire region'.[32]

Equally important on the Western agenda is the control of Libya's vast oil reserves—the largest in Africa at 47 billion barrels. Gaddafi long used Libya's oil to manipulate the international community, playing small companies off against the multinational giants, and US organisations against European ones. At the end of 2010 the state-owned Libyan National Oil Company provocatively announced that it would not issue any new oil concession licences in 2011; in March 2011 however, Gaddafi played the oil card during his battle for survival, urging Russia, China and India (who all opposed the NATO intervention) to invest in Libya's oil sector.

Threatening the West's interests in Libyan oil may have been Gaddafi's fatal mistake. After all, he had been thoroughly 'rehabilitated', having completed his nuclear disarmament commitments in December 2009; he had also deposited billions of dollars in Western-based bank accounts. The decision to back the opposition in Libya was made promptly, with the US suspending its diplomatic activities at its Tripoli Embassy on 25 February, just ten days after the first protests.

Following the introduction of the no-fly zone there were credible reports that US special forces were training rebel fighters and that British SAS troops were active in the eastern desert regions around Benghazi. Britain also hired private security firms to train and arm the rebels. Also in April, CIA asset Khalifa Haftar had arrived from the US. Haftar had been a commander in Gaddafi's forces during the Libyan war with Chad in the 1980s before leaving for Langley, Virginia.

The US and Europe clearly considered that the National Transitional Council (NTC) would form a West-friendly interim government—and to date that has been the case—with lucrative contracts for rebuilding the infrastructure devastated by civil war, as well oil exploration rights within its gift.

Initially Western media and security analysts predicted that the Arab Spring would damage AQAM, assuming that Western-style, liberal democracies would replace dictatorships. Instead, Islamist parties prevailed in the first rounds of voting in Tunisia and Egypt, demonstrating a recognition among the people of the Islamists' years of struggle against dictatorship and corruption as well as their welfare work among the poor and needy. However retrogressive it may seem to Western eyes, the voters revealed a deeply ingrained preference for Sharia-based governance in Muslim lands.

The West now faced a dilemma—if Islamist parties dominate the post-revolutionary political landscape in the Arab world, they may adopt an anti-Western agenda. More worryingly, in order to protect their revolution against internal and external enemies, such governments might tolerate the presence of *jihadi* fighters and training camps in a rerun of the 1990s in Afghanistan and Sudan.

The West has political, economic and diplomatic instruments at its disposal with which it may attempt to maintain its influence. It can use loans and aid to manipulate new governments and influence future investment. William Hague hinted at this in an editorial published in *The Times*:

> We need to redouble our diplomatic and long-term support to the region . . . [the Islamist parties] will be under pressure to stick by their pledges to share power and chart a moderate course. The scale of the economic problems they face is monumental. They will have to seek coalition partners and to reassure international investors if they are to meet the expectations of their people. . . . This makes our engagement with them all the more important.[33]

If diplomacy fails, the West could adopt a more nefarious approach, backing opposing militias or even the state army if it moves against the Islamists.

In an October 2011 statement posted on *jihadi* forums (one of seven 'Messages of Hope to the People of Egypt'), Ayman al-Zawahiri described the US as 'watching the political game from behind the curtains', and claimed that it would not hesitate to 'intervene when that game goes outside the prescribed boundaries'. Talking about the reluctance of Egypt's SCAF to relinquish power, al-Zawahiri notes that 'America supervised the transition of power from one wing to another . . . the leadership of the Egyptian military, which receives $1.3 billion in military aid from the US annually, is ready to preserve American interests and these are: the suppression of Islamism; preserving Egypt as a strategic power in service of America; Israel's security'.

If the people of the Arab Spring countries are denied their right to choose their own government the claim that Islamist ends cannot be achieved without violence will gain currency and there is a serious risk that support for AQAM would be boosted, enabling them to resume their historic role at the front line of resistance. As we will see in Chapter 6, the Algerian military's failure to cede power to the democratically elected Front Islamique du Salut (Islamic Salvation Front, or FIS) led to catastrophic civil conflict and the birth of one of the most violent Islamist groups—the Groupe Islamique Armé (Armed Islamic Group, or GIA).

Al Qaeda's Response to the Arab Spring

Al Qaeda did not anticipate the Arab Spring. Osama bin Laden admitted in audiotape released posthumously in May 2011 that, 'We were all taken by surprise when the sun of revolution rose from the Maghreb in the West.' Within AQAM debate raged as to the 'permissibility' of joining or supporting the revolutions and there was a wide divergence of opinion. Some clerics considered them *haram* (forbidden) because they were essentially secular, democratic events. The emir of the Islamic Emirate of the Caucasus (IEC), Dokku Umarov, participated in an online question and answer session in May 2011, expressing his antipathy—widely shared in *jihadi* circles—for 'the game of "democratic Islam" being played out in Tunisia and Egypt'.

Writing in the Taliban's *al-Samud* magazine (issue 62), hard-line ideologue Ahmad Bawadi was dismissive: 'nobody should think that a revolution over bread and unemployment will close the wine shops and nightclubs . . . the networks of singing, dancing prostitution and shamelessness will not be shut down by these revolutions . . . if democracy becomes the religion of the people and an alternative to *jihad*.'

The majority of AQAM leaders, however, celebrated what Ayman al-Zawahiri labelled 'the Blessed Revolutions' and the perceived opportunities they afforded. Now they sought to clarify their approach to the principle of elections. In a 2009 televised interview with as-Sahab Media, al-Zawahiri decried 'elections under a secularist constitution run by thieving, falsifying rulers' (in other words, the kind of rigged elections which were then occurring in the Middle East) but welcomed 'impartial supervision of balloting' in the context of an Islamic state.[34] In the light of the Arab Spring, al-Zawahiri's comments were revisited in an online question and answer session on the Centre of Jihad and Monotheism's website: a member was appalled by the idea that 'all Muslims, infidels and the ignorant, could participate in voting'. The group's 'legitimacy committee' explained that elections in an Islamic state would not be to choose a political or legislative system (that would, obviously, be Sharia) but to allow the people to 'express their opinions' and the 'ruler' to respect them.

AQAM was quick to emphasise the relevance of Al Qaeda to the revolutionary process. Much of the Spring 2011 edition of AQAP's English-language propaganda magazine, *Inspire*,[35] was devoted to what it labelled the 'Tsunami of Change'. The magazine offered analysis of the situation, its likely outcome and 'guidance' to Islamists as to the role they should seek to play in the revolution. The Arab Spring 'has proved that Al Qaeda's rage is shared by the millions of Muslims across the world', writes the magazine's editor 'Abu Suhail' (probably the American convert Adam Gadahn aka Azzam al-Amriki, who is one of the directors of the Al Qaeda media production house, as-Sahab). Certainly, many issues that have long exercised Al Qaeda are of equal concern to the Arab on the street, including their identification of the 'near' and 'far' enemies—the corrupt regimes and the West respectively—justice for the Palestinians and how to use the region's natural resources for the benefit of its citizens.

In a video marking the tenth anniversary of 9/11, Ayman al-Zawahiri claimed that the 'blessed raids' had paved the way for the Arab Spring, which was a 'new form of defeat for America'. Al-Zawahiri also made the intriguing suggestion that it was 'After the martyrdom of Osama bin Laden [that] the Islamic face of the Revolution was shown'. Given that bin Laden had written a letter to 'Sheikh Mahmud' about the Islamic nature of the uprisings (and the consequent opportunities they afforded for Al Qaeda) just a week before his death, this suggests that al-Zawahiri was either not in regular contact with the leader or was seeking to mark the revolutions with the stamp of Al Qaeda.

'Ibrahim Yahya', writing in the same issue, addresses the argument that Al Qaeda's armed struggle has been made redundant by the Arab Spring's peaceful protest. 'Al Qaeda is not against regime changes through protests,' he says, but points out, 'If the protestors in Libya did not have the flexibility to use force when needed, the uprising would have been crushed.'

How do AQAM see the Arab Spring producing outcomes that would benefit them? For the late Anwar al-Awlaki, it was an 'avalanche' that would open 'great doors of opportunity for the *mujahideen* all over the world'. He noted that there are 'thousands of Saudi *mujahideen* in prisons and elsewhere in the Arabian peninsula . . . [ready to] take off as soon as the regimes of the Gulf start crumbling'. 'Ibrahim Yahya' notes the impact regime-change in various countries would have on the Palestine–Israel question: 'The issue of Palestine is central to the Muslim *umma* and now that the masses have spoken, there is no doubt that it will be back to the forefront . . . there could be no freeing of Palestine with the presence of the likes of King Abdullah to the East, Hosni Mubarak to the West and al-Saud to the South.' For Dokku Umarov, the greatest potential for AQAM lies in the uprising in Yemen where 'The positions of the *mujahideen* are most promising and from where a serious military movement could start.'[36]

AQIM emir Abdelmalek Droukdal focused on the potential establishment of an Islamic state in Libya. The Libyan Islamic Fighting Group (LIFG)—whose members were heavily involved in the battle against pro-Gaddafi forces—was an early member of the new AQIM umbrella group in 2006–7. Droukdal released four encouraging statements to the fighters in Libya, finally offering: 'Congratulations on the Victory of the Grandsons of Omar al-Mukhtar' in October 2011, referring to the iconic Libyan Islamist martyr. AQIM's 'head of judicial authority' issued a warning to 'Muslims in Libya' to resist a NATO-backed secular regime being imposed and urging them to protect the 'victory of Sharia'.

Ayman al-Zawahiri also warns of NATO attempts to eclipse the Islamists' gains in Tunisia, Egypt and Libya: 'America does not like to deal with independent, honourable and free governments; they prefer those who are co-operative, puppets and agents.' Al-Zawahiri appears to be most interested in the potential (as he sees it) offered by changes in Egypt, Libya and the Sinai. Since the Egyptian revolution, security in the Sinai had been relaxed and two new AQAM groups have emerged—Al Qaeda in the Sinai Peninsula and Ansar al-Jihad in the Sinai. The gas pipeline running from Egypt to Israel has been targeted on numerous occasions and there have been skirmishes at Israeli border checkpoints. By April 2012 the pipeline had been attacked so many times that it was effectively out of action and the gas trade agreement with Israel was looking decidedly shaky.

AQAM had little or no actual involvement in the peaceful, unarmed protests in Tunisia and Egypt. This was not the case in Libya where the revolutionary process swiftly moved towards violent confrontation. Ayman al-Zawahiri—who has long been in charge of the Libyan cohort within Al Qaeda[37]—personally dispatched Al Qaeda men to Libya in the early days of the uprising to recruit and train additional fighters and to establish a 'bridgehead for Al Qaeda in Libya'—this core unit numbered around 200.[38]

Meanwhile *jihadi* cleric Sheikh Husein bin Mahmoud issued a fatwa that, 'Jihad in Libya now is an obligatory duty upon every capable person from the Libyans and the Egyptians and the Algerians and the Chadians and the Sudanese and the Nigerians, these lands around Libya. Whoever has a good weapon and can help the Libyans then he should do so quickly.'[39]

Also in the early stages of the Libyan uprising, a video message by radical AQIM cleric Sheikh al-Hasan Rachid al-Buleidi was posted on the protestors' official Facebook page (17 February Intifada).

Former LIFG leader Abdel Hakim Belhadj (aka Abu Abdullah al-Sadiq) was already in place, having been released from the notorious Abu Salim prison in 2010 after a 'rehabilitation' programme personally supervised by Saif al-Islam, Gaddafi's eldest son, during which he ostensibly renounced violent *jihad*. On the day of his capture by secular rebels in November 2011, Saif al-Islam spoke with great bitterness about his 'betrayal' by Belhadj, who had personally led the definitive attack on

Gaddafi's compound Bab al-Aziziyah. Saif warned that the LIFG and Islamists from Benghazi and Misrata would 'bring ruin' to Libya.

Other LIFG figures released with Belhadj (who was initially apprehended in Thailand in 2004) included his assistant, Abu Hazim, aka Khalid al-Sharif (who was held in Bagram before being handed over to the Libyan authorities by the US) and Abdul Wahab al-Qayad Idris, the older brother of Al Qaeda top brass Abu Yahya al-Libi. In the course of the conflict hundreds more *jihadis* were released from prison by the rebels.[40] A further AQAM contingent comprised Libyan *mujahideen* returning from abroad, the 'dear brothers, who fought in Iraq and Afghanistan' frequently lauded by presenters on the Benghazi and Derna rebels' radio station.[41]

Together with the LIFG men, the returnees formed an umbrella group in February 2011: Al-Harakat Al-Islamiya Al Libiya Lit-Tahghir (the Libyan Islamic Movement for Change—LIMC). The Derna armed group of the LIMC was named 'the Martyrs of Abu Salim Brigade' after the 1996 massacre of 1,200 Islamists at that jail in retaliation for an assassination attempt on Muammar Gaddafi. Led by long-term Osama bin Laden associate Abu Sufian Ibrahim Ahmed bin Qumu and ex-LIFG commander Abdul Hakim al-Hasadi, the brigade even announced the establishment an Islamic Emirate 'in the style of the Taliban' in Derna.

As the fighting in Libya came to an end in October 2011, AQIM's leader in the Sahel region—Mokhta Belmokhtar—was boasting that his organisation had greatly benefited from 'Libyan weapons'. He was referring to huge numbers of sophisticated hardware—including heat-seeking surface-to-air missiles—looted from unguarded stockpiles abandoned by pro-Gaddafi forces in the desert. Human Rights Watch Emergencies Director Peter Bouckaert visited one such depot near Sirte and reported that he 'could have walked away with hundreds of missiles and nobody would ever have known'.[42] According to records, Libyan arsenals contained 20,000 man-portable air defence systems (MANPADS), which are capable of shooting down helicopters and planes. Most remain unaccounted for.

Advice for the Libyan *jihadis* regarding attitude and behaviour was on offer during the conflict by AQAM colleagues. Concerned that the window of opportunity for an Islamic state would be lost, Sheikh Husein bin Mahmud, a *jihadi* scholar, warned against the high-handed attitude and extremism which had caused the late Abu Musab al-Zarqawi (leader of Al Qaeda in Iraq) to lose so much support. In his 'message to revolutionaries' at the end of September 2011 he recommended that 'Front line commanders should order their soldiers to avoid transgressions and sins as diligently as they evade Gaddafi's missiles and grenades . . . in humility before Allah.'

According to political commentator Saad al-Faqhi, 'Al Qaeda is gaining ground in Yemen through supporting the revolution but not trying to lead it.' AQAP has carefully navigated the country's complex tribal system to form some valuable alliances, particularly in the south where it has even operated in tandem with the liberal secessionist movement, Hirak. The present unrest, and the attendant loss of security, presented AQAP with opportunities to expand its influence and it seized control of towns around the capital, Sanaa, as well as much of Abyan province.

Osama bin Laden's father was a native Yemeni and the organisation has historically enjoyed support from many on the Yemen street where 40 percent of the population live below the poverty line and there are sixty guns per hundred people.[43]

Worryingly for key US ally Saudi Arabia, AQAP has also become involved in the sectarian conflict at its border, declaring war on the Shi'i Houthis in a gesture of solidarity with the region's Sunni tribes. In 2010 AQAP killed the Houthi spiritual leader Bader al-Deen al-Houthi, in September 2011 a suicide bomber killed up to a hundred Houthis and in December 2011 AQAP fighters killed military commander Abu Ali al-Hakim. Compromised security at the Yemen–Saudi border would facilitate the traffic of fighters and weapons between the two countries and there has been a marked increase in threatening rhetoric aimed at Saudi Arabia.

AQAP's activities during the uprising have undoubtedly strengthened the hand of the protestors by weakening the regime. There are almost daily attacks on government and security targets and in September 2011 a suicide bomber narrowly missed killing the Defence Minister (seven of his bodyguards died in the attack).

The US is clearly concerned about both the internal and external security implications of the protests. Drone attacks on AQAP targets inside Yemen, originating from drone stations in Djibouti, Abu Dhabi and the Seychelles, have escalated since June 2011 and are now at a level of more than one a day.[44]

The nature of Al Qaeda's involvement in Syria suggests that the leadership has had time to formulate a tailored strategy. In June 2011, Ayman al-Zawahiri began publically inciting the Syrians to rise up against Assad and by September 2011 a 52-page booklet offering guidance for the *mujahideen* in Syria (*A Strategy for the Land of Gathering (Syria): An Attempt to Pinpoint the Pivotal Aspects*[45]) had been produced by 'Abu Jihad al-Shami'. The booklet offers a revealing glimpse of how *jihadi* groups establish a logistical infrastructure and bases from which to operate.

Al-Shami considers the best locations for a 'safe haven' inside the 'newly opened door' to Syria, concluding that the Jabal al-Sheikh mountains and the Sunni area around the Nusayri mountains offer the best natural defences and resources for survival; being near the Lebanese border, flight is made easier. Cities, including the capital, are only suitable for 'non-kinetic secret cells' until the regime is much weaker.

Al-Shami advises *jihadis* already in Syria, and those arriving there, to 'establish secret logistics cells in the cities and mobile battalions in different regions . . . avoid centralisation, at least to begin with . . . but accept direction and guidance from the overall leadership'. The next stage of the insurgency is to 'attack the widest possible number of targets over as large an expanse of territory as you can . . . this will force the enemy to dilute their forces'.

With regard to the indigenous population, al-Shami notes with displeasure the high proportion of 'Sufis' among the Muslims—Sufis are considered heretics by AQAM. He suggests that the 'Arab tribes in the rough country' could be possible allies, as could the Kurds in the north, were it not for the fact that they are 'more concerned with their national heritage than their Sunni identity'.

Al-Shami points to the proximity of neighbouring Iraq as an advantage. 'When the front develops,' he advises, 'trainers, experts, leaders, arms and explosives can all be brought across the border.' He also points out that the *mujahideen* on both sides of the border can offer each other safe haven if they need to flee a losing battle or surveillance.

Because there is a strong military presence on the Syria–Turkey border, al-Shami advises against any attempts to use Turkey as a staging post. 'Any kind of activity inside Turkey is doomed to complete failure,' he says. He also reminds *jihadis* 'not to rile the Turks as long as they remain neutral with regard to our aims. We do not want to add to the list of our enemies unless for strategic reasons.'

Jordan is an inhospitable country full of spies, according to al-Shami, but the 'brothers' already active inside the country should start low-key operations against the government to destabilise the security situation which in turn will help the Syrian *jihadis*. The Syrian side of the border could be suitable for 'manœuvres' since it is not, at present, well policed, although he comments that this is only until 'the Jordanian regime realises the danger on its doorstep'.

Lebanon is an advantageous neighbour from al-Shami's perspective: 'it already has two effective, internal enemies in Hizbullah and the Christian militia. These weaken it and require a lot of attention from the security forces. . . . Open secret training camps in Lebanon,' he advises, 'and make it a rear operations base for planning and preparing attacks inside Syria.'

Al-Shami warns the *mujahideen* to expect large numbers of 'martyrs' at the hands of this singularly vicious regime and to ready the next generation of leaders to replace those who will be lost. Local leaders are urged to post YouTube videos on the Internet calling for volunteers, celebrating martyrs and narrating operations carried out by the *mujahideen* inside Syria. Pushing the *jihadi* worldview is also essential: 'We must re-awaken the *umma* by reminding them that the seat of the Abbassi Caliphate was Baghdad, and the Umawi Caliphate was based in Damascus.'

Al-Shami has funding suggestions too: *ghaniimah* (booty) such as taking 'enemy' oil tankers—'as the *mujahideen* do in Iraq'—is a lucrative activity, although the 'best source of liquid cash is kidnapping'. He suggests that 'Lebanon or other neighbouring lands might be suitable for such operations'. Weapons and explosives can be easily purchased from Iraq and Lebanon, al-Shami says. He suggests that safe houses could be equipped with 'sound-proof basements' for target practice, although mobile training units of five to ten men have been found to be the best option—especially if they operate near places where explosives and gunfire would normally be heard (a quarry or a hunting wood, for example).

Finally, al-Shami is hopeful that a *jihad* in Syria will benefit the Palestinians: 'an open *jihad* on the borders with Israel . . . will force the Israelis into a battle with the entire Islamic *umma.* Syria, like Iraq, will become a place from which the battalions will depart'.

Suicide bombs in Damascus in December 2011 marked the arrival of AQAM. 'The Osama bin Laden Brigades in Syria' posted calls for recruits and in February 2012 a group within the FSA announced the formation of the 'al-Bara Ibn Malik Martyrs' Brigade'—the name suggests this suicide wing is associated with Al Qaeda in Iraq which had a Martyrs' Brigade with the same name. In July 2012, the FSA claimed responsibility for the devastating suicide bombing at the heart of Assad's security establishment, which killed at least three key figures including the Defence Minister and Assad's brother-in-law.

Al Qaeda and the Post-Revolutionary Period

The post-revolutionary political landscape is complicated and chaotic; it is likely to be many years before the Arab Spring countries manage to negotiate new forms of governance that can comfortably accommodate all shades of opinion. For now let us consider what space the Islamists, and in particular AQAM, might carve for themselves in this uncharted territory.

Tunisia was one of the most liberal countries in the Arab world under dictator Zine el Abidinde ben Ali. Ben Ali's regime banned the *hijab* in educational facilities and government offices in 1981 and clearly wished Tunisia to be perceived on the world stage as a secular, modern, Westernised state. When the people went to the ballot box in October 2011, however, they voted in large numbers for the moderate Islamist party, Ennahda, which was banned under ben Ali. The most powerful post in the new government—that of Prime Minister—has gone to Ennahda's Hamadi Jbeli.

In December 2011, around 3,000 Salafists besieged Manouba

University near Tunis because it had refused to cede their demands that women should be allowed to wear the *niqab* if they chose to do so. There was a counter-demonstration by around 1,000 secularists and this schism between radical Islamists and the secularists threatens the societal cohesion that is necessary if a new, strong Tunisia is to emerge from the ashes of the ben Ali regime. The Salafists claim that the people voted for Islam when they chose Ennahda and that the secularists are attempting to impose their own form of dictatorship.

The same schism is already apparent in post-Mubarak Egypt where the young, largely middle-class and secularist leaders of the revolution have watched in dismay as the Muslim Brotherhood's newly formed political party, the Freedom and Justice Party (FJP), garnered nearly half of the votes in Egypt's parliamentary elections in January 2012. Another, more radical, Islamist party, the Salafist al Nour, gained 25.29 percent of the votes. Al-Wafd, the liberal party that one might have expected to do well, won just 8.9 percent. This result was predicted by Dr Saad al-Faqhi, interviewed for this book just before the elections. 'The Islamists will win because they have access to the roots of the people. The secularists with their Western influences cannot talk to the people. These countries are coming out of intensive care after fifty years of oppression.'

Writing in the spring 2011 edition of *Inspire* magazine the late Anwar al-Awlaki described Egypt as the 'cradle of today's *jihad* movement' and pointed out that the release, by the rebels, of *jihadis* who were imprisoned and silenced during Mubarak's regime represents 'a great leap forward for the *mujahideen*'.

Among those released were men with close links to Al Qaeda, such as the current leader of Egyptian Islamic Jihad (EIJ), Aboud al-Zumour, and his brother Tareq, who had been in prison for thirty years for their part in the assassination of Anwar Sadat. Ayman al-Zawahiri, himself a former leader of the EIJ, was also imprisoned for Sadat's killing and was Aboud al-Zumour's cell mate for four years until his controversial release; the two were close friends.

Release was not such a 'great leap forward' for al-Zawahiri's brother, Muhammad; he was among the fifty-nine *jihadis* set free in March 2011 but was rearrested just three days later by the State Security Investigation Service (SSIS) after he issued a fatwa opposing the political process and calling for the immediate imposition of Sharia.

The SSIS was meant to have been disbanded after Mubarak's departure from power but has continued operating in secret. This flags up another concern shared by Islamists and secularists alike—that foreign governments are interfering with the revolutionary process behind the scenes to ensure that a sympathetic regime comes to power. Ayman al-Zawahiri warned against 'incomplete revolutions', suggesting that America aims 'to replace these regimes and take new faces as a substitute for the old faces which delude the masses with slight reformation and freedom; however the interests of the supercilious and oppressive powers of the world remain maintained and well-protected'.[46]

In April 2012, as already noted, SCAF banned ten presidential candidates, among them two Islamists who were leading contenders for the post: Hazem Abu Ismail, a radical cleric, and Khairat al-Shater, the Muslim Brotherhood's candidate. Thousands took to the streets to protest in one of the biggest demonstrations since the fall of Mubarak.

Foreign aid is often used as a political tool to ensure the loyalty of regimes to the West. A Gallup poll in March 2012 showed that 80 percent of Egyptians opposed accepting US aid for this very reason.[47] The SCAF and Western governments were alarmed by the success of the Islamist parties in parliamentary elections, where they hold 70 percent of seats, and the implications this has for Western interests in the region and Israel.

Although the Freedom and Justice Party have said they will honour the peace treaty with Israel, they emphasised the proviso that Israel must honour its obligations towards the Palestinians too. In March 2012, with Israeli airplanes bombarding Gaza and twenty-five Palestinians dead, the new Egyptian parliament voted unanimously to sever diplomatic ties with Israel.[48]

June 2012 saw the standoff between SCAF and the Islamists escalate when the generals, acting on a decree from the Supreme Constitutional Court that the parliamentary elections had been legally flawed, dissolved parliament the day before the presidential election. SCAF also stripped the president of authority over the military, retained all legislative powers for itself and claimed the right to veto the constitution when it is drafted.[49]

Voters were offered just two presidential candidates in the second round: the Muslim Brotherhood's 'reserve', Mohammed Morsi, and Mubarak's last Prime Minister, Ahmed Shafiq. After a nail-biting, week-long wait, and a lot of horse-trading behind the scenes, SCAF announced that Morsi had won.

I was informed by a highly reliable source that SCAF initially intended to claim victory for Shafiq but were dissuaded from doing so by the US, who recognised that it would be unwise to impede the Islamists' democratic mandate and would almost certainly result in armed unrest led by a resurgent *jihadi* movement with the inevitable involvement of AQAM. Indeed, Al Qaeda flags had been flown in Tahrir Square as protestors called for the resignation of SCAF in December 2011. Radical speakers, many recently released from jail, attracted large crowds with anti-Israel and anti-US rhetoric and their demands for the immediate implementation of Sharia law.

Morsi's first action on taking office was to order parliament to reconvene, setting himself and the Muslim Brotherhood at loggerheads not only with SCAF but with the Supreme Constitutional Court. Morsi's undiplomatic, confrontational approach may have the unintended effect of making the region's electorate wary of voting for Islamist parties in future.

Having had no experience of democracy for more than forty years, the Libyans are starting from scratch as they attempt to establish the foundations of a modern state and here the schism between the secularists and Islamists is not the only impediment to a united country. Divisions along tribal lines are deeply ingrained while the country's Berber population have formed their own group—the Libyan Amazigh Congress. The NTC responded to this problem in April 2012 with a heavy-handed ban on all political parties based on religion, tribal loyalties or ethnicity, which it repealed the following month in response to protests from the Islamists.

Following the revolution, the NTC failed to either disarm the various factions which had joined forces to topple Gaddafi or bring them under the umbrella of a national army. As a result several warring militias have emerged in addition to the regular army. The most powerful is the Tripoli Military Council (TMC), which was formed by former LIFG leader, Belhadj, during the uprising in August 2011—at the same time as

600 *jihadis*, many of whom had fought in Iraq, were released from jail by the rebel armies. The TMC reportedly had around 20,000 fighters at the time of writing.

A further complication is the involvement of foreign powers: the national army has been subject to CIA tinkering—when their asset Khalifa Haftar failed to get the top job, another former Gaddafi general, Yussef al-Mangush, was appointed Chief-of-Staff. Belhadj, meanwhile, is supported and armed by Qatar. Another militia, the Zintan Revolutionaries, is supported by Britain and France. Other militias include the Tripoli Revolutionaries, led by Abdallah Nakir, the Misrata Brigades, the February 17th Brigade and the Benghazi Brigade. Sources in Libya say that various armed groups have seized control of parts of the country.

In January 2012 the NTC had lost control of the security situation to such an extent that it was obliged to hold its cabinet meetings in secret to evade grenades and bottles hurled by angry demonstrators.

Belhadj has renamed the LIFG the 'Islamic Movement for Change' and insists that he accepts the idea of 'democracy within an Islamic State'—a position much in keeping with Ayman al-Zawahiri's as outlined above. The key point here being that there must first be 'an Islamic state' established according to Sharia law.

Whilst it would be anathema to the liberal, secular youth who fought so valiantly for their freedom, it is quite conceivable that the majority of Libyans would actually welcome an Islamic state. In October 2011 Mustafa Jalil asserted that the future Libyan state would be predicated on Sharia.

Jihadi bulletin boards indicate the Islamists' areas of concern for the future of Libya. Ayman al-Zawahiri has posted several audiotapes warning, 'There are many scheming to snatch all or part of your victory away from you, headed by the NATO gang in the West . . . the first thing they will demand is that you give up your Islam . . . that you relinquish your desire for rule by Sharia and agree, instead, to abide by the West's ideological and legal systems.'

Libyans have long been sympathetic to the most radical ideology, supplying what a leaked diplomatic cable from 2008 described as 'a wellspring of Libyan foreign fighters for Al Qaeda in Iraq'[50] and several of the organisation's key leaders. I was not surprised when press reports from Benghazi described a 'sea of Al Qaeda flags' being waved to celebrate

Gaddafi's downfall.[51] A few days later the flag of the Islamic State of Iraq (ISOI) was also being flown.

The TMC and other militias are well armed, having commandeered whatever they could from Gaddafi's vast and sophisticated arsenals. As we have seen, AQIM has already benefited from these stockpiles and it is likely that *jihadis* within the country could supply other AQAM groups with weaponry. With AQIM in neighbouring Algeria and the Sahel countries and Boko Haram in Nigeria, an Islamic state in Libya would be a security nightmare for the West which is already concerned about the 'Africanisation' of Al Qaeda.

Another possible outcome in Libya would see the country divided into three autonomous federal states as it was pre-Gaddafi, with Tripolitania in the west, Fezzan in the southwest and Cyrenica in the oil-rich east (also called Barqa in Arabic). Indeed, in March 2012, a gathering of thousands of militiamen, tribal leaders, politicians and businessmen announced the independence of Barqa which would have its own parliament, judiciary and police, with Benghazi as its capital.[52]

Early indications of July 2012's election results suggest that the Alliance of National Forces party, led by the NTC's Prime Minister, Mahmoud Jibril, has prevailed over the Muslim Brotherhood's Justice and Construction Party. It is unlikely that the Islamists will accept such a result or that the militias will lay down their arms.

The electoral success of the Islamist parties in Tunisia, Morocco and Egypt revived old grievances in Algeria where the ruling elite, composed of politicians, generals and businessmen (collectively nicknamed *le Pouvoir*) deeply fear instability. The Islamist party Movement for a Peaceful Society (MSP)—the military junta banned parties from including any reference to Islam in their names—pulled out of the ruling coalition in January 2012 and formed the 'Green Alliance' with two others (al-Nahda and al-Islah) ahead of May 2012 elections. The alliance did not do as well as some expected, bucking the regional trend, and gained only 48 seats out of the total 462. Islamic Salvation Front (FIS) leader, Ali Belhajj—whose party has been banned since it won the 1991 elections—organised a boycott of the 2012 poll. Belhajj predicted a poor showing for the Green Alliance parties, suggesting that because they had all either supported or participated in the regime in the past they did not offer real change. The FIS has not gone away, however, with two satellite television stations broadcasting its message,[53] courtesy of the wealthy Gulf Cooperation Council which would like to see regime change in Algeria.

Contagion from the Arab Spring has extended into non-Arab Muslim countries where AQAM are active. In November 2011, TTP leader Hakimullah Mehsud addressed the Pakistani people, urging them to join his group's struggle and placing it within the framework of the Arab Spring: 'Allah has blessed this land with innumerable resources, but ... the selfish, greedy, amoral rulers have wronged a population of 180 million only to satisfy their unending desires. And behind all this are the institutions of *kufr* (such as the IMF and World Bank), America, Europe and other countries.' Bangladesh too (home to various Islamist groups including Hizb-ut Tahrir) is experiencing increasingly frequent and prolonged outbreaks of unrest.

In Nigeria, protests broke out in January 2012 when the government doubled the price of petrol at the pumps. Boko Haram was quick to identify with and join the protests, and local commentators have taken to describing this bloodthirsty group in Arab Spring-style rhetoric as 'the product of the dissatisfaction of the poor'.

In early April 2012, a military coup in Mali gave Tuareg rebels a window of opportunity to seize much of the northern part of the country where they declared an independent state called Azawad. The Islamist faction within the Tuareg armies was given armed support by AQIM's southern emir, Mokhta Belmokhtar, and members of Boko Haram.

Conclusion

The Arab Spring has brought dramatic regional change on a scale to rival the fall of the Soviet Union in 1991. The youthful protestors who made up the bulk of the opposition clearly wanted their demonstrations to be peaceful. The dictators used extreme violence, nevertheless, and in the case of Libya and Syria, armed resistance became necessary. What enabled the revolutionaries to overcome the much-discussed 'fear barrier' and to ultimately prevail was their willingness to die for their cause. To become a 'martyr'.

This vocabulary owes much (either consciously or subconsciously) to the cultural model established by the *mujahideen* whereby even the mightiest enemy can be defeated by what they believe to be a righteous, patient and brave adversary armed with faith in his/her cause. Nor should the desire for a shared identity be overlooked. The secular, nationalist, pan-Arab drive has been—to some extent at least—replaced by the notion of the Muslim *umma* which has proved itself to be a robust, resilient force on the world stage. The sense of humiliation and defeat (not least because of a failure to obtain justice for the Palestinians) which characterised the Arab world prior to the Arab Spring has been replaced by pride and hope.

Despite the widespread desire for calm and harmonious new societal models, the potential for violent conflict and the involvement of AQAM remains high. Civil war threatens the fabric of several countries, especially Libya and Syria, and schisms within new governments will weaken security and create the kind of chaos in which AQAM thrives. As we have seen, AQAM became militarily involved in Libya and Syria and armed Islamist insurgencies may ensue in several countries if the new constitutions do not reflect the will of the people or if there is foreign interference. In addition, the spectre of sectarian conflict stalks the post-revolutionary landscape and could ignite a regional war, pitting the Sunni states, led by Saudi Arabia, against the mighty Shi'i bloc headed by Iran.

In a return to a Cold War paradigm, Russia and China have already aligned themselves with Syria and Iran while the West champions oil-rich Saudi Arabia and the Gulf States. Such a polarisation might easily lead to proxy wars between superpowers and open the door for war with Iran. Having inadvertently handed control of Iraq to Iran, and given the emerging regional sectarian balance, the West would now prefer to see Sunnis at the helm in Syria and Afghanistan—we should not be surprised to find a slightly less radical Taliban not only back in government in Kabul, but invited into the international community.

A route away from violence might see AQAM and other *jihadi* groups engaging politically with the establishment of the new Arab states. This is not as far-fetched as it may seem. One has only to look at the recent history of Northern Ireland for a model whereby 'terrorists' become leading politicians. It is possible that the emerging model of Islamist politics will influence AQAM. An interesting—and potentially constructive—aspect of AQAM's response to the Arab Spring has been an unanticipated political pragmatism. Osama bin Laden warned the *jihadis* against 'confrontation' with the Islamist political parties, suggesting that they be allowed to consolidate their power in government before being 'guided' into a 'true Islamic understanding'.[54] Ayman al-Zawahiri advised his Egyptian colleagues to declare a willingness to coexist with the Coptic Christians and the organisation's wider leadership seems to have acknowledged a place for popular consultation within any putative Islamic state.

Coming at a time when the Taliban are establishing a diplomatic presence on the international stage, having opened offices in Qatar, this might mark the beginning of a new, less violent, era in Islamist history. The Arab Spring has already witnessed the willingness of some Islamist parties to present a more moderate face in order to gain power via the democratic process. Egypt's Islamic Group disbanded its armed wing and focused its efforts instead on its political arm, the positively named party called 'Construction and Development', and the LIFG rebranded itself the Islamic Movement for Change. However, attempts to block the progress of such parties within the emerging political infrastructure could backfire and see a reversion to violence.

The most significant network of political pragmatists are the Muslim Brotherhood who have branches in nearly every Middle Eastern country. The Muslim Brotherhood has rehabilitated itself to present a more accessible (and acceptable) face of Islamism through its political arm, the Freedom and Justice Party.

The Erdogan regime in Turkey has been an important influence in this respect. The difference is that Erdogan emerged via the democratic process over decades, whereas the Islamist politicians in Tunisia, Egypt and Libya—most of whom had been repressed or imprisoned for decades—suddenly find themselves in the driving seat with no experience of democracy or government.

However ideologically uncompromising AQAM may remain within the negotiating process as new societies are built in the Arab Spring countries, it will be on the political sidelines in most conceivable outcomes. Clearly a democracy dominated by Islamist political parties—as has already emerged in Tunisia and Egypt—is more useful to those seeking to establish an Islamic state than one dominated by the military or the secularists. Figures may emerge who are willing to participate in the political process and who are also capable of rapprochement with AQAM. AQAM's grassroots membership, however, retain a more radical approach towards the concept of democracy and we may see a conflict between increasingly pragmatic leaders and hard-line foot soldiers.

Whatever outcomes we eventually witness in the Arab Spring countries—and I have not relinquished hope that the region will develop its own, bespoke democratic model allowing all its citizens to coexist peaceably—the near and medium future are likely to be turbulent and chaotic: exactly the environment in which Al Qaeda thrives.

2

Al Qaeda in the Arabian Peninsula

Yemen has become the rear base for all jihadi work in the world.
Osama bin Laden, April 2011

Al Qaeda in the Arabian Peninsula has emerged as the most dangerous regional node in the global jihad.
CIA Director David Petraeus, September 2011

The Arabian Peninsula, comprising Saudi Arabia, Yemen, Kuwait, Bahrain, Qatar, UAE and Oman, is a land of contrasts. Here are the region's richest Gulf Cooperation Council (GCC) countries, with an average per capita GDP of over $60,000 and the region's poorest, Yemen, of just $2,500. The region is the repository of the world's largest oil reserves, and its elite indulge in the most lavish displays of wealth and seem to worship materialism. Yet Saudi Arabia is also home to Islam's holiest places, Medina and Mecca; the focus of the world's 1.6 billion Muslims' daily prayers; and the destination of up to 2 million pilgrims who undertake the *Hajj* each year—a spiritual experience of great intensity.

The Arabian Peninsula contains locations of the greatest strategic importance, with the Persian Gulf to the northeast, the Strait of Hormuz to the east, the pirate-infested Arabian Sea and the Gulf of Aden to the south. To the southwest and west, the Bab al-Mandeb Strait controls access to the Red Sea and the Suez Canal. No wonder, then, that the Arabian Peninsula has become a central battleground between the Islamists and the region's monarchies and autocrats; the latter shored up and armed by America and Europe, whose interests they protect.

When rumblings of the Arab Spring reached the Arabian Peninsula no force or expense was spared in maintaining the status quo. The GCC dispatched a small army to quell the uprisings in Bahrain, and the Saudi royal family handed over large amounts of money in pay rises, grants and unemployment benefits to placate their citizens. In Yemen, protests were met with great violence by President Saleh's regime, yet the West looked the other way because Saleh (albeit rather unwillingly) cooperated with the 'war on terror'. When Saleh eventually resigned (following a visit to Washington) his deputy, Field Marshal Abd-Rabouh Mansour Hardi, took over the presidency—a move backed by the Americans, with commentators describing him as 'a temporary malleable figure that is very acceptable to the US'.[1] Hardi is unlikely, then, to bring about the kind of real change the protestors have spilt their blood for, or to ensure anything approaching stability.

Al Qaeda in the Arabian Peninsula was formed in January 2009 by a merger between the Saudi and Yemeni offshoots of the organisation. It is considered the most significant terrorist threat to the region, to local Western interests and to the West itself. In April 2011, shortly before his death, Osama bin Laden noted with satisfaction that Yemen had become 'the rear base for all *jihadi* work in the world'.[2]

Leaked US diplomatic cables illustrate the depth of US concerns regarding AQAP: in addition to seeking permission for US drone strikes on AQAP targets inside Yemen, the Obama administration also sought permission to put troops on the ground in 2010, a request that President Saleh turned down. In August 2011 the UN Security Council announced that it, too, was 'deeply concerned at . . . the threat from Al-Qaida in the Arabian Peninsula'.[3]

AQAP is now headquartered in Yemen, the Saudi contingent having migrated following a severe crackdown on the other side of the porous border. In 2011 an offshoot of AQAP emerged, calling itself Ansar al-Shari'a, under emir Jalal Muhsin Balidi al-Murqoshi, alias Abu Hamza. Journalists reporting from southern Yemen in May 2012 affirmed that this is a rebranding exercise to present a more acceptable face of *jihadism* and that, while it has successfully boosted recruitment, the two names are used interchangeably by fighters and locals alike.[4]

AQAP have exploited the security vacuum created by the Arab Spring uprisings to seize control of parts of Yemen and have established an Islamic Emirate in the south, on the Gulf of Aden; this stronghold is perilously near the Bab al-Mandeb (Gate of Tears) through which up to 4 million barrels per day of the world's oil supplies are transported. On the other side of the Gulf of Aden sits Somalia where al-Shabaab (which announced it was part of Al Qaeda in February 2012) is in control of much of the country and where Somali pirates roam the seas. The US has its only official African base in Djibouti, Somalia's tiny northern neighbour. From here it monitors AQAP and al-Shabaab and launches its deadly unmanned drones in what Osama bin Laden referred to as 'the circle of espionage'.[5]

In addition to the threat AQAP poses to Yemen's own internal security, most recent plots against the West were devised in association with leading members of the group, including master bomb-maker Ibrahim Hassan al-Asiri and the late Anwar al-Awlaki. AQAP offers a safe haven to *jihadis* from many countries, as well as opportunities for training and battle. Like most AQAM groups, and indicative of a rising trend, AQAP includes a significant number of Western converts in its ranks.

The Yemeni government faces several other serious security issues, most significantly the Arab Spring protests demanding regime change, an ongoing uprising by Houthi rebels in the north and a secession movement in the south. AQAP has exploited the political turmoil and administrative chaos in Yemen, aided by tribal contacts, to become deeply embedded in the fabric of Yemeni society—a society where every man carries guns and even the youngest children know how to use them. In one of his letters retrieved from Abbottabad, Osama bin Laden betrays his Yemeni roots (his father was a native of Hadramut) with the declaration that, 'Men without weapons are incomplete.'[6] As AQAP battles to control further territory, town by town and village by village, thousands of civilians have been forced to flee the conflict. The country is disintegrating and many privately admit, as did an Aden-based UN official recently, that Yemen is 'Somalia in the making'.[7]

Saudi Arabia: Al Qaeda Under Pressure

AQAP was formerly ensconced in Saudi Arabia; several Saudi commanders fled the November 2001 US bombardment of Tora Bora and returned to the Kingdom in late 2001, where they established four *jihadi* cells under the banner '*Mujahideen* Military Committee in the Arabian Peninsula' (*Mujahideen al-Lajna al-Askiriya fi Jazirat al-Arab*), initially under the leadership of Yusuf Saleh Fahd al-Ayiri, who was killed by Saudi security forces in 2003. Ayiri was succeeded by Adbul Azziz al-Muqrin, who renamed the organisation Al Qaeda in the Arabian Peninsula (AQAP), and was himself killed in 2004.

Between 2003 and 2004 the Saudi branch of Al Qaeda carried out eight major attacks, mostly on Western targets within the Kingdom: the 12 May 2003 suicide bombings of three Riyadh compounds housing foreign workers, which claimed twenty-six victims, for example, or the Khobar massacre of 30 May 2004—a terrifying rampage by gangs of heavily armed men in which twenty-two people, mainly foreigners, were killed. The US Embassy in Jeddah itself came under attack on 6 December 2004 when a car bomb blew open the gates of the heavily fortified compound and fighters stormed the building, taking eighteen hostages, four of whom were killed along with four Saudi security guards.

Because of a general anti-US/Coalition sentiment among Muslims in the wake of the invasions of Afghanistan and Iraq, Al Qaeda enjoyed widespread support among Saudis from all walks of life at this time, including members of the royal family. This was to change, however. From late 2004, Al Qaeda started to attack security and police targets inside the Kingdom, assassinating police chief Lieutenant-Colonel Mubarak al-Sawat on 19 June 2005. Several Saudi commentators point out that this was an ill-conceived strategy which significantly weakened AQAP. Previously, the security services and the police force had been heavily infiltrated by Al Qaeda sympathisers. Once they became targets themselves, however, it was in their interest to clamp down on the *jihadis* and they started to help the regime in its efforts to eliminate or imprison AQAP personnel. The regime introduced an added incentive—a generous 'terrorism bonus', an extra payment for facing the risk of terrorism.[8]

The Saudi regime's clampdown on Al Qaeda took various forms, many learnt from the FBI. They started to publish photographic lists of the 'most wanted terrorists' in national newspapers, encouraging the population to be vigilant and offering rewards for information; these were updated regularly with information on successful detentions or killings and new suspects. There were two lists in 2003—one in May that contained nineteen names, of whom thirteen are now dead, and one in December with twenty-six listed, all but one of whom have been killed or captured. Another list in June 2005 named thirty-six, of whom twenty-three have been killed or captured.

More than a hundred sheikhs and Islamic scholars joined the propaganda effort, and in 2004 the regime began its ongoing deradicalisation programme (which it named the 're-education and re-habilitation programme') in special residential camps. Thirty psychologists provided 'counselling' and there were therapeutic workshops such as poetry and painting. Islamic clerics engaged captured *jihadis* (including several who had been released from Guantanamo) in intensive religious debates. Some 2,000 people have been through the programme; 700 renounced Al Qaeda and were freed, the remainder are still in detention. 1,400 refused to submit to the programme and they were put in regular jails. (This technique was later adopted in Libya in a programme overseen by Saif al-Islam Gaddafi—graduates included Abdel Hakim Belhadj, who later resurfaced at the head of an army of *jihadis* in the definitive battle against the Gaddafi regime in 2011.)

The Saudis also cracked down on 'cyber-*jihadis*', arresting several men who were running password-protected websites for the purposes of incitement or recruitment. While this tactic had some initial success, the younger generation of *jihadis* are well versed in cyber subterfuge and can usually outwit the authorities, given time.

Hopes that the Al Qaeda problem had been dealt with were dashed when the group carried out 'a spectacular' in 2006: the attempted bombing of the Abqaiq oil plant—the biggest such facility in the world which produces 60 percent of Saudi Arabia's oil. The attack set alarm bells ringing both in Saudi Arabia and in countries which rely heavily on its oil. President George W. Bush resolved to lessen America's dependence on Saudi oil, and demanded that the regime deal with Al Qaeda once and for all.[9]

The Saudi government were not natural allies of the US against Al Qaeda—in the past they had even funded bin Laden's group. British journalist Nick Fielding accessed court documents which allegedly support the claim that Osama bin Laden had received 'at least £200 million' from the royal family and that security chief Prince Turki al-Faisal had a long-standing friendship with the Al Qaeda leader whom he had 'hand-picked in the early 1980s . . . to organize Arab volunteers fighting the Russians in Afghanistan'.[10] Separate sources have told me that this friendship endured long into the 2000s.

A leaked US State Department cable claimed that, in 2009, 'Donors in Saudi Arabia constitute the most significant source of funding to Sunni terrorist groups worldwide'.[11] Despite Saudi monitoring of large deposits and transfers in the Kingdom's banking system, private individuals there are still the biggest source of finance for Sunni Islamist groups.

The Kingdom realised that another way it might rid itself of its *jihadi* population would be to export them; between 2003 and 2006 an estimated 3,000 Saudi fighters had already joined Abu Musab al-Zarqawi's group in the Iraqi insurgency. When a large group of pro–Al Qaeda clerics organised a December 2006 conference urging Saudi recruits to support the Sunni insurgency in Iraq, warning of a Shi'i and 'crusader' takeover, the regime turned a blind eye.

By 1 October 2007, however, the conflicted Saudi regime recognised that the *jihad* in Iraq was, in effect, a *jihad* against America, the main buffer against its own regional rival Iran. Now Grand Mufti, Sheikh Abdel al-Aziz bin Abdallah al-Sheikh issued a fatwa forbidding Saudi youth from engaging in *jihad* without the ruler's permission.[12] It is doubtful that such permission was ever sought.

There were few further attacks inside the Kingdom in 2007 and 2008, but now a new problem arose. Concerned about 'blow-back' from Iraq and Afghanistan—the phenomenon of trained and experienced indigenous *jihadis* returning home intent on resuming their fight against the regime—the Saudis started work on a sophisticated hi-tech security barrier to re-enforce the existing watchtowers and manned checkpoints along the border with Iraq.[13]

After a four-year gap, the Kingdom issued a new list of wanted Al Qaeda operatives on 3 February 2009 and the numbers had significantly increased. Comprising eighty-five men (eighty-three Saudis and two Yemenis), six of whom had been imprisoned in Guantanamo, this suggested that there were still large numbers of *jihadis* inside the Kingdom simply biding their time.

On 27 August 2009, Abdullah Hassan al-Asiri—who was on the Kingdom's 'most wanted' list—attempted to assassinate the Assistant Interior Minister Prince Mohammad bin-Nayaf bin Abdul-Aziz by detonating explosives concealed in his own rectum. Abdul-Aziz, who had led the fight against Al Qaeda in the Kingdom between 2003 and 2006, narrowly survived the blast.

Another crackdown by the regime was largely successful, sending large numbers of *jihadis* over the border into Yemen. However, there are still 'sleeper cells' in Saudi Arabia—groups of trained men or individuals waiting for a window of opportunity, or an instruction, to strike. On 6 August 2011, one such individual, following a command from AQAP's military chief Qasim al-Raymi, again tried to assassinate Prince Mohammad bin-Nayaf, opening fire on guards at his compound. Just how numerous these 'sleeper' operatives might be is suggested by the sheer volume of defendants—some 11,527—that Saudi courts tried between 2001 and 2011 for being members of Al Qaeda.[14]

Though headquartered elsewhere for the present, AQAP remains a serious threat to the Saudi regime, which faces additional internal security challenges: the spark of the Arab Spring has not been entirely extinguished despite the $120 billion the regime handed out to the general populace and there is an intermittent rebellion in the oil-rich east of the country, where the country's 2 million Shi'i are demanding their share of the nation's wealth and greater equality with their Sunni brethren.

The Yemen Connection

Al Qaeda thrives in a failed-state environment, especially one where the security apparatus has several calls on its attention. The organisation has established safe havens for seasons in Iraq, Afghanistan and Pakistan—countries which have consistently featured in the 'top ten Failed States Index' produced by US research institution Fund for Peace since 2005. Somalia—another hotbed of Al Qaeda–linked Islamist militancy as we shall see below—has topped the index since 2008 while Yemen has been steadily creeping up the ranks from twenty-fourth in 2007 to thirteenth in 2011.

Even before the Arab Spring uprising, which added to the security burden, President Saleh's regime had no control over around 60 percent of the country, with different areas being run by tribal leaders, rebels, separatists or *jihadis*. Historical factors have enabled Al Qaeda to thrive. Yemenis who migrated to Saudi Arabia for work during the 1970s oil boom were exposed to the country's radical Wahabbi form of Islam. In the 1980s, Yemeni fighters formed the second largest group (after the Saudis) within the estimated 25,000 Afghan-Arab *mujahideen* fighting the Soviet army in Afghanistan. It is worth recalling that Yemeni *mujahideen* were treated as returning heroes when that war was won—as were the Saudis, including Osama bin Laden.

President Saleh put the returning *mujahideen* to good use in the service of the regime: during the civil war in 1994 he enlisted their help against the southern secessionists and placed Islamists in positions of power in defeated southern provinces where they established a stronghold. One such *mujahideen* leader, Khaled Abdul Nabi Abdul Nabi, started the first Yemeni *jihadi* group in 1998—the Abyan-Aden Islamic Army which formed part of the 2009 AQAP merger. Nabi had been arrested as an 'Al Qaeda supporter' in a 2008 crackdown instigated by the US, only to be released a year later along with 175 other *jihadis*, having agreed to join the regime in its twin battles with a fresh separatist movement in the south and the Houthi rebellion in the north, ongoing since 2004.

Despite US aid to the tune of $60 million a year—intended to bring the Yemeni regime into the 'war on terror'—for many years Saleh did little to rout Al Qaeda, continuing, instead, to deploy them in his own battles. Indeed, Saleh craftily exploited the aid 'milk cow', a major source of income for the impoverished country, and would arrange for well-timed arrests of senior *jihadis* whenever the US complained of inaction.

Throughout the 2000s, Yemen served as a transit point for *jihadis* migrating from one battleground to another—from Iraq and Afghanistan to Somalia, for example—and as a training ground for inexperienced Saudi fighters who wanted to fight in Iraq. Saleh's approach was in keeping with the public mood. The Yemeni people regarded Osama bin Laden as their fellow countryman (his father being from Hadramut) and something of a hero. I recall being mobbed in Sanaa a few years ago by bin Laden fans because I had personally met 'the Sheikh'. Sermons and prayers broadcast through loudspeakers from local mosques are frequently radical and many Yemenis, when talking about the *jihadis*, refer to them as 'the believers'. The organisation has no shortage of recruits in the poorest country in the Arab world. In the south, AQAP has recently started working with the separatists who loathe the government and consider the Yemeni Army to be corrupt, brutal and an occupying force.

Increasing involvement by the US in Yemen's internal security, and high civilian casualties resulting from drone strikes—around 675 by 2012[15]—have also exacerbated anti-American feeling and boosted Al Qaeda's ranks. Yemeni journalist Abdulelah Shaea told colleagues that, following a US drone attack on an Al Qaeda base in which five civilians were killed, 'Relatives of the victims took their blood-stained clothes to Al Qaeda leaders and pledged their allegiance.' That Osama bin Laden's original Al Qaeda organisation had a large Yemeni contingent is evidenced both by word of mouth testimony and by the fact that, of the 172 prisoners still detained in Guantanamo, just over half—eighty-eight—are Yemeni.[16]

The country's geography favours clandestine guerrilla activity: it has 1,906 km of coastline on three sides (west, south and east); it shares a porous border with Saudi Arabia to the north in the aptly named 'Empty Quarter', the world's largest sand desert; the country's interior is otherwise composed of vertiginous, jagged mountains which are impenetrable to outsiders and security forces. Here are many possible hideouts and concealed training camps. The terrain offers the same strategic advantages that the *mujahideen* exploited to win two wars of attrition in Afghanistan, first with the Soviet Union (1979–89) and latterly with NATO.

The foundations for AQAP were laid years ago by Osama bin Laden. Even whilst fully occupied with the Afghan war against the Soviet Union, bin Laden had his eye on 'liberating' South Yemen from the Marxist National Liberation Front (FLN) which drove the British out of Aden in 1967, forming the People's Democratic Republic of Yemen in 1969 as a separate state and independent of its northern neighbour, the Yemen Arab Republic. According to Abu Walid al-Misri, an Egyptian journalist who had been close to bin Laden, the Al Qaeda leader foresaw 'the decisive confrontation in the land of Yemen. He wished to Islamize the cause internationally, after the Afghan example.'[17]

Osama bin Laden told me, when I met him in 1996, that if ever he had to leave 'Khorisan', as he called Afghanistan, he would like to live in the mountainous regions of Yemen where he felt he would be welcome. Tribal loyalties are very strong in the country where Mohammad bin Laden was born. In a 1998 meeting with the Taliban—who were on the brink of asking him to leave Afghanistan after the US Embassy bombings in Nairobi and Dar-es-Salaam—bin Laden expressed confidence that 'nearly all the tribes in the Arabian Peninsula are on my side . . . and every Al Qaeda member from Yemen has his tribe behind him'.[18]

He favoured Yemenis as his bodyguards, feeling that they were the most trustworthy; by 1999 nearly all the Al Qaeda leader's sixteen guards were Yemeni, chosen by the head of his security detail, Yemeni Nasser al-Bahri (also known as Abu Jandal), a former member of Al Qaeda who is now to be found driving a taxi in Sanaa.

Yemenis are known for their fighting spirit; they are born warriors who are used to carrying arms from an early age and whose culture is richly imbued with a sense of loyalty and vengeance. In an interview with *al-Quds al-Arabi*, al-Bahri recalled how Osama bin Laden handed him a special gun and two bullets, telling him: 'You must use them to kill me if ever I am surrounded by the enemy . . . I will never be taken alive by the Americans. I want to die a martyr with two bullets in my head.' As the whole world now knows, the Al Qaeda leader's death in Abbottabad was (reportedly) at the hands of his enemies after all.

Osama bin Laden started a deliberate push to increase Al Qaeda's foothold in Yemen around 2000, with a view to migrating there and establishing new headquarters. Plans for 9/11 were already under way by then and the Al Qaeda leadership was well aware that retribution was likely to be swift and devastating—they would almost certainly be bombed out of Afghanistan.

Bin Laden dispatched several envoys, including al-Bahri, to Yemen in 2000 to scout the terrain and to 'mobilise the tribes in favour of Al Qaeda'. He instructed al-Bahri to focus on those tribes that were not already sympathetic to Al Qaeda, in particular those of the eastern Shabwa province. Coincidentally or not, Shabwa is home to the Awlaq tribe from which AQAP's celebrated Anwar al-Awlaki hailed. Consisting of desert surrounded by mountains, Shabwa's geography is ideal Al Qaeda territory and has now become an Al Qaeda stronghold.

Al-Bahri was also instructed to win over Yemen's Muslim clergy. Several, like Sheikh Abdel-Majid al-Zindani (who founded and runs Sanaa's Iman

University), had been bin Laden's fellow travellers in Afghanistan. This connection was to prove useful to the organisation when Anwar al-Awlaki returned to Yemen from the US some time later, at Sheikh al-Zindani's invitation, and took up a teaching post at the university. Another sympathetic cleric al-Bahri contacted—Abu al-Battar, from the Ibb mosque—had recently been to visit bin Laden in Kandahar. Al-Bahri recalls how they asked the sheikhs and imams to voice their support for Al Qaeda during their sermons and that they obliged.[19]

To further enmesh the organisation with the fabric of Yemeni society, and in particular its tribal system, a strategic marriage was arranged for the middle-aged Al Qaeda leader by his close associate in Yemen, preacher Sheikh Rashad Mohamed Saeed Ismail, also known as Abu al-Fida. He chose a young Yemeni woman from Taez—Amal al-Sadah—to be bin Laden's fifth wife. Taez is Yemen's second largest city and, by marrying Amal, bin Laden secured the protection of her tribe for Al Qaeda members migrating to Yemen. Strategic marriages with Yemeni women to widen the network of Al Qaeda's tribal alliances were also arranged for other fighters, including al-Bahri; foreign *jihadis* in Yemen are urged to marry into local tribes for the same reason today.

Interestingly, the 2011 uprising against President Saleh originated in Taez and the region's tribes have been heavily involved in the attempt to oust him. The head of the region's tribal council, Sheikh Hammoud al-Mikhalfi, has committed his men to fighting with the rebels and he has also become a leader of the Islamist Islah party. In this way the *jihadis* might indirectly (or even directly) engage in the post-Saleh political process.

While the events of 9/11 may have alienated local support for Al Qaeda in most countries, they were widely celebrated in Yemen. Al-Bahri was in jail in Sanaa at the time and first learnt of the attacks on New York and Washington when he 'heard the Imam of a neighbouring mosque celebrating the fact that the Americans had been "struck"'.[20]

Al Qaeda had been active in Yemen long before the 2009 formation of AQAP and had carried out several major attacks there, the first as early as 1992 when a cell was dispatched to bomb the Golden Mohur hotel in Aden, where US troops were transiting on their way to Somalia.

In October 2000, suicide bombers in a small skiff attacked the huge US destroyer, USS *Cole*, moored off Aden, killing seventeen US sailors and blowing a massive crater in her hull. This David and Goliath victory delighted bin Laden and inspired the following verses from his pen:

A destroyer—even the brave fear her might
She inspires awe in the harbour and the open sea
She ploughs through the waves
Flanked by Arrogance, Haughtiness and Delusions of Power
To her doom she moves slowly
A dinghy awaits her, riding the waves[21]

Twenty-four hours later, a bomb was thrown over the wall of the British Embassy in Sanaa—nobody was hurt but Al Qaeda had declared war, not only on US but on European interests in the Arabian Peninsula too.

In October 2002, a small Al Qaeda boat laden with explosives attacked again, this time decommissioning a French oil tanker, the *Limburg*, and killing one crew member. After the attack, Al Qaeda issued a statement warning that 'this was not an incidental strike at a passing tanker, but an attack on international oil-carrying lines'.

The official franchise 'Al Qaeda in Yemen' (AQY) was founded after a daring 2006 Sanaa jail break in which twenty-three hard-liners escaped. These included the new group's emir Nasir al-Wahaishi—who had been inseparable from bin Laden in Kandahar where he served as his personal assistant for many years—and military commander Qasim al-Raymi.

AQAP Comes to Yemen

As hundreds of Saudi *jihadis* migrated over the border fleeing the crackdown, the two national groups and several smaller organisations decided to merge in January 2009. The leader would be al-Wahaishi who announced, 'We are uniting our efforts to cleanse the Arabian Peninsula from the occupiers' profanity and their treacherous agents, and then march towards our brothers in Gaza and Palestine.'

It is estimated that around 50 percent of the new organisation are

Saudi nationals[22] and funding continues to flow from Saudi and other Gulf-based 'businessmen who believe in *jihad*', as well as the members themselves and the tribes who are hosting them.[23] The group's new leaders, like its membership, were a mix of Saudi and Yemeni nationals. Soon they would be joined by native Yemenis returning from abroad, including the infamous Anwar al-Awlaki who would be killed by a drone strike in 2011.

In an interview with *Inspire* (issue 2, autumn 2010), the vice emir of AQAP, Abu Sufyan, described the foundation of AQAP: 'the base of the organisation and its leadership need to be in a protected place . . . this is why we chose Yemen. We do not accept these man-made borders between our countries and we consider the Arabian Peninsula to be one country. Our leader Abu Basir [al-Wahaishi], may Allah protect him, is approved by the general leadership of al Qa'ida in the land of Khurasan. Our goal is the establishment of an Islamic state.'

In common with all AQAM groups nowadays, AQAP is relatively autonomous and has built an organisation that can withstand the loss of its leaders. In 2009 AQAM consolidated its arrival in Yemen by taking control of Jaar province, a move that caused a ground shift in the *jihadis*' relationship with the Saleh regime. Hitherto, Saleh had had an unspoken agreement with the local Al Qaeda branch whereby his security forces allowed them breathing room in exchange for support in containing the southern secessionists and the Shi'i Houthis in the north. There were even reports that some members of Al Qaeda enjoyed 'close relationships with decision makers and people close to the President and his family'.[24] Now, however, AQAP presented itself as an additional challenge to the regime's security.

AQAP Leaders

The leadership of AQAP is unique among the franchises in that much of the 'top brass' has been close to bin Laden and al-Zawahiri for decades, intimately involved in the development of Al Qaeda and in plotting its most devastating attacks, including 9/11. Most commentators attribute the deadly 'success' of the group to the provenance of its leaders and the experience they are able to pass down to the younger generation.

Nasir al-Wahaishi—Emir

Abu Basir Nasir Abdel Karim al-Wahaishi was the emir of AQY from 2007 and became the leader of the new umbrella, AQAP, when it was founded in January 2009. He was born in Yemen's southern Abyan province (where AQAP presently hold sway) in 1976. His long-standing friendship with fellow AQAP man Qasim al-Raymi began at the Islamic Law Institute in Sanaa where the two men studied. They decided to leave Yemen together and head for Afghanistan where they hoped to join Osama bin Laden's Al Qaeda. They both enjoyed a rapid rise through the ranks of *jihadis*, with al-Wahaishi in particular becoming close to both Osama bin Laden and Ayman al-Zawahiri. Al-Wahaishi was put in charge of the day-to-day running of Tarnak Farm, the Al Qaeda compound that housed the leaders and various 'departmental' offices in Kandahar from 1998 to 2001, and was bin Laden's Chief of Staff. According to Nasser al-Bahri, al-Wahaishi was one of the handful of men bin Laden chose to take with him when he fled to his mountain hide-out in Tora Bora when the US bombarded Tarnak Farm in retaliation for 9/11. The others were al-Zawahiri, Othman al-Ghamdi (later to be a fellow AQAP leader) and 'a handful of Saudi guards'.[25]

In a May 2009 interview with Abdulela Haidah, al-Wahaishi described how the leadership was subsequently forced to evacuate Tora Bora. 'In 2002 I left Afghanistan and went to Iran where I stayed in the areas of the Sunni community inside Iran until the *rafidah* [a derogatory term for Shi'i Muslims] arrested me. The Iranians kept me in prison for one and a half months and then turned me over to the Yemeni authorities.'[26] Al-Wahaishi was extradited to Sanaa in 2003 where he was imprisoned. In February 2006, he and twenty-two other *jihadis* managed to escape during a dramatic jailbreak and he went on the run with Qasim al-Raymi.

His leadership of the newly formed AQAP in 2009 was endorsed by Ayman al-Zawahiri in a video posted online in 2009.[27] In turn, al-Wahaishi was the first AQAM leader to publicly pledge his allegiance to al-Zawahiri as the new emir of Al Qaeda in July 2011.[28] Al-Wahaishi is one of the new generation of leaders who are even more radical than their predecessors. He has a commanding presence in the videos which are regularly posted online and is reputedly a skilled politician and eloquent speaker. Like all AQAM leaders, he understands the power of the independent, online, media. Under his leadership the group has produced several issues of an online Arabic-language magazine, *Sada al-Malahim* (Echoes of Battle), developed the infamous English-language publication *Inspire* and established its own media outlet, the Madad News Agency.

Qasim al-Raymi aka Abu Hurayrah al-Sanaani—Military Commander and AQAP Spokesman

Al-Raymi was born in 1974 in the southern province of Rayma, the oldest of twelve children. He worked for a while in a restaurant to save money for the journey to Afghanistan. He didn't tell anybody where he was going and fellow villagers remember him as being a strong-willed youth who always carried a gun and frequently argued with his grandfather, who was the head of the family. During his time in Afghanistan he became well known for his ability to recruit for Al Qaeda. His family had assumed he was dead until his name appeared in newspaper reports as one of the twenty-three who had escaped in the 2006 Sanaa jailbreak.

Fahd al-Quso—Head of Operations

Al-Quso was killed by a drone in May 2012. He was born in 1974 and was from the same tribe as the late Anwar al-Awlaki, with whom he worked closely, planning the details and logistics of attacks. He was indicted in New York for his part in the 2000 bombing of USS *Cole* in Aden—he appeared in a spring 2009 video celebrating his role as a 'local coordinator' in the attack and threatening more. He also allegedly participated in planning meetings for 9/11, based at the time in Malaysia. The so-called underpants bomber, Umar Farouq Abdulmutullab, visited him whilst he was in Yemen preparing for his failed suicide mission. In late 2011 a Yemeni journalist spent the day with him in his mountain hide-out in Shabwa province where he was being protected by the Awlaq tribe.[29]

Ibrahim Suleiman al-Rubaysh—Mufti (Religious Adviser)

Saudi al-Rubaysh was a trainer at the infamous Al Qaeda/Taliban al-Farouq camp in Afghanistan where he was arrested in 2001. Having spent five years in Guantanamo, he was transferred into the deradicalisation programme in December 2006. On his release he fled to Yemen and joined Al Qaeda in Yemen.

Othman Ahmad al-Ghamdi—Operational Commander

In his late thirties, al-Ghamdi is another former Guantanamo detainee and graduate of the Saudi deradicalisation programme. Prior to leaving for Afghanistan—where he fought with the Taliban in the civil war and subsequently joined Al Qaeda—he was a soldier in the Saudi national army.

Anwar al-Awlaki

Although al-Awlaki was killed in September 2011, he remains one of the most influential figures not only in AQAP but in Al Qaeda or AQAM as a whole. Nicknamed 'the bin Laden of the Internet', al-Awlaki has left a significant online legacy of *jihadi* writings, publications, sermons, audio and video broadcasts—much of it in English. Because his work is still accessible in cyberspace, he eerily transcends his physical death.

His sermons, many in English, were posted on web forums from the late 1990s onwards and proved extremely popular. Collections on cassettes and CD became bestsellers in Islamic shops around the world. According to his father, Dr Nasser al-Awlaki, 'Five million preaching tapes of Anwar al-Awlaki have been sold in the West alone.'[30] This level of exposure ensured that al-Awlaki became very well-known within the international *jihadi* community, even before he surfaced in Yemen among the AQAP leadership. Awlaki apparently wished to follow in the footsteps of Yusef al-Ayiri, Al Qaeda's first webmaster and an influential ideologue who wrote thirty books.

Awlaki senior, Dr Nasser al-Awlaki, moved to the US to study in 1966. Anwar was born in New Mexico, in 1971. When the family returned to Yemen in 1978 Nasser decided not to live in his tribal homelands in Shabwa because he 'didn't want to live in the socialist south'. Nasser became a member of the ruling General People's Congress in 1982 and 'worked with Saleh for many years' but later expressed his disgust at corruption among the ruling elite.[31] Following unification in 1990 the family had returned to Shabwa where their tribe, the Awlaq, live. It is significant that Anwar's great-grandfather was the leader of the Awlaqs who today number some 2 million—presumably this ensured the support of the tribe for Anwar's Al Qaeda activities.

In 1991 Anwar al-Awlaki returned to America to study at Colorado University, where he graduated in civil engineering. He spent his 1993 summer vacation in Afghanistan—an experience which, he said, increased his religious zeal—and on his return he applied for the post of imam at the Denver Islamic Society where his fluency in English and skill as an orator secured him the job. Two years later he became the imam of San Diego's al-Ribat al-Islami mosque.

Awlaki's eloquence and enthusiasm for his religion attracted a large following; among those who came to the mosque were two of the 9/11 hijackers, Nawaf al-Hazmi and Khaled al-Mihdhar. According to the 9/11 commission records, al-Awlaki and his followers helped the pair open bank accounts, find housing and get to know the area. Hazmi told friends that al-Awlaki was their 'spiritual leader'. Also in San Diego, al-Awlaki was on the board of a charity that the FBI now believe was a front for raising Al Qaeda funding. Through the charity he met Omar Abdel Rahman, who was implicated in the failed 1993 World Trade Center bombing.

Al-Awlaki's next clerical appointment was as imam at the dar al-Hijrah mosque in Falls Church, Virginia, in early 2001. Al-Hazmi followed him there and brought another 9/11 hijacker to see him—Hani Hanjour—and the Commission report says that he helped the newcomer obtain identity documents. Al-Awlaki had another connection to the 9/11 plot—German investigators who raided Ramzi Binalshibh's Hamburg flat shortly after the attacks on New York and Washington found al-Awlaki's phone number among his possessions. Binalshibh was from Hadramut in Yemen.

Al-Awlaki was very careful never to endorse violence and it is possible (though rather unlikely) that he did not know what the 9/11 team were about. Indeed, al-Awlaki was a past master of the art of dissembling—he did not admit he was a member of AQAP for years. In Virginia, he immediately condemned 9/11 and became part of the media face of 'moderate Islam'. Nevertheless, he was under FBI scrutiny and his sermons began to focus on the link between the suffering of Muslims in Iraq—where one million had died as a result of sanctions—and the *jihadi* impulse. Al-Awlaki moved to London in March 2002 and was nearly arrested on a trip to the States in the October when he was accused of putting false information on his passport.[32]

Al-Awlaki returned to Yemen in 2004 and became a lecturer at al-Imam University in Sanaa, run by the veteran Sheikh al-Zindani, who had been Osama bin Laden's spiritual adviser in Afghanistan. He was arrested by the Yemeni security services and interrogated by the FBI in 2007 about his involvement with the 9/11 hijackers. It was after this interrogation that Awlaki began openly inciting violence against the US.

By 2008 he had made an impact on Nasir al-Wahaishi, now the head of Al Qaeda in Yemen; al-Wahaishi discussed his protégé with Osama bin Laden and it was decided to appoint him 'head of external operations'. The Internet is not widely available in Yemen, so while al-Awlaki had a significant online profile, the average Yemeni had no idea who he was. The security forces were unaware of Awlaki's real interests and therefore disregarded the immense risk he was posing to both Yemeni and global security. Al-Awlaki continued to focus his efforts on developing a strong online presence, building his own and other *jihadi* websites, magazines and forums and entering into e-mail correspondence with followers, possible recruits and—as it later emerged—lone-wolf *jihadis* intent on carrying out an 'operation' against the West.

Al-Awlaki insisted for many years that he was not in Al Qaeda. It was not until the first edition of *Inspire*, which appeared in summer 2010, that he publicly announced that he was not only a member but had a leadership role in AQAP. Al-Awlaki was the mastermind of the most significant attacks and failed attacks by any AQAM group between 2009 and his death in September 2011. He had a lengthy e-mail correspondence with Nidal Malik Hasan, the US army psychiatrist who killed thirteen when he opened fire on colleagues at the Texan Fort Hood military base on 5 November 2009. Awlaki subsequently described him as 'a hero', justifying the killings with the comment that 'Nidal killed soldiers who were about to leave for Iraq and Afghanistan to kill Muslims.' He was also in e-mail contact with the so-called underpants bomber, Umar Farouq Abdulmutullab. In 2010, al-Awlaki was part of the team who devised a method for packaging bombs in printer cartridges before freighting them via UPS cargo planes, timing them to go off as the planes neared their Western, urban, destinations. A trial run out of Dubai succeeded in downing the aircraft, killing two crew, but the actual attack was, thankfully, intercepted in London. Al-Awlaki was undeniably 'extraordinarily dangerous', as US Treasury spokesman Stuart Levey described him.[33]

Ibrahim Hassan al-Asiri

Considered the 'most dangerous man in the world' by Western intelligence, the master bomb-maker was born in Saudi Arabia in 1980. His father was an officer in the Saudi Army and Ibrahim spent his youth in Riyadh, showing no signs of Islamic extremism until the US invasion of Iraq in 2003 when he was arrested trying to cross the border to join the insurgency there. Ibrahim spent nine months in jail and was under heavy surveillance within the Kingdom thereafter.

When AQAP was formed Ibrahim and his younger brother, Abdullah, moved to Yemen. It was here that Ibrahim al-Asiri honed his explosives skills, mostly using pentaerythritol tetranitrate (PETN), which is very hard to detect. Ibrahim has worked at devising bombs which are tiny but deadly—the explosives he persuaded his brother to carry in his rectum weighed just 100 g.

It is rumoured that he is currently working with *jihadi* doctors on surgically implanting small bombs inside suicide attackers, specifically to bring down civilian aircraft destined for the West. He might also place bombs inside pets being carried in the hold. A double agent handed over a bomb made by al-Asiri to forensic experts in April 2012; a more sophisticated version of the original 'underpants bomb' which Umar Farouq Abdulmutullab failed to detonate in a passenger plane over Detroit, it concealed 300 g of PETN and had two detonators (in case one failed)—one chemical and one manual.[34] It is likely that al-Asiri will be the target of a drone strike sooner or later but, as we have seen, AQAM groups always ensure that key members have at least two deputies and al-Asiri is certain to have shared his expertise and trained his successors.

Allegiances—Tribes and Society

The presence of Al Qaeda and affiliated groups is widespread throughout Yemen, largely due to tribal allegiances. Interviewed for *al-Sharq al-Awsat*, Anwar al-Awlaki claimed, 'There is support from vast areas of people here in Yemen whether it be in Abeedah or Dahm or Wailah or Hashid or Bayqal or Khawlaan, whether it be in Hadramaut or in Abyan or in Shabwa or Aden or Sana'a.'[35]

The Al Qaeda leadership realised early on that without significant tribal connections and support the organisation would never get a foot-hold inside Yemen. Indeed, loss of tribal support, or alienating the tribes, would endanger the survival of AQAP more than US drones. Osama bin Laden, as we have seen, sent envoys to Yemen as early as 2000, urging them to concentrate on winning the support of the tribes there. Dr Ayman al-Zawahiri addressed Yemen's 'noble and defiant tribes' in a February 2009 al-Sahab Media video called 'From Kabul to Mogadishu', urging them to rise up against President Saleh and 'support your brothers the *mujahideen*'. Many tribal areas in Yemen are no-go areas for government forces; meanwhile Al Qaeda's efforts to win the tribal people over include basic welfare programmes and other forms of material help to the region's most impoverished families. AQAP has developed a method for insinuating itself in the towns and villages it has taken over which avoids confrontation with the tribes. First, a small group establish a *dawa* (outreach) centre, handing out leaflets, CDs and DVDs, gathering a small indigenous group of sympathisers who then invite larger numbers of Al Qaeda men into their community and vouch for them with their elders.

As Yemeni expert on *jihadi* groups Abdul-Elah Haidar wrote: 'The state cannot overcome the tribes. Even if the tribes knew who are members of Al Qaeda they would not betray this information. Would the tribes then report their own sons who live with Al Qaeda and have been trained by them? This is impossible in tribal values.'[36]

Anwar al-Awlaki's told an interviewer that AQAP was helped and supported by his tribe, the Awlaq, 'and also others in Yemen . . . because the people hate the Americans'; in the same interview he recounted how 'tribal pressures' had secured his release from jail in Sanaa. The current Sultan of the Awlaq, Fareed bin Babakeer, openly admitted to *Guardian* journalist Ghaith Abdul-Ahad in 2010 that Anwar al-Awlaki's compound was in his village, Saeed.[37]

Yemen's tribal system, like that of several Middle Eastern countries, predates Islam. The tribal structure is complicated. Econometric researcher Daniel Egel discovered that, in Yemen, 'The average number of tribes per sub-district, which have an average 6,500 residents, is nearly five. And the average district, which has around 50,000 residents, has nearly thirty-five tribes and almost ten tribal confederations.'[38]

The tribes are exceptionally strong, well armed and independent, with their own administrative, judicial and military systems. As with the Pashtun tribes of Afghanistan, the code of honour and the protection of guests is an unerring precept. Nevertheless, inter-tribal relationships can be changeable and tend to be based on the pragmatic concerns of the moment. As a result, alliances are volatile. During his many years in office, Saleh purchased the temporary loyalty and cooperation of some tribes with 'salaries' (often for a non-existent post), luxury vehicles and positions of power in central government. Saleh was wily when it came to manipulating tribal support; he could remember important, or potentially useful, individuals' tribal origins as well as the constantly changing network of inter-tribal allegiances. He tried the same method with members of Al Qaeda but it backfired since the *jihadis* mostly kept the money and used it to buy weapons to further their own power base.

The two main tribal confederations in the north of Yemen, the Bakil and Hashid, are followers of Zaydi Islam, which is a Shi'i sect. Nevertheless, AQAP has established a foothold in Jawf, where it is engaged in battle with the Houthi rebels.

In the south and centre of the country, AQAP has several major strongholds which are largely supported and defended by Sunni tribes. These include Mareb (where leader al-Wahaishi is believed to spend most of his time) and Abyan, where the *jihadis* declared an Islamic Emirate with Zinjibar as its capital in May 2011. Local reports suggest that tribal militias, including the separatist Hirak militia, joined forces with AQAP to consolidate its hold on Abyan. Saudi leaders Qasim al-Raymi and Said al-Shihri are based in Zinjibar and AQAP run a training camp outside the capital which is home to around a thousand recruits—rumoured to include Australians and Germans—with their women and children living in a self-sufficient community.[39]

In Shabwa, tribal leader Mullah Zabara is the late Fahd al-Qusu's cousin. In Hadramut, Mohammad bin Laden's home town, eighty Al Qaeda prisoners were able to escape from al-Mukla jail on 17 July 2011, which local people say would not have been possible without the collaboration of staff sympathetic to Al Qaeda.

President Saleh's close relative, General Mohsen Saleh, defected during the Arab Spring uprising and joined forces with the Abyan tribes and AQAP. Mohsen has historically close ties with Al Qaeda, having recruited more than 5,000 Afghan veterans back in the early 2000s to fight with the regime in the civil war against the south; he later recruited *jihadis* for the war against the Houthis too.

Not all tribes are sympathetic to AQAP by any means, and one gets the impression from talking to people on the ground that in some cases—particularly in the early days, before they developed the *dawa* approach outlined above—Al Qaeda imposed its presence through military force rather than being invited in. In *Inspire*, 4, there is a vivid account of a chaotic AQAP encounter with rival tribesmen in Abyan by one 'Abu Zakaria al-Eritri':

> Within a few minutes, the news reached everyone in the town that the *mujahideen* had succeeded in killing al-Baham. Immediately after, people from his tribe and the tribe of the Governor of Abyan, Ali Maysari, went to the house of one of the brothers and told him to come out and give himself up. We sent a message to the brother to never give up and sent a group of brothers in his defence. When they reached the scene, they couldn't find a way to enter the neighbourhood because of the surrounding tribes who wanted to kill him were in every street corner. Then the brothers decided to sacrifice themselves for their brother's sake. The brothers started shooting bullets in the air as a warning to the tribes. None of them resisted and proceeded to comply with the *mujahideen*'s demand. Most of the tribal members left the neighbourhood and the *mujahideen* were able to take the brother away.

There have been several abortive attempts by tribal elders in Abyan to join forces and expel the *jihadis* from their midst. Two suicide bombers attacked one such gathering in August 2011, killing eleven.[40] The US hoped to repeat the success of its Iraqi 'Awakening' campaign in Yemen but attempts to pay the tribesmen off have not, as yet, succeeded.

Conclusion: The Future of AQAP

In 2012 AQAP, by then also going by the name of Ansar al-Shari'a, celebrated its 'third anniversary' by posting a round-up of what they consider to be their achievements on *jihadi* forums; the following are quotes from that posting, with my comments in square brackets:

1. *Successfully fighting three wars simultaneously*: the *Mujahideen* of AQAP have not only been engaged in a fierce battle with the Apostate forces [i.e., Saleh's regime], but have also been directly attacking the Crusading Americans AND the Rejectionist polytheists in the north [i.e. the Houthis].

2. *Exposing* the so-called Zaidi Houthis as being the lowly agents of the Iranians... the brothers in AQAP have launched many devastating attacks against the criminal Rejectionists, and even managed to eliminate the chief criminal Badr ud-Deen al-Houthi in a martyrdom-seeking operation. [A deliberate campaign to escalate sectarian tensions and bring Iran into the equation is clearly a worrying development.]

3. *Dislodging Ali Abdullah Saleh from power*: make no mistake—Saleh being forced from office has nothing to do with popular protests, or Western concern about the regime killing civilians... the Americans only insisted that Saleh be forced from office when it became clear that he could not control the country, as village after village fell to the *Mujahideen* of AQAP.

4. *Inflicting massive damage to the Crusader [i.e., Western] economies*: the operation of Umar Farouk Abdulmutallab was said to have cost the American economy $30 billion; it is likely that the operation involving the cargo planes [i.e. the UPS ink cartridge bombs] cost as much, if not even more.

   And while America was the first to act to ramp up their security measures in response to these operations, let us not forget that the other Crusading nations have also followed suit—for they know that as they are also at war with Islam they could just as easily be the next target of the *Mujahideen*.

The brothers have shown that with only a small investment, catastrophic damage can be done to the Crusader economies, when the targets are carefully selected. ['Economic *jihad*' has been a consistent strategy within AQAM for many years now, and was one of Makkawi's seven stages as discussed in the Introduction above.]

5. *The Mujahideen* of AQAP have captured vast swathes of land in southern Yemen, and have set about establishing the Shariah in the lands they have captured, enjoining what is good and forbidding what is evil. The brothers have been careful not to over-extend themselves, and have focused on consolidating their control of one area before moving on to the next area.

Despite the chaos and near failed-state environment in which they are operating in Yemen, AQAP have adhered to a well-planned strategy. In 2010 the group announced 'operation haemorrhage', a relentless series of relatively small-scale attacks designed to damage internal security and harm the US economy. These attacks cost little to carry out but billions to guard against. By 1 January 2011, AQAP had claimed responsibility for forty-nine attacks since June, most of them targeting security headquarters, checkpoints and military patrols (particularly round the Marib oilfields).

When the Arab Spring protests erupted, AQAP acted quickly to exploit the security vacuum with attacks on domestic military and security targets reported every day. By working with the protestors, AQAP turned the situation to their advantage.

The inauguration of President Saleh's successor Mansour Hardi on 25 February 2012 was greeted by a suicide attack at a presidential palace in Mukalla which killed twenty-six security personnel. In March 2012 AQAP carried out its most bloody attack to date when it attacked the Yemeni Army base in al-Koud, killing at least 185 officers and soldiers; in May 2012 a similar attack saw a suicide bomber blow himself up in the middle of a Yemeni Army battalion, killing at least ninety-eight soldiers and maiming hundreds. The group also made away with a significant quantity of Yemeni Army military hardware including a tank and anti-aircraft missiles. Yemeni journalist Hakim al-Masmari told Al Jazeera that such an operation would be impossible without the collusion of government officials, hinting at a new alliance between disaffected elements of the Yemeni military and Al Qaeda. The absence of a satisfactory outcome following the Arab Spring protests in Yemen may lead to increased support for AQAP from unexpected quarters.

Throughout the Arab Spring unrest, AQAP continued to expand its territory, emulating the Taliban in weakening the country's security apparatus by constant attacks and seizing areas of control little by little. It is notable that AQAP have often withdrawn from a town or village because they do not feel they can secure it for the long term.

I believe that AQAP intend to create a corridor of contiguous zones under their control through Yemen, from the south to the Saudi border. This would facilitate the passage of fighters both inside Yemen and those arriving in the southern ports—from Somalia for example. There is already evidence of a growing alliance between al-Shabaab in Somalia and AQAP. Aggravated by the arrival of the US into the fray in Yemen, al-Shabaab leader Mukhta Robow abu Mansour declared as long ago as January 2010: 'We tell our Muslim brothers in Yemen that we will cross the water between us and reach your place to assist you.'[41] Under such circumstances the *jihadis* would represent a renewed threat to Saudi Arabia where unknown numbers of sleeper operatives may be biding their time. In May 2012 Ayman al-Zawahiri began inciting unrest in Saudi Arabia, perhaps in preparation for a new AQAP infiltration northwards.

Thousands of people have fled towns and villages overrun by AQAP, although AQAP has made discernible efforts to reach accommodation with local tribes and community leaders. Fawaz al-Hadari, a Yemeni journalist, described the following incident that took place in January 2012. A group of AQAP fighters, led by Anwar al-Awlaki's brother-in-law, Tarek al-Dahab, took over Rada, a town 130 km south of Sanaa. The group announced that they had come to 'reform the situation by implementing God's law and removing corruption and the corrupt officials'. As thousands of residents fled in panic, local tribes set up a committee to negotiate with AQAP and the two sides spent three days in talks. The committee shared AQAP's desire to weed out corruption and it was decided to establish an administrative committee of Rada residents to replace local officials. AQAP wanted the release of fifteen of their number who were held in the local jail and when this was conceded they agreed to withdraw from the town and returned to al-Manara, al-Dahab's home village. Amid noisy celebrations in the newly liberated town the chant went up, 'Affesh, it's no use! The people of Rada are united.' (Affesh was President Saleh's original family name but he never used it because it means 'thug' in the local dialect.[42]) The political pragmatism of AQAP in this strange narrative was linked, in the public consciousness, with the Arab Spring.

In February 2012, following a failed military offensive to dislodge AQAP from Abyan, an Al Jazeera television report showed Al Qaeda flags and banners flying all over Zinjibar.[43] An Ansar al-Shari'a spokesman claimed that people were welcoming their imposition of Sharia as a welcome antidote to the chaos engulfing the rest of the country in the wake of President Saleh's departure. According to another report, AQAP was working with newly established 'national committees' and intended to hand over local administration to them in due course.[44]

Dissatisfied with the outcome of their revolution, many in Yemen may see AQAP as a vanguard in the continuing struggle; having displayed some political pragmatism in the course of the revolution and in their dealings with the people, it is possible that in the next decade AQAP may enter the debate about improved governance solutions rather than seeking influence through violence.

AQAP has political connectivity through individuals who are sympathetic to Al Qaeda and are also leading members of the Islamist political party, Islah. In addition, Dr Nasser Awlaki (father of Anwar al-Awlaki) is member of the National Dialogue Committee, the most organised political opposition group. He had served under Saleh as Minister of Agriculture for several years.[45]

In the short term, however, it is difficult to see how Yemen can avoid disintegration. With so many opposing factions—the tribes, the sectarians, the separatists, the *jihadis*, the protestors—any prospect of peaceful nation-building seems remote and many commentators fear that Yemen is another Somalia in the making. Another failed state.

3

Somalia's al-Shabaab

If Afghanistan was too far away, or if the way to Iraq was closed to you, if the doors to Algeria were locked . . . here is Somalia, just beginning . . . so hurry with the lightness of a bird without making excuses or procrastinating.
Abu Yahya al-Libi, 14 September 2011

It's only a matter of time before we see terrorism on our streets inspired by those who are today fighting alongside al-Shabaab.
Jonathan Evans, Head of MI5, March 2010

The Horn of Africa countries are Somalia, Sudan, Ethiopia, Eritrea and Djibouti. The region has long been steeped in violent Islamism; indeed one could argue that the 1998 Global Islamic Front manifesto, which effectively launched the notion of global *jihad*, actually had its roots seven years earlier, in Sudan.

In 1991, the leader of Sudan's ruling National Islamic Front, Hassan al-Turabi, organised the first Popular Arab and Islamic Conference. I attended this event which brought around 500 people from forty-five countries together under the roof of a Chinese-built conference centre in Khartoum. This was like no other conference I had ever attended since most of the delegates were infamous 'terrorists' including Abu

Nidal, Carlos 'the Jackal', PLO leader Yasser Arafat, Afghan *mujahideen* leader Gulbedin Hekmatayar, Palestine *jihad* leader Fatih al-Shakaki, Hizbullah's military chief of staff Imad Mughniyah (who would be assassinated by the Israelis) and, key to our subject, Osama bin Laden and Ayman al-Zawahiri. It was strange to see these men (all unarmed) filing out of the main hall for tea breaks, or lining up to collect their lunch, wondering who they should sit next to.

The British delegation was led by Yusuf Islam (formerly known as Cat Stevens)—I am not convinced that he was really aware of who his fellow conference-goers were but he was very pleasant and diplomatic. On the first evening, Sudanese President Bashir gave a banquet for all the leaders of the various movements which I also attended. It was here that Yusuf Islam sang for the first time since he abandoned his career as a successful pop star, having converted to Islam. He sang unaccompanied; I can still hear that beautiful voice singing *tala'a al badar alina* (the full moon rises over us) about the Prophet Muhammad coming to mankind with the message of Allah. Many of the world's most hardened terrorists wiped away tears.

The aim of the conference was to form a confederation of Arab nationalist groups and radical Islamist groups to counteract the growing US military presence in the Gulf. At that time, bin Laden and al-Zawahiri did not display any sectarian prejudices and were happy to engage Hizbullah officials in conversation. (Indeed, when I interviewed bin Laden in 2006, several of his closest aides were Zadi Shi'i from Yemen.)

There was another gathering the following year but the confederation did not survive due to the emerging rift between Turabi and Bashir and pressure from the US and Saudis to abandon this—potentially highly dangerous—project. Nevertheless, contacts were made at these conferences, and alliances formed, that would later bring many militant groups under the Global Islamic Front (Al Qaeda) umbrella or into an affiliation with Al Qaeda.

When Afghanistan descended into civil war in 1992 many disenchanted *mujahideen* who were unable to return home for security reasons chose to migrate to Sudan where Osama bin Laden had been based since 1991 at Turabi's invitation.[1] Bin Laden dreamt of an international Islamic Army and it was in Sudan that he formed the Islamic army *shura* to coordinate and develop links with organisations around the globe. The idea of a network of collaborative franchises and alliances—which AQAM would later become—has its roots at this time.

Ethiopia and Eritrea have both produced various Islamist groups and used them as proxies in their bitter rivalry with each other. The Eritrean Islamic Jihad Movement (EIJM), was a major force in the 1990s as was the Ethiopian branch of al-Ittihad al-Islami which had a stronghold in the Ogaden region, largely populated by Somalis. Eritrea has armed and funded Islamist groups in Somalia; Ethiopia, on the other hand, backed by the US, set itself against the Islamists in Somalia and invaded the country to oust the Islamic Courts Union (ICU) in 2006. Al-Ittihad al-Islami later rebranded itself the Raskamboni Brigades which in turn came under the newly formed, Al Qaeda–affiliated, al-Shabaab umbrella in February 2010.

In this chapter we are going to focus on Somalia, where al-Shabaab is in control of significant zones in the centre and south of the country. On 8 February 2012 a video featuring al-Shabaab emir Ahmed Adbi Godane (aka Mukhtar Abu al-Zubeyr) and Ayman al-Zawahiri announced the 'glad tidings' that '*al-Harakat al-Shabaab al-Mujahideen* has officially joined Al Qaeda'.[2]

Situated opposite Yemen across the Gulf of Aden, the security situation in Somalia is of great concern to international shipping and the oil-producing nations of the Gulf. The two countries, both partly under the control of AQAM groups, effectively control traffic to and from the Bab al-Mandeb—a narrow (30 km) strait between the Red Sea and the Gulf of Aden through which more than 3.3 million barrels of oil are shipped every day en route, via the Suez Canal, to Europe and the US.

In 2008 independent analysts produced a report for Lehman Brothers identifying five 'Global Oil Choke Points':[3] the two that caused them most concern were the Suez Canal and the Bab al-Mendeb. The 190-km-long Suez Canal, which connects the Red Sea with the Mediterranean, is in turn located to the west of the Sinai where another AQAM group, Al Qaeda in the Sinai Peninsula (AQSP), has also emerged. At its narrowest point, the Suez Canal is just 300 m across and can be easily blockaded—as it was in 1967 during the Six-Day War. Super-tankers are unable to transit the Suez Canal, and since 1977 a 320-km oil pipeline called Sumed has provided an alternative method of channelling oil to shipping in the Mediterranean.

Moving more than a million barrels per day, Sumed too is vulnerable to attack. Somalia is also a global crossroads for air traffic, with ninety flights a day crossing its airspace. Another security threat issuing from Somali are the pirates who terrorise the region's waters. As we will see, there is growing cooperation between the pirates and al-Shabaab.

Because al-Shabaab attracts large numbers of foreign, including Western, *jihadis* to its ranks, it also poses a certain level of security risk to Western homelands. Battle-hardened and experienced fighters bearing Western passports might return home to establish sleeper cells or be sent back to conduct an attack.

Western security experts are increasingly concerned about the 'Africanisation' of AQAM, with groups active in Algeria, Libya, Mali, Mauritania, Niger, Kenya and Nigeria. The US has long sought to establish a military presence in Africa, with little success due to resistance from local governments. Djibouti, Somalia's tiny northern neighbour, houses America's only permanent military base in Africa; the Combined Joint Task Force-Horn of Africa (CJTF-HOA) at Camp Lemonnier has more than 2,000 military staff in residence and is the base from which the CIA launches drone strikes inside Yemen and Somalia. The US has some facilities in Kenya—from where the most recent counter-terrorism efforts inside Somalia have originated.

A Failed State

Somalia has topped the Failed States Index since 2007. The index is compiled by NGO Fund for Peace based on nations' security, stability, human rights record and other indicators.[4] Although Somalia's present woes began in 1991 when the Marxist dictator, Barre, was overthrown, we will need a wider perspective to properly understand why Somalia is so uniquely out of control and why the Islamists have been able to gain so much power.

The Somali people number around 16 million and inhabit most of the Horn of Africa. Apart from Somalia they also live in the Ogaden region of southeastern Ethiopia, constituting the majority population at 4.6 million, and form a sizeable part of the populations of southern Djibouti (350,000) and the northeastern province of Kenya (900,000). There are also an estimated 1 million Somalis living in Yemen and approximately 2 million in the diaspora.

Due to the clannish nature of their society, the Somali people have historically resisted being united under any political system and national governments are usually rapidly overthrown. There are six clan 'umbrellas' under which sixty-six major sub-clans are grouped. The 'umbrella' clans are the Dir, Isaaq, Darod, Hawiye, Digil and Rahanweyn. The latter has thirty-three clans in a loose alliance.

In the 1880s both Britain and Italy established protectorates, dividing the territory along the lines of clan alliances and groupings, while the French took what is now Djibouti. On independence in 1960 the protectorates merged to become the United Republic of Somalia under President Aden Abdullah Osman Daar.

Marxist dictator Mohamed Siad Barre staged a coup in 1969, introducing what he termed 'Scientific Socialism'. Long-standing tensions between Somalia and Ethiopia erupted in 1977 and continued in 1978, with the Soviet Union arming both sides. Somali dissidents living in London formed the Somali National Movement (SNM) in 1981, probably encouraged by Britain and the US, who wanted to remove Soviet influence in the strategically sensitive Horn of Africa. Northern Somalia rose up against Barre in 1981 and in 1982 the SNM, operating out of Ethiopia, also attacked the government forces. The civil war cost the lives of 40,000 people and a further 400,000 fled to Ethiopia.

Barre clung onto power until 1991, having constructed his government exclusively with members of his own Marehan tribe. This alienated and enraged the other tribes who were effectively excluded from power; his rivals finally overran his palace in the capital, Mogadishu, and he was forced to flee for his life.

At this point, Somalia became even more fragmented with up to thirty warring sides all struggling for power. The northeast part of the country declared itself 'The Independent Republic of Somaliland'. Neighbouring Puntland also became an autonomous state in 1998.

US President George H. W. Bush had spotted an opportunity in the chaos—the US was looking for a foothold in the region—and sent aid (for famine victims and those fleeing conflict) in 1992, swiftly followed by troops on the ground participating in 'Operation Restore Hope'. The move was bitterly resented by certain warlords and in particular

Mohamad Farrah Aideed, the leader of the Habr Gedir clan and self-proclaimed next president of Somalia.

On 3 October 1993 nineteen US aircraft, twelve armoured vehicles and 160 men headed for Mogadishu from their base outside the capital, intending to capture Habr Gedir's leaders. The attack ended with the downing of two Black Hawk helicopters by warriors using simple RPG launchers—these men included Al Qaeda operatives, according to bin Laden himself when I interviewed him in 1996.

Eighteen US troops were killed and more than seventy wounded but the operation cost as many as 700 Somali lives when the surviving US soldiers blasted randomly into the surrounding crowd. When the crowd got hold of the dead body of a US marine, they dragged it through the streets in a gruesome display of jubilation broadcast on television screens the world over. When the US withdrew five months later, Aideed and Al Qaeda claimed this was their victory.

UN peacekeepers remained but they too were withdrawn in March 1995, at which point Aideed took control of Mogadishu and declared himself president. In August 1996 Aideed was gunned down by militia-men under the command of his own brother. Aideed's son, Hussein, was hailed as the new leader but bitter in-fighting continued; the country was further blighted by natural disasters including widespread floods in 1997 and 2000.

In 2000 the first government in over a decade of civil conflict was sworn in under a new president, Abdiqasim Salad Hassan; he himself was deposed in 2006 by a coalition of hard-line Islamist groups—the Islamic Courts Union (ICU).

Ethiopian troops, backed by the US, invaded, dislodged the ICU and installed the Transitional Federal Government (TFG) under Abdullah Yusuf. Some of the more moderate ICU members formed another group, the Alliance for the Re-Liberation of Somalia (ARS)—which would later align itself with the TFG—while others went into temporary exile. The ICU's militant youth wing, al-Shabaab, now picked up the baton and started to fight the Ethiopian troops. The Ethiopian invasion had an unanticipated effect, as revealed by leaked 2008 US Embassy cables from Mogadishu: 'the unpopular Ethiopian "occupation" of Somalia is causing Somalis to hail al-Shabaab gunmen as heroes and freedom fighters.'[5]

In January 2009 Ethiopia withdrew its troops and a civil war erupted between Islamist groups polarised around al-Shabaab, and former ICU chief Sheikh Sharif Sheikh Ahmed's new ally, the TFG.

Sheikh Sharif Sheikh Ahmed (who is also the spiritual leader of Sufi sect the Idrisiyah) became President of Somalia and is the present incumbent, but al-Shabaab control a significant portion of the country—much of the centre and nearly all of the south and southwestern parts. There is some level of cooperation between al-Shabaab and the northeastern autonomous region of Somaliland which includes the coastal area opposite Yemen and borders Djibouti.[6] Various reports have linked the President of Somaliland, Ahmed Silanyo, and the Interior Minister, Dr Mohama Abdi Gaboose, with the *jihadis*.

Neighbouring Puntland, also devolved, accuses Somaliland of trying to undermine its security by supporting militant elements in Puntland, including the militia belonging to Mohamad Saeed Atom which joined the al-Shabaab–Al Qaeda nexus in December 2010.

The Al Qaeda Connection

As we have already seen, Al Qaeda's first military involvement in Somalia took place as long ago as 1993 when some of the organisation's fighters took part in the so-called Black Hawk Down attack. Between 1996 and 1998, bin Laden bodyguard Nasser al-Bahri was sent on a series of fact-finding missions to Somalia; the Afghan-based Al Qaeda leadership were thinking of relocating to either Yemen or Somalia and had received a serious invitation to install themselves in the latter from tribal warlord Sheikh Hassin Harsi. In 1998, following the bombings of two US Embassies in Nairobi and Dar-es-Salaam, an element within the Taliban was agitating for Al Qaeda to be expelled, fearing American retribution. According to al-Bahri's recollections, Osama bin Laden intended to move his entire organisation to a large Al Qaeda base he was planning in southern Somalia at Kambouni, near Kismayo on the Kenyan border. The base would comprise a landing strip and also make use of a local harbour. Osama bin Laden had grand plans, intending to join forces with sympathetic clan leaders and 'take over the country' which would then be used as a base for wider *jihad* in Africa and Arabia.[7]

Al-Bahri was not impressed by the Somali *jihadis* he met in 1998, describing them as 'amateurish' and obsessed with money. Al-Ittihad al-Islami were 'a mixture of Islamists and tribal leaders, each giving the other legitimacy and protection, but uniquely for financial benefit'. They asked al-Bahri for money but had a 'negative vision of Al Qaeda' and he doubted their 'commitment to fighting and establishing Sharia'.[8]

In the event, Mullah Omar's faction within the Taliban prevailed and Al Qaeda were encouraged to stay in Afghanistan. The idea was revisited in 2000, however, when plans for 9/11 were well under way. Now al-Bahri discovered that Hassin Harsi wasn't trustworthy; he had sold all the arms Al Qaeda had given him and pocketed the money.[9]

A Somali parliament in exile, the Transitional Federal Government (TFG), was formed in Kenya in 2004, but would not meet in Somalia until February 2006, when it convened in a grain shelter in the town of Baidoa. Meanwhile, as we have seen, the Islamic Courts Union (ICU) took power in June 2006, having overcome the US-backed group of secular warlords, the Alliance for the Restoration of Peace and Counter-Terrorism.

Evidence of Al Qaeda influence within the ranks of the ICU came with two 2006 suicide bombs against TFG targets in Baidoa; statements from Osama bin Laden and Ayman al-Zawahiri praised their efforts and called them the 'lions of Somalia'. Al Qaeda media outlets started posting audiotapes in the Somali language and videos featuring Arab and Somali recruits training side by side.

Thousands of *jihadis* from many countries poured into Somalia to prop up the ICU. Rich individuals and groups in the Gulf provided generous finance. When the Israelis invaded southern Lebanon in July 2006, the ICU sent around 700 specially selected fighters to support Hizbullah; only 105 returned.

This export of Somali muscle, especially against Israel, alarmed Western security agencies, as did the ICU's openly expressed expansionist ambitions for a Caliphate throughout the whole Horn of Africa. The US tapped into Ethiopia's anxieties and backed an invasion by its army, which succeeded in pushing the ICU out of its strongholds, allowing the TFG, accompanied by Ethiopian troops, to enter Mogadishu unopposed on 28 December 2006.

The UN mandated US-trained and -backed African Union Mission in Somalia (AMISOM) troops to maintain internal security and keep

President Sheikh Sharif Sheikh Ahmed (elected by parliamentary vote in January 2009) in power. Of the 17,000 AMISOM troops mandated, many countries have either fallen short of the number required or have failed to provide any troops at all. Around 10,000 soldiers, almost all from Uganda (5,210) and Burundi (4,400) are deployed in Mogadishu. In 2011 and 2012 Kenya and Ethiopia finally provided some troops for AMISOM. Kenya—which has justifiable fears of an incursion from Somalia—has set up a buffer zone in the Jubaland area in southern Somalia but lack an exit strategy, making them unable to progress any further and more vulnerable to attack.

Al-Shabaab and AQAM

Harakat al-Shabaab al-Mujahideen, more commonly known as al-Shabaab (the youth), was originally the militant youth wing of the ICU and was active in the battle against invading US-backed Ethiopian forces in 2006. When the Ethiopians prevailed in December 2006, the group broke away from the more moderate elements of the deposed ICU. Locally, al-Shabaab are known as the 'veiled men' because they wrap red scarves around their faces to hide their identities and to present an intimidating appearance.

Al Qaeda watched the group's emergence with keen interest; several members of al-Shabaab, including one of its leaders, Ahmed Adbi Godane, had fought with Al Qaeda in Afghanistan. The group formally pledged allegiance to Al Qaeda in 2007 and would officially join the organisation in February 2012. Meanwhile, Hassan Dahir Aweys, erstwhile leader of the ICU, started a rival Islamist group called Hizbul Islam.

When the Ethiopians withdrew in January 2009, the fortunes of the TFG deteriorated rapidly and al-Shabaab were able to take control of large swathes of southern and central Somalia, including most of Mogadishu. Al-Shabaab declared its intention to expand into Somali-majority areas in Ethiopia and Kenya and establish an Islamic Emirate.

In 2008 Godane explicitly threatened to attack the US, which marks a shift from local concerns to global ones, in line with Al Qaeda ideology. An Internet courtship between al-Shabaab and Al Qaeda was conducted on Islamist websites from 2006. In 2008 Al Qaeda formally acknowledged al-Shabaab as the champions of a perceived Somali ambition to become an Islamic state. On 28 February 2008, the US officially designated al-Shabaab as a terrorist organisation.

In December 2008, AQAP cleric Anwar al-Awlaki released a statement in support of al-Shabaab and highlighted the 'opportunities' for *jihadis* considering migration to Somalia: 'The university of Somalia will graduate an alumni of judges, administrators, enjoiners of good and forbidders of evil, capable and tested leaders, teachers, imams, and fighters who are hardened by the field and ready to carry on with no fear and hesitation. It will provide its graduates with the hands-on experience that the *umma* greatly needs for its next stage . . .'[10]

When Sheikh Sharif Sheikh Ahmed was elected president of the TFG in January 2009, al-Shabaab immediately declared war on the new government and TFG ministers have since been frequent targets. On 18 June 2009 a bomb in Beledweyne killed Security Minister Omar Hashi Aden and thirty-four others; on 3 December 2009 three government ministers were among twenty-five killed in the suicide bombing of Hotel Shamo in Mogadishu. The TFG and al-Shabaab have battled for control of Mogadishu since May 2009 when the latter—having joined forces with Hizbul Islam—took control of most of the capital.

In 2009 three statements by top Al Qaeda leaders praised and supported al-Shabaab's actions. Osama bin Laden devoted one of his only five statements in 2009 to al-Shabaab and placed their struggle in the context of global *jihad* by calling it a battle with the 'Crusaders'. This increased the organisation's credibility and helped its recruitment process.

In the latter part of 2009 it became obvious that al-Shabaab was aiming to become part of AQAM. In September 2009 an al-Shabaab video posted on *jihadi* sites showed the reclusive then leader, Ahmed Adbi Godane, offering to become Osama bin Laden's 'soldier'. Next, the group displayed their engagement with the global *jihadis*' central cause—Palestine. On 1 November 2009, when the Palestinians and Israelis were fighting over Jerusalem's al-Aqsa mosque, al-Shabaab announced that it had formed an 'al-Quds (Jerusalem) Brigade' which would target Israeli interests in Africa. Its leader is Abdifatah Aweys Abu Hamza.

In January 2010 a statement signed by senior rebels including Godane and Sheikh Hassan Turki, the commander of the Raskamboni militia, read: 'We have agreed to join the international *jihad* of Al Qaeda.... We have also agreed to unite al-Shabaab and the Raskamboni *mujahideen* to liberate the Eastern and Horn of Africa communities ... to revive the military strength, finances and politics of our *mujahideen* and stop the war created by the colonisers.'

Becoming part of the Al Qaeda 'brand' clearly gave al-Shabaab more credibility within the *jihadi* community. In order to establish their international credentials, the group launched their first attack outside Somalia—on 11 July 2010, suicide bombers struck in the Ugandan capital, Kampala, simultaneously targeting a rugby club and an Ethiopian restaurant while people were watching the World Cup final. These horrific attacks, which killed seventy-four and injured seventy, were linked to the deployment of AMISOM troops (mostly composed of Ugandan and Burundian soldiers). Al-Shabaab spokesman, Ali Mohamud Rage, claimed responsibility and added, 'We are sending a message to Uganda and Burundi ... if they do not withdraw their AMISOM troops from Somalia, there will be more blasts and it will happen in Bujumbura [the Burundi capital] too.'[11]

Al-Shabaab redoubled attacks inside Somalia, killing more than 300 in Mogadishu in August 2010. In December 2010, Aweys's Hizbul Islam officially merged with al-Shabaab and by May 2011 it was estimated the umbrella group had nearly 15,000 fighters.[12]

Al-Shabaab's military tactics are similar to those employed by AQAP. The group has carried out some large 'spectaculars', usually against international or government targets: for example the October 2008 coordinated suicide bombings which rocked the UN compound and Ethiopian Embassy in Mogadishu and the presidential palace in Hargesis, and the October 2011 suicide bombing of the Ministry of Education in Mogadishu which killed nearly a hundred people.

Since Ethiopian troops re-entered Somalia in 2012, al-Shabaab has also engaged in 'operation haemorrhage'–style, persistent, wearing, smaller attacks which occur almost every day; these include car bombs, grenades, armed raids and, more recently, IEDs (suggesting Al Qaeda training). In Mogadishu and larger towns the group also engages in street fighting with guns, RPGs and mortars. In February 2011, in keeping with other groups in the AQAM stable, al-Shabaab launched its own press office, production house and television news channel al-Kata'ib (Brigades) which issues daily reports on its operations.

Al-Shabaab has become infamous for its hostile stance towards Western NGOs and aid agencies. In 2011 it set up its own 'Office for Supervising the Affairs of Foreign Agencies' (OSAFA) and banned the UN, the WHO, UNICEF and eleven NGOs, saying the groups were misappropriating funds, using field data for 'dubious' purposes and 'working with international bodies to foster secularism, immorality and the degrading values of democracy in an Islamic country', among other 'crimes'.[13] In January 2012 it banned the newly opened UN Political Office for Somalia based in Mogadishu, which a press release described as 'an impediment to the attainment of lasting peace and stability in the country', claiming that it 'aimed to foment dissent and ill-will among the local tribes, thereby keeping the Somali state in a perpetual cycle of conflict and disharmony'. Later the same month, OSAFA banned the Red Cross from helping famine victims, because '70 percent of the food stored for distribution was deemed unfit for human consumption'—something the Red Cross, incidentally, confirmed, the grain having been kept in storage too long due to distribution problems.

The explanation for this conduct may have some connection with ongoing efforts by Islamists in Somalia to prevent the tragic famines which often blight the country. In 2006, Somali farmers enjoyed a relatively good harvest; unfortunately, just as they were bringing their grain to market, the UN's World Food Programme (WFP) decided to hand out its entire year's grain aid for the country. Thousands of tons of free grain stole away the farmers' chances to sell the food they had worked so hard to grow in the most difficult conditions. Incredibly, despite agreeing not to repeat the mistake it admitted it had made, the WFP did exactly the same in 2007—with Ethiopian troops on hand to protect its workers.

As a result of this blow to Somali agriculture, al-Shabaab evicted the WFP from the areas they control and in 2009 banned all imported grain with the intention of boosting Somalia's own grain production. The first harvest was a success but widespread drought in both 2010 and 2011 precipitated al-Shabaab into full-blown conflict with the aid agencies. At the end of 2011, an estimated 3.6 million Somalis were dependent on international food aid. Al-Shabaab allowed local relief workers to distribute aid but their operations were frequently attacked and forty-two people were killed. Sources in Somalia say that al-Shabaab's recent conduct towards those providing desperately needed aid has turned many who previously supported them against the group. It also occasioned a split within the group as we shall see below.

In February 2012 as-Sahab released a video featuring Ayman al-Zawahiri and al-Shabaab's leader, Godane, announcing that al-Shabaab had formally become part of Al Qaeda; the press office within al-Kata'ib Media issued a statement explaining that the move was intended to make 2012 'the year for all the other *mujahid* groups to fight in the army of the *umma* under one banner ... and pave the way for the blessed Caliphate'. Later postings claimed that the merger occasioned widespread celebrations and a video showed a gathering of 150 clan leaders wildly applauding al-Shabaab leaders flanked by Al Qaeda flags.[14]

Fighters, Leaders and Clans

Before I focus on the indigenous members of al-Shabaab I will briefly discuss the large number of foreigners among its ranks which indicates how linked up the group is with global *jihad* and AQAM in particular. Al-Shabaab have released several videos urging fighters to 'make *hijra*' and join them in Somalia.[15] Regional specialists say there more than 2,000 foreign recruits, many from Arab countries as well as other African countries and Pakistan; there is also a significant cohort of Westerners.

The proportion of foreign fighters in al-Shabaab is reflected in the make-up of its central *shura*—of eighty-five members, forty-two are non-Somalis. These include Muhammad Abu Fayad, a Saudi who is in charge of finances, and Abu Musa Mombasa, a Pakistani citizen, al-Shabaab's security chief. The infamous al-Shabaab military commander and propagandist, Abu Mansour al-Amriki ('the American') will be discussed later in this book.

In January 2012, an al-Shabaab commander, Bilal al-Berjawi, was killed by an American drone in Mogadishu; his parents revealed that he was from West London. In December 2011, UK International Development

Secretary Andrew Mitchell was quoted in *The Times* saying, 'There are probably more British passport holders engaged in terrorist training in Somalia than in any other country in the world.'[16]

There are 2 million Somalis in the diaspora and vigorous attempts have been made to recruit them to al-Shabaab, both to fight in Somalia and to form 'sleeper cells' in their adopted countries. There are 100,000 Somalis in the United States and there have been several press reports regarding recruitment drives for al-Shabaab, especially in the Minneapolis–St Paul area—the biggest Somali community in the US—where twenty young men joined al-Shabaab and left for Somalia.

The UK is home to the largest Somali community in Europe, with 250,000 officially settled. Community leaders have estimated that up to 100 men and women have returned to Somalia to join al-Shabaab. Sweden, Denmark, Australia, Canada and Germany have reported similar proportions of their Somali communities leaving to join al-Shabaab. The numbers are small but significant and it is an ongoing problem. These foreign fighters also pose a danger when they return to their Western homes. In August 2009 Melbourne Police uncovered a plot to attack Sydney's largest barracks involving two men of Somali origin with links to al-Shabaab (their two co-conspirators were Lebanese).

In 2010 the head of Britain's MI5 spy agency, Jonathan Evans, said, 'It's only a matter of time before we see terrorism on our streets inspired by those who are today fighting alongside al-Shabaab.'[17]

Al Qaeda itself sent several high-ranking people to Somalia to further al-Shabaab's development, including its emir for the Horn of Africa, Comoros-born Fazul Abdullah Mohamed, who became al-Shabaab's commander-in-chief. He was killed in June 2011. Issa Osman Issa, who was born in Kenya, is a veteran Al Qaeda man who took part in the 1998 US Embassy bombings in Nairobi and Dar-es-Salaam among other attacks; he is in Somalia to aid recruitment. Mahmud Mujajir, a Sudanese citizen, recruits al-Shabaab's suicide bombers.[18] Although Somalis are notorious for their dislike of foreign interference, al-Shabaab seem to have assimilated these foreign co-travellers. There also an estimated 1,000-strong contingent of fellow Somalis from neighbouring Djibouti and Kenya.

As one would expect, clan rivalries, ideological differences and other disputes—about whether the organisation should focus on the 'near' or 'far' enemy, for example—continue to undermine the stability of the group and it has already had four changes of leadership. The first leader, Adan Eyrow, was appointed by fellow clansman ICU leader Hassan Dahir Aweys; both men are from the Habr Gedir clan (part of the central and southern Hawiye umbrella)—the same clan as Mohamad Aideed. There are an estimated 2,400 fighters from this clan.[19] Eyrow trained in Al Qaeda's Afghan camps in the late 1990s. Eyrow was killed by a US drone attack on 1 May 2008 and replaced by Mukhtar Robow, alias Abu Mansour, whose tenure lasted just one year before he was replaced by Ahmed Adbi Godane. Robow is a member of the Rahanweyn group of clans and remained a prominent and influential figure in al-Shabaab. Over 4,000 fighters are from the Rahanweyn, the main tribal group in southwestern Somalia.[20] Ahmed Adbi Godane is from the Arab sub-clan of the northern Isaaq clan group (which accounts for 1,702 members of al-Shabaab[21]); he spent time in Afghanistan, training and fighting with close friend Ibrahim al-Afghani, who became his rival for the leadership.

In December 2010, Hassan Dahir Aweys announced that his group, Hizbul Islam, would merge with al-Shabaab. Now Godane and Robow fell out over the future direction of al-Shabaab and the role Aweys would have within the new group. Godane was against Aweys having much power and influence, whereas Robow thought he should join the leadership. Also in support of Aweys was hard-line leader Fuad Mohammed Qalaf (a Somali with Swedish nationality). Qalaf was the head of education in the ICU before becoming a senior leader in al-Shabaab where he presided over some draconian punishments including the widely reviled stoning to death of 13-year-old Asho Duhalow, who had been raped. He also personally amputated the hand of a man accused of theft.[22]

With Robow and Godane unable to reconcile their differences, Robow sent his fellow clansmen—the biggest contingent in al-Shabaab—out of Mogadishu and returned to Baidoa with them. In December 2010 the Al Qaeda leadership intervened, trying to impose al-Afghani as leader. Al-Afghani, like Godane, is from the Isaaq clan group but from a different sub-clan—the Saad Muse. Al-Shabaab rejected Al Qaeda's choice of leader, however, and it is highly significant that the person who appears alongside al-Zawahiri in the February 2012 video announcing the formal merger between Al Qaeda and al-Shabaab is Godane. Robow returned to the fold in the interests of unity and is currently the deputy leader.

Other key figures in al-Shabaab include Sheikh Ali Mohamud Rage who seems to act as a tribal coordinator—it is he who accepts pledges of allegiance from tribal chiefs.[23] Hassan Abdullah Hersi al-Turki brought his Raskamboni Brigades (formerly al-Ittihad al-Islami) into al-Shabaab in February 2010 and Mohamad Saeed Atom, a Puntland warlord and arms trader, announced that he and his men had become part of al-Shabaab in June 2010.[24]

Organisationally, the group has emulated the Taliban and Al Qaeda by establishing a system of ministerial departments, committees and regional governors. The various departments the 14,000-strong group operates give a strong idea of their modus operandi: there is a special department for tracking NGO activity; another department is dedicated to kidnapping foreign workers for ransom and another to 'liaising with the pirates'; there's also a department which supervises 'assassinations'; the head of fatwas is Mukhtar Abu-Moslem and the chief judge is Dahir Gamaey Abdi al-Haq; Ali Roti is the man in charge of 'burying children killed in the war'.

The Somali Pirates and Al-Shabaab

As with all AQAM groups, funding comes from a variety of sources but the advice from Al Qaeda 'central' is always to find as many local sources as possible. Al-Shabaab have been implicated in various swindles including around $10 million which disappeared from the bank accounts of forwarding company Dalsan International, causing its bankruptcy. The brother of the late al-Shabaab leader Adan Eyrow was working for the company at the time and is said to have transferred the funds into the group's own accounts.

In 2010 the UN's International Monitoring Group (IMG) found that the Eritrean government was supporting al-Shabaab with money and weapons despite sanctions imposed on it the previous year. Other sources include Gulf individuals, which probably explains why Al Qaeda 'central' sent a Saudi to head the group's finance department.

But al-Shabaab's most novel milk-cow is its recent deal with the Somali pirates who have made millions in ransom demands. The pirates are the stuff of terrifying newspaper reports and they have carried out some brutal executions and attacks. However, the background to their story is entirely overlooked in the Western media and many of these men were originally fishermen whose living was ruined by unscrupulous foreigners.

With Somalia in turmoil and with no effective central government throughout the 1990s and into the new millennium, foreign trawlers exploited the absence of a coastguard (or any form of policing) in the Indian Ocean off the coast of Somalia to illegally poach tons of seafood and fish. Much worse was the arrival of ships intent on dumping hazardous toxic waste in the clear blue waters. The Italian Mafia specialises in this 'industry' and many of the vessels came from Italy but other foreign businesses also sent container-loads of waste to be jettisoned into the sea.

Rumours of this ugly and tragic practice were confirmed in the aftermath of the 2004 tsunami when rusty containers were washed up on the shores of Puntland. United Nations Environment Programme spokesman Nick Nuttall told Al Jazeera that they testified to a 'frightening activity' that had been going on for many years. Nuttall confirmed that uranium nuclear active waste, lead and heavy metals like cadmium and mercury had all been found in Somali waters, as well as industrial, chemical and hospital waste.[25]

A UN report into the aftermath of the tsunami reported on the health problems, caused by toxic waste spills, experienced by Somalis living on the coast. These include 'Acute respiratory infections, dry heavy coughing and mouth bleeding, abnormal births, abdominal haemorrhages, unusual skin chemical reactions, and sudden death after inhaling toxic materials'.[26]

In March 2011 Somalia's Minister of Aviation and Transport, Mohammad O. Ali, belatedly announced a state of toxic danger alert and described how he had witnessed for himself the 'calamitous impact it was having on marine life and the fishing community', with residents of the coastal areas telling of hundreds of dead fish washing ashore each day.[27] A 2005 report by Britain's Department for International Development 'conservatively' estimated that toxic waste and illegal fishing had already cost the Somali economy—one of the weakest in the world—£100 million in lost fishing revenue.[28] This then is the backdrop to the recent spate of piracy that began in earnest in 2005.

As one of the pirate leaders, Sugule Ali, explained to Al Jazeera, 'We don't consider ourselves sea bandits. We consider sea bandits those who illegally fish, and dump waste, and carry weapons in our sea.' The pirates prefer to be called *badaadinta badah* or 'saviours of the sea' and originally took on the moniker 'National Volunteer Coastguards'. Initially their purpose was to frighten foreign 'illegal unreported and unregulated' (IUU) vessels away from the Puntland coast and they used to take to the sea in small speedboats, armed with machine guns. They started charging 'fines' before they realised the potential for extorting large sums of money with no moral justification whatsoever. Hijacking and demanding ransoms for kidnapped crew and passengers have now taken precedence and piracy has become a highly lucrative business.

Somali pirates operate over an increasingly wide territory. In July 2010 they captured a chemical tanker in the southern part of the Red Sea and 2011 brought reports of incidents as far south as the port of Beira in Mozambique. According to the International Maritime Board, which monitors piracy events as they occur, Somali pirates were involved in 237 incidents in 2011: they hijacked twenty-eight vessels and took 470 people hostage, of whom they killed fifteen.[29]

Piracy in the region costs the world economy around $15 billion a year in increased shipping costs (rerouting ships round the Cape or through the Suez Canal), increased insurance premiums, stolen goods, loss of trade, hijacked ships and ransoms. An international task force composed of thirty national navies has so far been unable to curtail the Somali pirates' activities and they are becoming increasingly daring, ruthless and violent. The pirates are well armed with machine guns and RPGs purchased in Yemen; they are also equipped with the latest satellite navigational equipment.

The pirates bring in hundreds of millions of dollars a year. So lucrative is their business that they have even set up a form of stock exchange where people can buy shares in forthcoming hijackings and receive handsome rewards on their original investment. Trades are reported to be in the region of $150 million a year, with much of the interest coming from ex-pat Somalis based in the Gulf and the West.[30]

In April 2009 the Somali pirates shocked the US military establishment by capturing a ship that was part of the state-funded US Maritime Security Program (MSP). The MSP maintains sixty 'commercially viable, militarily useful, privately-owned vessels to meet national defense and other security requirements' according to the US Transport Department website.[31] The container ship in question, the *Maersk Alabama*, is believed to have been carrying arms and the pirates may not have realised what a significant target they had boarded. The story became headline news when the captain, Richard Philips, offered himself as hostage in exchange for the freedom of his men and the pirates accepted. When the US government refused to negotiate a ransom with the pirates, three of them set off in a motor-powered lifeboat towards land with Captain Philips still in captivity. The lifeboat ran out of fuel and the pirates and their captive were adrift for three days under the blazing sun. When a US warship hove into view the pirates thought they had come to rescue them but they were all shot dead by US Navy SEAL snipers as soon as they took a tow. The pirates were deeply angered by the murders and spokesman Jamac Habeb told Associated Press, 'US forces have become our number one enemy. . . . From now on, if we capture foreign ships and their respective countries try to attack us, we will kill them [the hostages].' Al-Shabaab fighters showed their sympathy for the pirates by attempting to shoot down a plane carrying US Congressman Donald Payne out of Mogadishu the following day.

Enormous ransoms are now demanded and received. The record to date, according to the Mariners' Club, is the $12 million paid for Panama-flagged Kuwaiti-owned crude oil tanker MT *Zirku* and her twenty-nine crew members on 10 June 2011. Ransoms are delivered by helicopter drop or parachuted onto the deck of the stolen vessel. To ensure no forged notes are present, the pirates have invested in currency-counting machines of the kind used in commercial banks.

Piracy has replaced fishing as the main economic activity in Puntland. In their main base, the town of Harardhere in the Mudug Province, a local leader told Reuters that the pirates pass on a percentage of the ransoms to fund schools and hospitals. Pirates have become the local elite, driving expensive cars and marrying the most beautiful women; many young men aspire to join them—including defectors from al-Shabaab. There were reports of increasingly rowdy, unruly and completely un-Islamic behaviour among the pirates.

Al-Shabaab, empowered by its merger with Hizbul Islam and its newly consolidated relationship with Al Qaeda, took control of the major sea ports of Southern Somalia—including pirate stronghold Harardhere and Kismayo—at the end of 2010. Sources on the ground say that the al-Shabaab 'officers' immediately set about trying to control the pirates, whose on-shore activities were becoming a problem for the local community. Pirates were regularly drunk on wine and spirits found on the ships they had hijacked and had taken to firing randomly into the air or frightening local residents by taking aim at them.

In February 2011, Reuters confirmed stories that were emerging of a deal between the pirates and al-Shabaab. Al-Shabaab would allow them to continue operating out of Harardhere on the condition that they donated 20 percent (some say 25 percent) of every ransom to their *jihad*. According to local leader Ahmed Wardhere, who attended the negotiations on behalf of the local community, 'Pirates who previously belonged to al-Shabaab signed the agreement first and then the others agreed . . . a small group of pirate gangs who refused the agreement moved away with their ships towards the deep shores of Hobyo.' Al-Shabaab then established a 'marine office at Harardhere to liaise with the pirates'.[32]

By May 2011, al-Shabaab appeared to be actively encouraging the pirates to expand their level of operations. The UN Office on Drugs and Crime reported increasing numbers of raids out of al-Shabaab-controlled Kismayo and an al-Shabaab officer told a local news agency (hiiraan.com) that the pirates were now working in full cooperation with the Islamists: 'If there was no relationship between us, there is no way the pirates would be able to operate, or carry their weapons within zones we control.'[33]

Al-Shabaab's close involvement with the pirates has had another, dangerous, repercussion—the formation of a '*mujahideen* navy' patrolling the Somali coast. An al-Kata'ib press release on 20 November 2011 described how 'Elements from Harakat al-Shabaab al-Mujahideen Naval Forces, using high-power speedboats and under cover of darkness, launched a carefully planned attack on two Kenyan naval vessels patrolling the Somali coast . . . one was set on fire when hit by Rocket Propelled Grenades.'

Conclusion: Squabbles or Survival?

Like the Taliban in the 1990s, al-Shabaab has gained support among some of the people and clan leaders by bringing a version of law and order, as well as basic welfare, to towns and villages where there had been none for decades. A January 2012 pledge of allegiance by the Gaaljecel clan acknowledged that 'What distinguishes the *mujahideen* is justice between the people and fairness to the poor and snatching their rights from those who plundered it, because the Islamic courts in the Wilayas resolved cases which some were unresolved for nearly twenty years and souls and blood were gone for it and families were displaced as an effect of that [*sic*].'[34]

The group is well funded and armed but the seeds of its destruction may lie in the in-fighting and factionalism which have characterised it thus far. While some of the causes for disagreement have been petty, others, such as the draconian nature of the more extreme wing's 'punishments' and their prevention of international aid agencies bringing relief to famine victims, are not. Further, Somalia's social structure and history suggest that permanent cohesion and cooperation between members of a large group composed of members of different, rival clans is unlikely. These are difficulties that Ayman al-Zawahiri and senior Al Qaeda leaders will be acutely aware of. It remains to be seen whether they can exert sufficient influence on their Somali cohort to focus on the AQAM agenda rather than their own squabbles.

Al-Shabaab's lucrative collaboration with the pirates—on which the group largely depends in financial terms—is another tinderbox. Unsupported by ideological or religious unity, lethal in-fighting over the huge amounts of money involved is almost inevitable.

There is no obvious end to Somalia's chaos in sight. Regardless of the future of al-Shabaab, Al Qaeda is likely to find operating room in this failed state for the foreseeable future.

4

The Taliban–Al Qaeda Nexus: Afghanistan

America's involvement in Afghanistan is just like someone who is losing at gambling. He keeps playing hoping to win but, in the end, rather than achieving anything he loses everything he owns.
Jalaluddin al-Haqqani[1]

I will not swear on Washington as my qibla nor will I bow to Bush. . . . My beliefs and my Pashtun pride teach me this;
I sacrifice my head and my blood for the oppressed people;
But I will not even pretend to be humble in front of Pharaoh
Tariq Ahmadzai, Taliban poet, January 2007[2]

The core alliance at the heart of the AQAM phenomenon is between Osama bin Laden's original Al Qaeda and Mullah Omar's Taliban. Al Qaeda was under Taliban protection as it plotted and then carried out the 9/11 'raids'. In the intervening years the two groups have become inextricably involved organisationally, operationally and ideologically. Several commanders, like Sirajuddin Haqqani, are on the central *shura* of both organisations.

A leaked NATO report on 1 February 2012 conceded that the Taliban enjoyed a renewed popularity among the people, having reinvented themselves as more tolerant and progressive. Not only that, the Afghan military—to whom the US intends to hand over security when it withdraws—are increasingly supportive of the Taliban and provide them with weapons. It is almost inevitable that, when the US withdraws in 2013 or

2014, the Taliban will return to government in Kabul either as part of a coalition or alone. America's withdrawal from Afghanistan, whether sooner or later, will be processed by the Taliban as a military and moral victory.

That the Taliban have been able to gain any ground against the world's greatest superpower has been due, in part at least, to its alliance with Al Qaeda. Over the past five years the Taliban has adopted many of AQAM's trademark tactics and weapons—most notably suicide bombing and improvised explosive devices (IEDs)—with deadly effect. It has also developed a highly efficient intelligence capability of using infiltrators and double agents. This has resulted in several dramatic attacks, including the murder of seven specialist CIA agents including the leading Al Qaeda expert, and the downing of a Black Hawk helicopter in which thirty men from the same SEAL team that assassinated Osama bin Laden were killed. In the first four months of 2012 alone, sixteen Afghan policemen or soldiers, either Taliban infiltrators or sympathisers, turned on their NATO trainers or colleagues, killing twenty-two of them. In addition, the Taliban has joined the propaganda war, having observed the effective use AQAM makes of the Internet. In the past the group eschewed technology as *haram* but now it has developed a strong online presence which we will consider in more detail in a later chapter.

Most reasonable commentators could see by 2008 that NATO was unlikely to defeat the Taliban and an allied network of AQAM groups. Furthermore, the financial crisis in the West, which began the same year, was not unrelated to the enormous sums being spent on the war—by July 2011, America's bill was at least $3.7 trillion and was predicted to rise to as much as $4.4 trillion.[3] The terrible cost in human lives has also increased year on year; 2010 and 2011 saw the highest fatalities yet, bringing the total dead to 14,700 civilians and 1,796 NATO troops; in addition there are 3 million Afghan refugees and nearly half a million displaced persons inside the country.

The ten-year conflict has been waged to uphold President Karzai's government, established in haste at the 2001 Bonn conference by the US and Afghan warlords. But in 2011 it was found to be the third most corrupt regime on the planet, worse by far than any of those deposed in the Arab Spring and only marginally better than North Korea and Somalia.

In the summer of 2011, President Obama declared NATO's 'success' in the battle against the Taliban and Al Qaeda and announced his intention to start withdrawing all 130,000 NATO troops. The Taliban responded with a surge of attacks including a twenty-hour siege of Kabul's Green Zone. A heavily armed group of men fired mortars, RPGs and automatic weapons, while car bombs and suicide bombers targeted NATO headquarters, the US Embassy, the International Security Assistance Force (ISAF) headquarters, foreign and local intelligence services and other government and military buildings. Sixty-nine people lost their lives in the onslaught, according to Taliban sources. In a statement posted on the Internet, the Taliban explained their motives for the attack: 'The move was to show the US, NATO and their allies that *mujahideen*'s resolve has not weakened through the 10-year-long battle, on the contrary, it strengthened and the morale among *mujahideen* is higher than before.'[4]

Meanwhile the US was engaged in makeshift diplomacy with the Taliban, using former Afghan president, Burhanuddin Rabbani, as go-between. Given that Rabbani was a leader in the Northern Alliance, against which the Taliban had waged a bitter civil war, this was not a wise choice. The Americans suggested the establishment of a Taliban consulate in Qatar, implying the group's rehabilitation as a plausible element in a future post-conflict government and one that would be acceptable to the international community.

Despite the siege of the Green Zone, Afghan President Karzai asked Burhanuddin Rabbani to persist with diplomatic overtures to the Taliban. On 20 September 2011 they thought these had succeeded when a turbaned man turned up at one of their meetings saying he had an important message to give Rabbani from the Taliban. As he hugged him in greeting, the messenger detonated a bomb hidden in his turban, killing Rabbani and himself. General John Allen, the American head of US and NATO forces in Afghanistan, told *Time* magazine, 'The face of the peace initiative has been attacked.'[5]

Paradoxically, American hopes for an imminent withdrawal of her troops from Afghanistan are now dependent on successful peace negotiations with the Taliban—whom they came to topple in 2001. The US is keen to withdraw from its fruitless and cripplingly expensive Afghan adventure but its precondition, that the Taliban break entirely with Al Qaeda, is unlikely to be met.

The Taliban are currently faced with a difficult choice: do they fight on until NATO exits, with a view to regaining control of the whole country—a course which would almost certainly result in a rerun of their civil war with the Northern Alliance—or do they accept a negotiated settlement which would see them in control of certain administrative areas in a federal system of the type already being discussed with Western negotiators by January 2012?[6] The Islamist parties which are dominating the post-revolutionary political process in the Arab Spring countries would be more likely than their secular predecessors to endorse a Taliban-run Islamic state in Afghanistan. In this chapter we will consider the origins of the Taliban, how the Taliban–Al Qaeda nexus evolved and how it has altered regional security and the balance of power.

Afghanistan: Graveyard of Imperial Ambitions

The Taliban spring from a fierce culture not given to surrender. They are mostly Pashtun, from the dramatic mountain ranges straddling the Afghan–Pakistan border and abutting the Himalayas. This is difficult territory, vertiginous and mostly impenetrable, especially during the exceptionally harsh winters.

In 1893, the territory—and people—was artificially divided by the British along the so-called Durand line[7] to fix a border between Afghanistan and what was then Northern India, and is now Pakistan. This division still remains a source of resentment towards the West. The Pashtun are the largest ethnic tribal group in the world. They number 42 million, are the majority population group in Afghanistan, where they constitute 40 percent of the population, and also represent 15.5 percent of Pakistan's population. Hamid Karzai (himself a Pashtun) presides over the first Afghan government in centuries not to be dominated by Pashtun. The present government is composed mostly of Tajiks—the majority ethnic group in the Northern Alliance that aided the US in overthrowing the Taliban in October 2001.

The British went to war thrice with the Afghans in the name of securing or expanding their empire, and thrice they were roundly defeated.[8] In 1897 Sir Winston Churchill, then a 23-year-old lieutenant in the British Army, had his first taste of combat when Pashtun warriors laid siege to the colonial garrison at Malakand in what is now Pakistan's North-West Frontier Province (NWFP). Writing a report for the *Daily Telegraph*, he noted their 'warlike nature . . . their hatred of control' and concluded that, among the Pashtun, 'every man is a soldier'.[9]

Agitation for a breakaway, independent 'Pashtunistan' started in 1949 on both sides of the border and has revived of late with a widespread poster campaign in the NWFP. The desire for independence, coupled with constant feuding between the sixty major tribes and 400 sub-clans, have combined to produce a singularly unstable, all-but-lawless region.

When the Soviet Union invaded Afghanistan in 1979 the Pashtun united against a common enemy, forming the majority of the *mujahideen* who rose up against them. The mighty Soviet Army, like the NATO forces two decades later, could never have anticipated that these tribesmen would hold them off for ten years, kill 50,000 soldiers and finally rout them in a defeat that contributed to the demise of the Soviet empire.

The *mujahideen* were greatly helped in their efforts against the Soviet Union by interested foreign governments. Afghanistan enjoys an important strategic position as the 'navel' of the Greater Middle East, having borders—many of them porous—with six other countries: Pakistan, China, Turkmenistan, Uzbekistan and Tajikistan.

Between them, the CIA and Pakistani Inter-Services Intelligence (ISI) trained and armed an estimated 1,614,000 *mujahideen*, establishing more than 100 training camps inside Pakistan.[10] The US and Saudi Arabia funded the Afghan resistance to the tune of $3.5 billion.[11] It was to these battlefields that the so-called Afghan-Arabs were called, along with the other Muslim fighters who came from many countries in their thousands to join the *mujahideen*. Among the Afghan-Arabs, of course, were Osama bin Laden, Ayman al-Zawahiri and many others who would later form the core of Al Qaeda. Afghanistan was to offer these international fighters their training and first experiences in guerrilla warfare.

The Taliban Emerge

The Soviet troop withdrawal from Afghanistan on 15 February 1989 led to a period of civil war. Initially, the Cold War alignment continued: the Soviets upheld the brutal regime of Mohammed Najibullah, who had been head of the secret police, the Khadamat-e Etela'at-e Dawlati (KHAD). The US and Pakistan backed the *mujahideen*.

With the demise of the Soviet Union in December 1991, Afghanistan was plunged into further disarray. Those who had fought together now split into warring factions and the country was torn between violent rival warlords—many of them ex-*mujahideen* leaders. When I interviewed him, Osama bin Laden told me that he initially intended to move back to Afghanistan in late 1991 but was so disappointed by the disintegration of, and in-fighting among, the *mujahideen* that he went instead to Sudan.

Burhanuddin Rabbani, the Tajik leader of Jamiat-e Islami—the most powerful of the *mujahideen* factions—became President of Afghanistan in 1992. However, Rabbani's policies reflected long-standing Tajik pro-Indian sympathies, setting him at odds with his erstwhile comrades who would assassinate him in 2011. Meanwhile Pakistani and American regional aspirations began to diverge. Backed by the US, Rabbani would later become a leader of the Tajik-dominated United Islamic Front for the Salvation of Afghanistan—known in the Western media as the Northern Alliance—which pitted itself against the Taliban.

Mullah Omar first came to public attention in 1994 as the leader of a group of Islamic students and Pashtun military commanders, many from the Pakistani side of the Durand line. They called themselves the Taliban—'students'—and many had been trained in the *madrassas* (religious schools) which flourished in Pakistan from 1980. By 2004, according to Pakistani expert Amir Mir, there were 6,761 Deobandi *madrassas* in Pakistan 'of which 200 are *jihadi* types or are affiliated with *jihadi* organizations'.[12] The schools are encouraged and often funded by the ISI which has historically exploited militancy in its proxy battles with India, in Kashmir for example.

The Taliban's aim was to restore stability and enforce their interpretation of Sharia law. Given that they emerged in a period of chaos with no effective central government, no effective police and no security apparatus, their brand of Islamic justice—and the swift manner in which they administered it—appealed to the Afghan people. The Pakistani government began to support the Taliban, via the ISI, with arms and training. It was, and remains, in their interest to have a sympathetic, Sunni fundamentalist government in Kabul providing secure routes into Central

Asia as well as a buffer against India and Shi'i Iran, the western neighbour of both Pakistan and Afghanistan.

Despite the efforts of the Northern Alliance, the Taliban took Kabul in September 1996, having gained control of 90 percent of the country, and established themselves as rulers under Sharia law. Mullah Omar was invested as *Amir ul-Mimineen* (Commander of the Faithful) and was draped in Kandahar's most precious relic, the mantle of the Prophet Muhammad. This moment is of great significance to the *jihadis* who regard Mullah Omar as their spiritual leader. Since the death of Osama bin Laden, Mullah Omar has become the most iconic and unifying figure in the movement.

The Taliban's claim to government was recognised only by Pakistan, Saudi Arabia and the United Arab Emirates (UAE), all of whom accepted the credentials of Taliban ambassadors. In off-the-record conversations, several Western politicians have opined that it might have been more effective to allow the Taliban to participate on the world stage, and dilute their extremism through diplomacy, rather than face a long-term military confrontation. History may now provide a second chance.

The Haqqani Network

The Haqqani Network (HN) is a powerful, autonomous organisation under the Taliban umbrella. Its military commander, Sirajuddin Haqqani, is a member of the Taliban's central *shura*. Operating as a kind of hub for various *jihadi* groups, the network has facilitated the evolution of the Pakistani Taliban and its nexus with the Afghan Taliban and Al Qaeda. TTP leader Hakimullah Mehsud began his *jihadi* 'career' fighting under Haqqani commanders in the Loya Paktia region.

Its power base is in the strategically important mountainous area between Pakistan and Afghanistan, which contains the major supply routes including the Khyber Pass. HN is strong in Pakistan's North-West Frontier Province (NWFP) and the Federally Administered Tribal Areas (FATA)—a vast, mountainous area larger than Portugal. On the other side of the border HN dominates the southeastern part of Afghanistan, particularly in the provinces of Paktika, Logar, Gazni and Khost. HN is composed of smaller, semi-autonomous units based on family and tribal links, but generally accepting the command of the leadership.

Born in 1950, leader Maulvi (Mullah) Jalaluddin Haqqani was a senior *mujahideen* leader during the Afghan–Soviet war. His links with Al Qaeda date back to 1996 when Osama bin Laden persuaded the then justice minister to leave Rabbani's government and join forces with the Taliban instead. This was as significant to the eventual Taliban victory as Gulbuddin Hekmatyar's Saudi-backed switch of allegiance, since these military commanders brought well-trained officers and men with them, as well as tanks and war planes. When the Taliban seized power in Kabul in 1996, Jalaluddin was appointed Minister of Tribal Affairs.

The HN influence extended over the border into Pakistan, particularly after the US began its bombardment of Afghanistan in November 2001. North Waziristan became so thoroughly dominated by militants under HN that it declared itself an Emirate and received *de facto* recognition by the Pakistani government when it named the 'Islamic State of Waziristan' as one of the parties in the peace agreement of 5 September 2006. Realising Haqqani's significance and influence, the US bombed his compound on 8 September 2008, killing his wives, grandchildren and several other female relatives. WikiLeaks cables reveal that Haqqani and his right-hand men then moved to other houses in Islamabad, Rawalpindi and Peshawar. Now in his sixties, Jalaluddin has delegated military command to his son Sirajuddin who in turn operates under the command of Mullah Omar's Quetta *shura*. According to Sirajuddin in a September 2011 Reuters interview, the group has more than 10,000 fighters.[13]

Much of the network's power and influence derives from its long-standing connections, honed over forty years, and its diplomatic abilities. The HN has aided the Taliban to expand the area under their control: most Taliban leaders are from the lowland tribes of Loya Kandahar whereas the HN is the strongest Islamist group among the tribes of the mountainous Loya Paktia region. The HN leadership is renowned for its diplomacy, adept at talking effectively with opposing sides in a conflict or squabble but rarely falling prey to factionalism itself. It has been key to uniting tribes and different *jihadi* groups to fight common enemies (at present NATO and Coalition forces) and pursue shared goals (to live under Sharia law and establish a global caliphate).

The group has historic associations with the Pakistani Army and the ISI dating back to the 1980s and has long been used as a proxy by the Pakistani state to carry out strategically significant strikes (for example, the 2008 suicide bombing of the Indian Embassy in Kabul) and to manage the fractious tribes in the FATA.

A secret NATO report leaked on 1 February 2012 revealed that the Haqqani compound in Islamabad is in the immediate vicinity of ISI headquarters, affirming the level of collusion between the Pakistani security services and the Taliban–AQAM nexus which was also evident in the location of Osama bin Laden's compound in Abbottabad.[14] The HN facilitates operational collaboration between the Taliban and Pakistani Taliban (TTP) at the same time as it acts as a go-between for the Pakistan security apparatus and the TTP.

The Afghan *jihad* brought fighters of all nationalities and backgrounds to Jalaluddin's headquarters in Zawara—it was here that key Al Qaeda men Abu Hafs and Abu Ubaydah al-Banshiri first met. The ties developed then formed the basis of the global movement, based around Al Qaeda, which has now evolved into the much wider AQAM network. Osama bin Laden was a close associate of Jalaluddin Haqqani—Al Qaeda's legendary al-Farouq training camp was located at Haqqani's base in Zawara, for example, and the two groups shared military training personnel.

This long-standing connection would prove useful when bin Laden was obliged to leave Sudan in 1996. It was through the mediation of the Haqqani network that the ties between Al Qaeda and the Taliban were strengthened in the 1990s, preparing the way for bin Laden's return to the country in 1996. Nasser al-Bahri recalls how, once Al Qaeda was installed in Kandahar, he often had to provide a security detail for Osama bin Laden when he went on one of his frequent visits to 'his friend Jalaludin Haqani'.[15] This connection is also the reason why the Al Qaeda leadership fled to Haqqani territory in Waziristan during the US bombardment of Tora Bora in retaliation for 9/11—Ayman al-Zawahiri's wife and children were killed in an air strike on a Haqqani-owned house on the Afghan side of the border in late 2001.[16]

One could argue that Al Qaeda and the Haqqanis introduced a wider, international agenda to the Taliban, although Mullah Omar's primary focus remains the battle to oust the occupying NATO forces. Despite rarely making any public pronouncements in support of attacks carried out by Al Qaeda (including 9/11), in an interview posted on as-Sahab, a Haqqani commander, Mawlawi Sangeen, says that there are no ideological, operational or strategic differences between Al Qaeda and his group. 'We are one,' he concludes.[17] HN members were the first to carry out suicide bombings in Afghanistan; the Taliban had not previously resorted to this Al Qaeda–inspired tactic.

In a rare interview in September 2011 Sirajuddin told Reuters that the group was actively expanding the Taliban's area of influence in eastern Afghanistan where it found itself in conflict with a rival group of insurgents, erstwhile comrade-in-arms Gulbuddin Hekmatyar's Hizb-e-Islami. 'I asked the *shura* if we should allow them to operate in areas under our control. They said no, so I ordered Hekmatyar's fighters to either join the Taliban or leave Khost and they left the area,' Sirajuddin reported.[18]

Al Qaeda in Afghanistan

Under pressure from the US, Sudanese President Omar al-Bashir asked Osama bin Laden to leave Khartoum and in May 1996, the Al Qaeda leader, his two sons Saad and Omar, and a handful of *mujahideen* boarded a privately chartered plane bound for Afghanistan, which was to become Al Qaeda headquarters. Initially there was a level of mistrust on the part of both the Taliban and Al Qaeda, exacerbated by cultural differences and the lack of a common language which meant all communications between leaders necessitated a translator. Al-Bahri notes that meetings between the one-eyed Mullah Omar—who was as tall as bin Laden—and the Al Qaeda leader rarely lasted more than half an hour and that both spoke 'in short sentences in serious tones'.[19]

The Taliban feared Al Qaeda's extremist rhetoric—routinely handed out in press releases—and their threatened attacks on foreign targets. Mullah Omar reasoned that if the US (or any other foreign force) retaliated, the Taliban would be in firing line too. Nor did the Taliban particularly want to incur the hostility of the international community at a time when they were seeking credibility for their regime on the world stage. Al Qaeda, meanwhile, misled by certain members of the Northern Alliance, worried that their hosts were 'neo-marxists'.[20] Abu Musab al-Suri (one of Al Qaeda's main ideologues at the time) also voiced his complaints about the Taliban's reverence for tombs and cemeteries, which he considered un-Islamic.[21]

Despite their mutual reticence Mullah Omar's men protected their Al Qaeda guests in line with Pashtun rules governing hospitality, providing them with safe houses and security and intelligence back-up. When there was an assassination attempt on bin Laden in 1997, for example, it was the Taliban's secret services who tracked down the culprits and arrested some, killing others.[22]

At the end of March 1997 Mullah Omar's men insisted that Al Qaeda make their headquarters in Kandahar, a Taliban stronghold, for their protection. Al-Bahri relates how the helicopter flight from Jalalabad to Kandahar nearly ended in disaster for the organisation: bin Laden's second son, Abdelrahmane, then aged 16, was carrying several hand grenades in a belt. 'In mid-air, one of the safety catches snagged on his seat; fortunately the pin didn't come out. Abdelrahmane held on to it for dear life; he showed the grenade to Abu Hafs who clasped his hand over it too . . . everyone was terrified . . . all the Al Qaeda leaders except bin Laden and Saif al-Adel were on the plane.'[23]

The Taliban provided Al Qaeda with several training camps, among them Wal Jihad, al-Farouq and Abu Bakr al-Siddiq (which both al-Bahri and L'Houssaine Khertchou assert was run by the infamous Khaled al-Fawwaz, better known as bin Laden's 'Ambassador to London', in which capacity I met him in 1996). They also gave them an agricultural complex 30 km outside Kandahar, known as Tarnak Farms. Boasting little in the way of material comfort and initially without any running water, electricity or sanitation, the series of brick buildings was capable of housing fifty fighters and their families—around 200 people. Having built a brick wall around the houses and the central mosque, Al Qaeda was securely ensconced. Fighters dug a well and purchased an electricity generator (which bin Laden ordained should operate for only four hours a day). 'We want to live a primitive life,' he often repeated. Neighbouring Taliban warned them of danger by firing three shots into the air.[24]

When Al Qaeda bombed the US Embassies in Nairobi and Dar-es-Salaam in August 1998 the relationship between the group and the Taliban reached a critical point. The Taliban had not been forewarned and there was a faction in the group who wanted Al Qaeda to leave. Indeed, bin

Laden had an escape plan in place which would have taken around 1,000 fighters with him to Somalia.[25] US threats against the Taliban for sheltering Al Qaeda had the opposite of their intended effect, however, and after some internal dispute (mainly between two mullahs: Moutawaqil, who was opposed to Al Qaeda, and Jalil, who supported them) they resolved to support their 'brothers in the Islamist cause'.[26] It was only at this point that Osama bin Laden announced that he had officially sworn *bayat* to Mullah Omar who was now, in effect, his leader—the 'emir of the faithful'.

A tragic event in August 1999 would cement the bond between the two groups. A booby-trapped car exploded outside Mullah Omar's house, killing one of his wives and his son. Al Qaeda had a neighbouring guest house and two of its commanders, Abu Hafs and Saif al-Adel, were the first to rush in to help, ordering their men to set up checkpoints around Kandahar to trap the assassins. The perpetrators were discovered to be Afghan refugees from Iran who had been sent to avenge the killing of eight Iranian diplomats at Mazar e-Sharif in 1997.[27]

By 2001 Northern Alliance forces, now backed by the CIA, represented a very real threat to Taliban rule. Two days before 9/11, Al Qaeda suicide bombers, posing as journalists, assassinated Northern Alliance leader General Ahmed Shah Massoud by setting off a bomb hidden in a TV camera. In this way, bin Laden won the undying gratitude of Mullah Omar and his followers.

Many prominent figures in Al Qaeda opposed the planned attacks on New York and Washington, fearing the severity of America's response. They were right to do so because the subsequent US bombardment of Tora Bora and its environs, followed by a full-scale land invasion, spelt the end of both Al Qaeda's safe haven and, by December 2001, the Taliban's rule. After some ill-fated attempts at resistance, surviving fighters from both groups dispersed. Mullah Omar, Osama bin Laden and Dr Ayman Al-Zawahiri did not, in fact, go far, finding refuge in the mountainous tribal area on one side of the Pakistani border or the other.

Insurgents Resurgent

While the majority of Al Qaeda fighters dispersed over the border into Pakistan, a cohort remained active in Afghanistan, maintaining a loose alliance with the Taliban who, by summer 2002, had already begun to garner support for a renewed *jihad*. Kandahar, the spiritual home of the Taliban, became a focal point for renewed violence including the attempted assassination of new president, Hamid Karzai, on 6 September 2002. Reports at the end of 2002 spoke of a secret Taliban recruitment drive in Pashtun villages on both sides of the border, using leaflets and word of mouth. In the winter months these areas are inaccessible to outsiders, offering ideal conditions for plotting a summer offensive. A UN report in December 2002 confirmed rumours of Al Qaeda–run mobile training camps in the area.[28]

Al Qaeda's operational focus shifted to Iraq in the months following the US-led invasion of that country (March 2003); its fighters started to migrate there in their thousands. Iraq, a secular state, had little prior history of extremism. Iraq's main Islamist group, Hizb al-Islami (an offshoot of the Muslim Brotherhood), had been banned under Saddam Hussein and joined the US project at the earliest opportunity. Its leader, Tariq al-Hashimi, is now Iraq's vice president.

No sooner had US President George W. Bush claimed victory in Iraq on 1 May 2003 than a full-scale insurgency began with Al Qaeda at its centre. Thousands of Iraqi civilians, as well as large numbers of military commanders and soldiers loyal to Saddam, were now exposed to the global ideology of bin Laden's *jihad* and the lessons of guerrilla warfare.

Meanwhile, attacks in Afghanistan by a resurgent Taliban began in earnest through the summer of 2003. In August, NATO took control of security in Kabul—the first such operation it had ever undertaken outside Europe. September 2004 saw another assassination attempt on President Karzai when a rocket was launched at his helicopter. Taliban attacks steadily increased until, in June 2006, NATO announced it would also oversee the fight against the burgeoning insurgency in the south—a move which angered the Taliban and sparked renewed support from the Al Qaeda leadership. In October of the same year NATO, under US leadership, expanded its area of command to the whole of Afghanistan.

Al Qaeda would face its own problems in Iraq due to the conduct of its emir, Abu Mus'ab al-Zarqawi, who became increasingly fanatical. Al-Zarqawi's vicious sectarianism alienated all but the most hardline element among the insurgency, as did his insistence on 'Islamic' punishments (including chopping off the fingers of smokers), the indiscriminate nature of his attacks—which resulted in the deaths of hundreds of ordinary citizens—and his presumption that he could talk on behalf of indigenous Iraqi insurgents. He was effectively demoted by Osama bin Laden in April 2006, and by early June had been tracked down and killed by the Americans.

Al-Zarqawi's errors helped the Americans' 'Awakening' effort, which encouraged Sunni tribesmen and disaffected insurgents to join a militia called the 'Sons of Iraq' aimed at rooting out Al Qaeda. In January 2007, the US committed 21,500 extra troops to Iraq for the so-called Surge offensive under General David Petraeus, which put even more pressure on the insurgency.

Al Qaeda's attention now reverted to Afghanistan and the protection that the Taliban, by now in control of the south of the country, could once again afford. On 11 February 2007 Ayman al-Zawahiri made a broadcast exhorting the *mujahideen* to join the Taliban's fight against NATO under the leadership of the 'commander of the faithful', Mullah Omar, to whom, he announced, he had given his *bayat*.[29]

On 31 October 2007 Al Qaeda's production wing, as-Sahab, broadcast an interview with the late Mullah Mansour Dadullah, the Taliban military commander in Helmand province, as a sign of the renewed operational closeness between the two organisations. In his Internet-based open question and answer session released in April 2008, Ayman al-Zawahiri declared that he and bin Laden were the Taliban leader's 'soldiers'.[30]

A new *hijra* got under way, bringing fighters back to Afghanistan—mostly from Iraq—between 2006 and 2009. The ISOI was established on 15 October 2006 under the leadership of Abu Omar al-Baghdadi and included men from Saddam Hussein's Republican Guard who joined the insurgency after the US invasion. Sources have spoken of 'scores' of highly trained officers from Saddam Hussein's Republican Guard who turned up running militant training camps in the tribal regions on both sides of the Afghan–Pakistan border. These included General al-Bashir al-Jabouri, who was the ISOI defence minister. Having fought with Al Qaeda in Iraq, these men have converted to their brand of Salafist Islam and adopted the lifestyle of the global *jihadi*. The presence of these professional soldiers is evidenced by the increase in IED roadside bombs which began at the same time. The Republican Guards were specialists in IEDs, particularly those with highly sophisticated accessories such as infrared trip wires and 'daisy chain' detonators (whereby one remote detonator can set off a whole line of explosions capable of destroying an entire NATO convoy). The ex-Republican Guards clearly shared their 'expertise' with the Taliban just as they had done with Al Qaeda in Iraq. IED attacks doubled in the year 2008–9 to 8,200 and by the end of 2010 had increased to a massive 14,661. The trend continues and is the biggest single cause of death for Coalition troops in Afghanistan.

Former ISOI emir Abu Ayub al-Masri, whom many believed was captured or killed in May 2008, also resurfaced in Afghanistan in the summer. In September 2008, Osama bin Laden's late son and heir apparent, 24-year-old Saad bin Laden, relocated from Iran, initially to the 'Islamic Emirate of Waziristan' on the Pakistani side of the border. This was Haqqani-dominated territory where Al Qaeda had installed a regional commander, Mustafa Abul Yazid (who would be killed by a drone in June 2010). Saad bin Laden was accompanied by another high-profile Al Qaeda leader, Sayf Al-Adl—one of Osama bin Laden's closest aides.

As well as the increased use of sophisticated IEDs discussed above, the influx of Al Qaeda operatives was also evidenced by the use of suicide bombers; in 2004 there were only four such attacks in Afghanistan, with seventeen in 2005. In 2006 and 2007, however, there were 136 and 116 respectively; numbers soared in 2008 with 146 suicide attacks; 2009 and 2010 both saw 140 such attacks[31] and 2011 saw an escalation of attacks as the year progressed, with 40 attacks by the end of August having killed 470.[32]

In 2008, another new tactic imported from the Iraqi insurgency saw Taliban fighters disrupting NATO supply lines by attacking convoys on the Khyber Pass. On 7 December, 300 Taliban armed with automatic weapons and RPGs attacked two supply depots, the Portward Logistic Terminal and the Al Faisal Terminal in Peshawar, destroying all 160 NATO vehicles parked there, including lorries laden with supplies for the troops and seventy Humvees.[33] On 8 December a further fifty trucks were destroyed at Peshawar's Bilal Terminal. Supplies for NATO troops in Afghanistan have to travel via Pakistan because Afghanistan has no coast, most of them via Peshawar and then over the mountains via the Khyber Pass. In a victory for the Taliban, the attacks prompted Pakistani officials to close the Khyber Pass for several weeks.

Following an escalation of violence in 2009, US President Obama sent 30,000 extra troops to Afghanistan in an attempt to reproduce the success of the 'Surge' in Iraq. The Taliban were squeezed out of Helmand but migrated the insurgency into other provinces further north such as Kunduz and Bahghlan.

In January 2010, when the increase in US troops should have improved the security situation, the biggest Taliban operation to date saw twenty suicide bombers and as many gunmen attack in the heart of Kabul's heavily protected Green Zone. Having won another term in an allegedly rigged election, President Karzai was swearing in his new cabinet when the attacks occurred.

Security in Kabul had been formally handed over to Afghan troops in August 2008. The fact that such a large number of gunmen and bombers were able to go through the checkpoints carrying weapons, ammunition and explosives indicates the extent to which the Taliban have infiltrated the capital's security apparatus.

In 2011 the Taliban started a campaign of systematic assassinations. These included the 12 July killing of the President's brother, Ahmed Wali Karzai, who was shot dead by his bodyguard, Sardar Mohammad, a trusted friend and a member of Karzai's extended family clan, the Popalzai, who had worked in security for them for more than a decade. The Taliban say they convinced Sardar over a period of many months to betray his boss and called the assassination 'one of our greatest achievements'.[34]

Police chiefs, government ministers, local dignitaries and military leaders were the most common targets along with rank and file members of the security services; according to the Afghan Interior Minister, between March 2009 and March 2011 2,770 police were killed and 4,785 wounded, and 1,052 soldiers were killed with 2,413 wounded. Correspondents for *al-Quds al-Arabi* on the ground estimate that the Taliban and other *jihadi* fighters number in excess of 100,000. Given that there were a million armed Taliban at the height of their power in 2001, this seems reasonable.

In Afghanistan and the tribal areas of Pakistan, Al Qaeda is secure. The international *jihadis* are seen as guests as well as comrades in arms by sympathetic tribes, most of whom are Pashtun. Pashtun culture is governed by a code of honour, *Pashtunwali*, which explicitly forbids the betrayal of guests. This contrasts with the mentality among Iraqi Sunni tribesmen which allowed the Awakening campaign to gain currency, and which also led to the betrayal of Saddam Hussein by his own cousin.

From 2007 to the present, *jihadi* websites sympathetic to Al Qaeda have enjoined Muslims to support the Taliban's battle. Al Qaeda has also been actively fundraising for the Taliban, mostly via the Internet. Since the death of Osama bin Laden, Mullah Omar is increasingly seen as the spiritual leader of the entire AQAM network. His power will increase exponentially as an end to the war with the US nears. Any lasting settlement will almost certainly see the Taliban in total or partial control, with greatly enhanced credibility, operating room and funding. In 2011, leaders of groups from AQAP to Boko Haram emphatically and publically pledged their allegiance to Mullah Omar.

Leadership

The Taliban leadership structure is mirrored by all the main *jihadi* organisations including Al Qaeda. It has a central leadership council—the *rahbari shura*—with four regional *shura* (mainly for planning and carrying out military operations) and ten committees. The *rahbari shura* is more commonly referred to as the Quetta *shura*, being based in the Pakistani city of that name.

As with all AQAM groups, the Taliban leadership has been designed in such a way that roles are widely delegated and younger men are trained as deputies, ready to step into the shoes of 'martyred' or captured colleagues. When Mullah Omar's deputy, Mullah Abdel Ghani Baradar, was captured in Karachi in February 2010, for example, two successors were named—Adel Qayim Zakir (who had been released from Guantanamo in 2007) and Akhtar Muhammad Mansour. A Taliban spokesman told the BBC that this was designed to send out the message that 'one arrest will not affect our movement'.[35]

All four regional military *shura* are based in Pakistan from where they conceive of, and direct, attacks inside Afghanistan. They are located in Quetta (overseeing operations in the south and west of Afghanistan),

Peshawar (overseeing eastern and northern Afghanistan), Miramshah (several provinces and Kabul) and Gerdi (Helmand province).

There are ten committees to deal with: military matters; religious matters (the *Ulema* council); finance; political affairs; culture and information (propaganda and the Internet); interior affairs; prisoners and refugees; education; recruitment; and repatriation (the latter refers to those Taliban who fled abroad during the US invasion).

In early 2010 the Pakistani government, under pressure from the US and Saudi Arabia, acted against the Quetta *shura*, arresting nine out of its eighteen members. Pakistan's policy had previously been to protect Mullah Omar and his government in exile in anticipation of an eventual NATO withdrawal.[36] It would appear that the former status quo has now been resumed.

Intelligence Network

Since 2009 incidents involving double agents and imposters have soared and the Taliban has infiltrated the security apparatus of both Afghanistan and Pakistan. The head of the Taliban Intelligence Service, Hafiz Abdul Majid, is a leading member of the Quetta *shura* and Al Qaeda frequently reminds its adherents of its belief that 'war is deceit'. As a result the Afghan Taliban–TTP–Al Qaeda nexus is increasingly focusing on the intelligence aspect of its planning.

Intelligence is well organised and has several different 'divisions'. The Lashkar-e-Khorozan for example was formed in 2010 in response to the increasing accuracy of US drone strikes on both sides of the border. According to reporters, it has 300 members and seeks to identify local 'spies' who are collaborating with US and Pakistan security and execute them.[37]

The most dramatic intelligence-related incident, on 31 December 2009, resulted in the deaths of seven CIA intelligence operatives, including the organisation's top Al Qaeda specialist, Jennifer Matthews, who had just flown in from CIA headquarters in Langley, Virginia. A suicide attacker—Jordanian triple agent, Doctor Humam Khalil al-Balawi—struck in the heart of the main CIA base in Afghanistan which is concealed inside Fort Chapman in Khost. His Jordanian General Intelligence Department

(GID) 'handler' was also killed in the blast. The attack was the greatest disaster for the CIA since the 1983 Beirut US Embassy bombing. US intelligence community journal *Stratfor* said it was the security equivalent of 'sinking an aircraft carrier in a naval war'.

The logistics of the Khost plot point to a serious, evolving and increasingly interconnected AQAM–Taliban intelligence network throughout AQAM's operational territory. The GID believed they had recruited al-Balawi, who had been sentenced for running a *jihadi* website, in an Amman jail in 2008. It is clear, however, that Al Qaeda men in Jordan were in on the 'sting' from the outset since al-Balawi was able to give the GID, and subsequently the CIA, 'actionable intelligence' to boost his credibility.

Claiming that he was on the track of Al Qaeda deputy, Ayman al-Zawahiri, al-Balawi was moved to Pakistan under cover of pursuing his medical training. Instead, he continued to pen *jihadi* articles under the pseudonym al-Khourasani (the Afghani) and boasted online that he had joined the Afghan Taliban—who would later identify his Khost target and carried out the necessary reconnaissance.

Through his contacts in Al Qaeda and the Afghan Taliban, al-Balawi was able to access the Pakistani Taliban (TTP) leadership with whom he would plan the suicide attack and who would subsequently furnish him with explosives. The extent of collaboration, and the complicated web of logistics and intelligence, was fully revealed in al-Balawi's videotaped 'will and testament'. In it, he is seated next to TTP leader Hakimullah Mehsud (who does not speak Arabic) and explains that his mission is in retaliation for the US drone attack that killed former TTP emir, Beitullah Mehsud, in August 2009. Those drone attacks were launched from Fort Chapman.

The video and a transcript (translated into several languages) was immediately available from Al Qaeda's Global Islamic Media Front. All three *jihadi* organisations—the Afghan Taliban, Al Qaeda and TTP—separately claimed responsibility for the attack. They were announcing in the most dramatic way possible that the distinct elements of the nexus were working in full collaboration with each other.

Prior to al-Balawi's attack, there had been two incidents of Taliban infiltrators killing NATO troops: just one month before, an Afghan policeman opened fire on his British trainers at an outpost in southern

Afghanistan, killing five of them. In October 2009 another Afghan policeman shot dead two US marines who were training him near Kabul.

The *New York Times* received a classified Coalition report which found that between October 2009 and May 2011 there were fifty-eight such killings in twenty-six separate incidents and that officers on the ground expected the problem to escalate.[38] The first four months of 2012 saw sixteen such attacks, among them an incident in January 2012 where an Afghan 'trainee' opened fire on French soldiers, killing four and wounding more than a dozen[39]—an event which prompted President Sarkozy to prepare for a French withdrawal from Afghanistan.

Perhaps the most dramatic evidence of Taliban infiltration was the 25 April 2011 breakout of 546 prisoners—most of them Taliban, including some top-level commanders—from Kandahar's Saraposa prison. The men had maps and plans of the jail and had dug tunnels over a five-month period. When the moment of escape came they also had keys to cells and were able to supervise a mass, well-organised exodus which took several hours and which the guards seemingly failed to notice. In November 2011, the Taliban gleefully announced that their spies 'inside the government of Karzai' had brought them maps and minute details of the security plans for the imminent Loya Jirga.[40]

The Taliban and AQAM are themselves frequently subject to infiltration by security services and deal with spies in a ruthless manner. Ayman al-Zawahiri notoriously tried and executed two teenage spies (one aged just 13) in Sudan in 1995; the Taliban are no more forgiving as this announcement from the Islamic Emirate of Afghanistan on 25 October 2011 demonstrates: 'Javid, the son of Abdul Malook and the grandson of Akbar Shah was killed by *mujahideen* today on spying charges after a judicial hearing. The spy was an Afghan-born American from Farah province and was living in Texas with his family and only arrived recently to Kandahar as an American agent before his capture.'

In May 2012, Saudi intelligence, the CIA and MI6 managed to place a spy right in the heart of AQAP. The Saudi-born British citizen managed to furnish forensic specialists with a fully prepared suicide bomb, concealed in a pair of underpants, which he had convinced AQAP he was going to detonate on a US-bound passenger airplane.

Conclusion: The Future of the Taliban

The Taliban–TTP–Al Qaeda nexus is well funded. The US was able to block much of the $150–200 million donated annually by individuals and organisations in the Gulf, but the Pashtun have traditionally made large sums of money by taxing smugglers bringing drugs, arms and even people over the border. The Taliban also levies a 'tax on harvests' from Afghanistan's opium producers (who supply 93 percent of the world market). The UN estimates that the Taliban's drugs revenue is up to $500 million per annum; the Taliban also benefit from US-funded rebuilding and transportation contracts by levying a percentage from local firms. In 2011 CBS news reported that the US taxpayer had spent $206 billion in civil projects in Afghanistan, with an estimated $360 million going to the Taliban.[41]

In addition it is well equipped and armed, seemingly able to continue to unleash an unbroken string of attacks whose power to harm is undiminished. The Taliban is not in any hurry, then, to enter peace talks with either the discredited Karzai government or the West. Nevertheless, the Taliban are seeking greater credibility and respectability on the world stage as a prelude to regaining, or sharing, power. If violence is no longer necessary, we may see a new era of political pragmatism emerge within the Taliban which, in turn, may affect the wider AQAM groups.

At home, the Taliban have made efforts to present a less extremist image. They lifted bans on televisions, kite-flying, music and dog-fighting in the 'emirate' under their control (around two-thirds of the country). A published *La'iha* (code of conduct) is in place to ensure good relations between the Taliban and local civilian leaders and it is strictly enforced.[42] In addition, they have posted information sheets in public places asking villagers and townspeople to complain if their local Taliban commander was not to their liking and providing a telephone number for the purpose. Reports of draconian public punishments have been fewer in recent years, although women continue to suffer savage retribution for alleged sexual misdemeanours. Sources say that, whereas before they would have beheaded captured government officials, police and military personnel, the Taliban now offer them amnesties. They are asked to switch sides and sometimes return to duty as an infiltrator.

A November 2011 poll found that 82 percent of the population now hope for a political accommodation with the Taliban.[43] According to sources on the ground, the Taliban have set up an efficient media machine in order to control their image and are even embedding journalists with their brigades.

The Taliban is clearly intent on regaining power in Afghanistan and Al Qaeda has proved a formidable ally in their fight to do so. The strategic implications of a Taliban return for AQAM cannot be underestimated; as Osama bin Laden wrote in an April 2011 letter, '*Jihad* in Afghanistan is the path towards conducting the larger duty, which is liberating the one-and-a-half billion-strong *umma* and reclaiming its Holy Places.'

Paradoxically, as the balance of power in the Middle East changes as a result of the Arab Spring and a Cold War–style alignment is resumed along sectarian lines, the US might prefer a hard-line Sunni government in Kabul to counteract Shi'i Iran's growing regional hegemony and ally with Saudi Arabia. After all, this is more or less the situation that existed in the 1980s when the CIA was training the *mujahideen* as their proxy in the *jihad* against the Soviet Union. In December 2011, after ten years of war, thousands of deaths, millions displaced and trillions of dollars squandered, President Obama's Vice President Joe Biden declared, 'The Taliban is not our enemy.'[44]

5

The Taliban–Al Qaeda Nexus: Pakistan

Pakistan will prove to be, Allah willing,
a stronghold of the Islamic Caliphate.
Hakimullah Mehsud, November 2011

Pakistan's tribal regions are the epicentre of terrorism.
Admiral Mike Mullen, August 2011

Pakistan is the political product of two British-brokered, artificial borders. The 1947 partitioning of India created what would become, in 1956, the 'Islamic Republic of Pakistan'—a nation predicated on religious conflict with its Hindu southern neighbour. It is in this context that Pakistan's numerous *jihadi* groups have emerged, and that the uniquely dangerous collusion between the state's security apparatus and violent extremism has evolved. Indeed, several of the most dangerous *jihadi* groups were created, armed and funded by the Inter-Services Intelligence (ISI) as military proxies.

As we recalled in the previous chapter, the Afghan–Pakistan border was also imposed by the British, along the Durand line, in the latter part of the nineteenth century; unsurprisingly, tribal connections and loyalties here remain strong on both sides. Pakistan and Afghanistan are further bound by Islam and, latterly, *jihad*. When the US started its bombardment of Afghanistan in November 2001, an estimated 10,000 individuals from the Pakistani North-West Frontier Province (NWFP) crossed the border to offer their services to the Taliban.[1]

More recently, an indigenous Taliban organisation has emerged on the Pakistani side of the border, greatly expanding the territory for NATO's nemesis—a factor which has undoubtedly influenced the direction of the Afghan conflict in the Taliban's favour. The Tehrek-e-Taliban Pakistan (TTP), established in 2007, is an umbrella grouping of twenty-eight like-minded *jihadi* organisations. There is also a Taliban movement in the Punjab incorporating major *jihadi* groups including Lashkar-e-Taiba (LeT), which carried out the 2008 Mumbai atrocities. There are many other *jihad* groups which largely support, both ideologically and operationally, the TTP and Al Qaeda.

Estimates vary but sources claim, and it seems credible in a country with a population of 180 million, that the number of Taliban sympathisers in Pakistan is around 4 million, with 80,000 of these armed fighters.

As of 2010 Pakistan only slightly lags behind Somalia as the country most affected by terrorism in the world.[2] Pakistan has also been exporting violence. With the introduction of Al Qaeda's global ideology, the threat to the West from Pakistan-based *jihadi* groups has greatly increased. According to a study carried out for the New America Foundation by analyst Paul Cruickshank, 'More serious plots emerged in the West in 2010 linked to established *jihadi* groups in Pakistan than in any year since Al Qaeda built up its operations in FATA in the early 2000s.' Cruickshank also considers that, 'Al Qaeda's safe haven in Pakistan has actually become more dangerous [than Yemen] in recent years . . . of the thirty-two *jihadi* terrorist plots launched against the West between 2004 and 2011, 53 percent had operational or training links to Pakistani-based *jihadi* groups whereas only 6 percent had links to Yemen.'[3]

One well-publicised and, happily, failed TTP-claimed attack was the 1 May 2010 Times Square car bomb. Would-be suicide bomber Faisal Shahzad, an accounts analyst who earned $50,000 per annum, said in his 'will and testament' that his attack was in revenge for all Muslim martyrs, al-Zarqawi in particular, and that he looked forward to the day democracy would be defeated.[4]

Counter-terrorism cooperation between Pakistani and US agencies continued through 2010 and 2011 in the Federally Administered Tribal Areas (FATA) but America's use of unmanned drones provoked public outcry due to the high cost in civilian casualties—957 civilians were killed in 2010 alone. Following the death of bin Laden in May 2011, Pew

Global Attitudes polled the Pakistani public: 63 percent disapproved of the killing and 70 percent considered the US an enemy.[5] In November 2011, a drone killed twenty-four Pakistan soldiers at the Salala border post, resulting in Pakistan withdrawing permission for the US to use its airspace—a ban which lasted just fifty-five days.[6]

Relations between the two countries had already seriously deteriorated after bin Laden's death, with the ISI and Pakistani Army accusing the US of breaching their national sovereignty and failing to inform them of their plans. The US meanwhile accused the Pakistani Army and the ISI of having offered the Al Qaeda leader safe haven. President Zardari protested his innocence but it is perfectly conceivable that he was not informed of the situation. The 'accidental president' was elected on a wave of public sympathy following the assassination of his wife, Benazir Bhutto, in 2007. In October 2011, he allegedly sent an anonymous memo to the American State Department (via Pakistani envoy Hussein Haqqani) begging for US help to 'curb the Army'; a move which prompted Pakistani Army chief, General Ashfaq Parvez Kayani, as well as ISI chief, Ahmed Shuja Pasha, to accuse the president of 'conspiracy'.

The evident antipathy between the ISI and CIA can only work to the *jihadis*' advantage. In October 2010, the Pakistani media 'leaked' the identity of the CIA's Islamabad station chief—the most important CIA operative in the country, a covert military commander who runs the drone programme and processes the most urgent and significant tip-offs. He was obliged to leave the country immediately following death threats. The ISI—almost certainly the source of this information—frequently plants stories in the Pakistani press, and has journalists on its payroll. On 10 May 2011, just a week after bin Laden's death, the name of the new CIA chief was leaked to the press. The CIA has repeatedly ignored requests for information from the Zardari government's 'Enquiry Commission into the Abbottabad Operation'.

Pakistan is a hive of *jihadi* organisations and they are an intrinsic part of society in some regions, providing basic welfare, employment and education in *madrassas*. Just how 'everyday' they are is evident in the Pakistani-published book, *A–Z of Jehadi Organizations in Pakistan*, which not only lists well over 200 such groups but includes the names of the regional leaders and the addresses where they might be found![7]

Many of these groups, as well as *jihadi* groups in Kashmir, have joined what Pakistani expert Muhammad Amir Rana called 'the bigger alliance of holy warriors led by Al Qaeda' in a January 2012 report on the security situation in Pakistan. Rana also identified an escalation of Sunni–Shi'i sectarian violence and expected this to constitute an ongoing security problem, 'because there are now strong nexuses among sectarian groups, the Taliban and Al Qaeda'.[8]

Of interest in the context of the Arab Spring, and the question of political engagement by radical Islamist groups, is the fact that many of Pakistan's *jihadi* groups have a political wing, or are connected with a political party, and take an active part in the political process. Rana notes that 'Many of the banned sectarian organisations wear political hats in order to take part in electoral politics... through this practice these groups gain political legitimacy.'[9]

Rana mentions the Islamist party Sipah-e-Sahaba (SSP) as an example. The SSP had a role in the Pervez Musharraf–led government and has political influence nowadays in the Punjab government. A leaked 2009 cable from the US Embassy in Islamabad noted that a key figure in the Pakistani Taliban (TTP), Qari Hussein Mehsud, was also a member of the SSP, as were many of the Taliban's foot soldiers. In the NWFP a coalition of Islamist parties, with an undisguised anti-US agenda, Muttahida Majlis-e-Ama (MMA), won local government elections just three months after 9/11.

Tehrek-e-Taliban Pakistan

Though the Afghan and Pakistani Taliban are organisationally distinct, their agenda is almost identical: the establishment of an Islamic emirate under Sharia law throughout the region. The majority of the region's militant training camps are now in Pakistan; most of the Afghan Taliban leadership, including Mullah Omar, is believed to be based in Quetta, whence it organises and launches attacks within Afghanistan, apparently undisturbed by the Pakistani security apparatus.

According to Pakistani expert on *jihadi* organisations Muhammad Amir Rana, Quetta is a hive of *jihadi* activity, housing offices for five major Pakistani outfits including Lashkar-e-Taiba, Al-Badar, Harkat-ul-Mujaheddin, Harkat-ul-Jihad and Hizbul Mujaheddin International.[10]

The tribal regions first became radicalised during the 1980s' *mujahideen* war against the Soviet Union when they helped channel weapons across the border to Afghanistan. As a consequence, the tribesmen were well armed and battle-ready when the TTP emerged.

The TTP's power base is in the Pashtun-dominated tribal areas: mainly the NWFP and FATA—areas of influence it has in common with the Haqqani network.[11] The Taliban are also expanding their influence in parts of Balochistan.

From early 2002 the tribal areas underwent a rapid 'Talibanisation' as the Pakistan Army, under pressure from the US, attempted to flush out the Islamist influence. The TTP see themselves as the 'saviours of Pakistan'[12] in the face of an 'apostate' government intent on doing America's bidding.

In a March 2012 interview Wali-ur-Rehman Mehsud, the TTP's regional commander in Waziristan, underlined the group's view of Pakistani society in terms that resonate strongly with the Arab Spring protestors: 'Every single institution or organisation in Pakistan from a normal police constable to the highest government officials, everyone is corrupt... they have eaten up the rights of the poor in every way possible. The rich are getting richer and the poor is getting poorer,' he declared. The TTP see themselves as the 'saviours of Pakistan' and believe that 'Islam is the only solution to these problems. Manmade rules based on the western model have failed.'

In the same interview, Wali-ur-Rehman Mehsud describes the group's origins, confirming a long-standing relationship with Al Qaeda: 'In 2003 the Arab *mujahideen* transferred into our area... we were told either to deliver the *mujahideen* to the Pakistani government or send them out of our areas.' Wali-ur-Rehman makes a direct comparison with the dilemma faced by the Afghan Taliban in the face of US demands that they hand bin Laden over: 'in the same way that the *amir-ul-Momineen* [Mullah Omar] fought against those demands without worrying about the consequences and refused them so we had the same response to the demands of the Pakistani government... this is why the war was imposed on us in our areas, simply to achieve the American agenda and interests'.[13]

Tribally affiliated Taliban groups sprung up in North and South Waziristan, Oraksai, Kurram, Khyber, Mohmand, Bajaur and Darra Adamkhel. The districts of Buner, Upper Dir, Lower Dir, Bannu, Lakki

Marwat, Tank, Peshawar, Dera Ismail Khan, Mardan and Kohat also produced Taliban forces.

The following account of what happened in the lawless Swat district, home of the Yusufzai tribe, gives us a vivid picture of how the group established itself in the region over a period of time. In 2007, a local Taliban leader, 32-year-old Maulana Fazlullah, consolidated his control over fifty-nine villages by installing his own government. Fazlullah's men hoisted the black and white Taliban flag in place of the Pakistani national flag outside police stations and established Islamic courts. Reports suggest that the Taliban takeover was welcomed by the populace whilst dissenters feared speaking out. Some locals told reporters that the Taliban's brand of justice was an improvement on the ponderous state apparatus it replaced; the women of one village gave Fazlullah 4 kg of gold after he arrested and punished three people who had kidnapped another local woman.[14]

At just 17 percent for men and 3 percent for women, the tribal areas have the lowest rate of literacy in the world. These areas have always been considered ungovernable by outside agencies, although FATA is still ostensibly controlled by the Frontier Crimes Regulations (FCR) which were established under British colonial rule; the NWFP has a regional administration. In recent years, largely due to an increasingly 'webbed-up' network of AQAM groups in Pakistan, the TTP has allies and operational capacity throughout the country.

The Leadership

The first TTP emir, Baitullah Mehsud, declared war on the Pakistani government and is said to have orchestrated the suicide bombing that assassinated Pakistani President Benazir Bhutto in December 2007. Baitullah himself died in August 2009, either killed by a US airstrike, as the government claim, or of 'a serious illness' if his comrades are to be believed. Rival contenders for his position were prevented from fighting each other when Haqqani Network leader, Sirajuddin Haqqani, reminded them of the need for unity to combat their common enemies—the Pakistani regime and America.

This is not intended to be a comprehensive list but a sketch of the TTP leadership which has, in any case, been damaged by the concerted

US drone campaign. These are the main leaders we believe to be still alive at the time of writing.

Hakimullah Mehsud

Hakimullah Mehsud is the current emir and was close to the original leader, and fellow tribesman, Baitullah Mehsud. Born Jamshed Mehsud around 1979 in a town called Jandola in South Waziristan, Hakimullah had little formal education, joining Baitullah in *jihad* at an early age. He served as Baitullah's bodyguard before making his name in a series of daring raids, including his hallmark bombardments of NATO supply lines which were followed by triumphal parades of captured lorries and Humvees. In 2008 Hakimullah demonstrated the ruthlessness for which he has become infamous when his men managed to kidnap an entire platoon of 300 Pakistani paramilitary soldiers. In exchange for the release of 100 Taliban from prison, Hakimullah set most of the paramilitaries free ... but not all; he killed five of them and returned their mutilated bodies. These incidents have boosted Hakimullah's popularity, and not only with the hard-line element in the Taliban; videos on YouTube show him being feted as a hero in towns and villages as he and his men ride in on stolen Humvees, brandishing Kalashnikovs and RPG launchers.

A BBC correspondent who has met Hakimullah describes him as 'personable ... but radiating danger'[15] and relates a hair-raising journey with Hakimullah at the wheel which ended with a screech of brakes inches from the edge of a precipice.

His appointment as emir suggests that the more radical, hard-line element holds sway within the TTP. As reports circulated of imminent talks between the government and 'moderate' TTP representatives in January 2012, fifteen Pakistani soldiers kidnapped by Hakimullah in the Khyber Agency were murdered in cold blood and their bodies sent back as another grim warning to the regime.[16]

Qari Hussein Mehsud

Qari Hussein Mehsud (Mehsud is a tribal, rather than family, name) is Hakimullah's deputy and is considered an expert trainer—especially of suicide bombers. He taught Faisal Shahzad how to build the car bomb which ultimately failed to detonate in Times Square, 1 May 2010. Qari was the spokesman on the TTP video claiming responsibility for the attack. With long-standing connections to Al Qaeda, he was also key to the Fort Chapman CIA attack and is believed to have trained the Jordanian triple agent Balawi for his suicide mission. He is believed to be based in the Mir Ali region of Waziristan. The Pakistani government frequently announces the deaths of TTP leaders and claimed that Qari had been killed in October 2010. He resurfaced soon afterwards, however, and was added to the US State Department's list of global terrorists in January 2011.

Wali-ur-Rehman Mehsud

Wali-ur-Rehman Mehsud is the leader of the Movement of the Taliban in Pakistan in the Mehsud tribal area of South Waziristan. In his early forties, he is well educated and from a middle-class family. He was a member of the Jamiat Ulema-e-Islam, an Islamist political party, but joined the Taliban movement in 2003. He is reportedly the TTP's chief military strategist and is in charge of its finances.

Faqir Mohammed

Faqir Mohammed is the TTP regional leader in Bajaur and is believed to be overall second in command. Like most of the TTP leadership his death has been reported on several occasions by the Pakistani regime. The last time this happened was March 2010 but Faqir surfaced again with a radio broadcast from Afghanistan in July 2011. He is reputed to be close to Al Qaeda leader Ayman al-Zawahiri (who has long been rumoured to be based in Bajaur). Bajaur is used as an Al Qaeda forward base for operations in northeast Afghanistan.

Qari Zia Rahman

Qari Zia Rahman (not to be confused with Attiyah Abdel Rahman) is a commander in both the TTP and Al Qaeda and is also based in Bajaur. He leads a group of multinational *jihadis* from many Arab countries as well as Chechnya, Uzbekistan and Turkmenistan. He is an intelligence expert and also trains female suicide bombers, according to sources. He may have been captured by Pakistani security in July 2011 but has often been reported dead or captured.

In addition to the above, leaders fulfilling the extremist sectarian agenda include Maulvi Noor Jamal (aka Maulvi Toofan) and Fazal Saeed Utezai, hard-liners who have been spearheading sectarian attacks against the Shi'i tribes in Kurram province. In addition, Mufti Ilyas, based in Darra Adam Khel, has formed a group with the specific aim of assassinating Shi'i leaders.

The TTP/Afghan Taliban/Al Qaeda Connection

In November 2011 Hakimullah Mehsud posted a 'statement of policy' on *jihadi* websites in which he described the relationship between the TTP and Afghan Taliban:

> The Muslim *umma* is one body, and as Muslims we do not accept the divisions of the Durand Line or any other borders. We are all the loyal soldiers of the *Emir al Mominen*, Mohammad Mullah Omar. He is our leader and guide. The services and sacrifices made by Tehrik-e-Taliban Pakistan for the Islamic Emirate of Afghanistan have long been proven and our link with them will only grow stronger.

Hakimullah thanks the Pashtun tribes for their 'loyalty' and 'support', lists several TTP attacks on Pakistani soil and claims that 'Many areas have returned to our control'. He reasserts his Islamic credentials saying, 'The *mujahideen* are under the strict guidance of the scholars of the movement, who ensure that all work is done in line with Islam and the Shariah.' He concludes with the wish that 'Pakistan will be a stronghold of the Islamic caliphate', emphasising that the TTP have embraced the global *jihadi* ideology of Al Qaeda.

The Al Qaeda connection is long-standing: Ayman al-Zawahiri spoke of his love for Pakistan in his 11 September 2008 broadcast and revealed that he had lived in Peshawar on and off for six years in the 1980s. In 2002 and 2003, under continuous American bombardment of militant strongholds in Afghanistan, Al Qaeda and Taliban fighters—as well as millions of refugees—fled over the porous border into Pakistan. Most found refuge in Waziristan and the FATA while others migrated to Pakistani cities far from the northern border, indicating an ease of movement and a network of friendly agencies within Pakistan as a whole. 9/11's Khaled Sheikh Mohammed, for example, was eventually captured in Karachi, as was Ramzi Binalshibh.

Thousands of Arab *jihadis* have made their home in Waziristan and many have married the Pashtun widows of Taliban fighters, ensuring that they will enjoy the continued loyalty and protection of local tribespeople.

In August 2011 the Libyan Attiyah Abdel Rahman, a prominent Al Qaeda leader, closely associated with Ayman al-Zawahiri, was killed by a CIA drone strike near Mir Ali, in North Waziristan, Pakistan. Rahman had been very active in Iraq alongside al-Zarqawi and had migrated first to Afghanistan in 2006, fleeing the 'Surge'; he was a key coordinator in many operational collaborations with the Taliban (and other groups), including Fort Chapman. We were surprised to see just how many messages of condolences from AQAM emirs his death garnered on *jihadi* websites, incidentally—as many as that of Osama bin Laden himself. Attiyah must have been extremely significant to the *jihadi* community.

The FATA area is a magnet for foreign *jihadis* sympathetic to the Taliban and Al Qaeda. Thousands of foreign fighters from most Arab countries, North Africa, Uzbekistan, Chechnya, western China and even Europe and America moved to both sides of the border in the tribal areas. By 2008 reports suggested there were already 4,000 British-born fighters[17] and hundreds of Turks—an unprecedented phenomenon.[18] In September 2009, the *Daily Telegraph* reported that there was a whole 'German village' among the Taliban fighters in Waziristan.[19] In his December 2009 'will and testament', Jordanian suicide bomber al-Balawi spoke of the 'emigrants who were hosted by Beitullah Mehsud', confirming that the TTP is welcoming foreign *jihadis* into its ranks.

There were almost no suicide attacks inside Pakistan until 2002, when Al Qaeda started training fighters in this method.[20] Another grisly innovation from Al Qaeda is the use of female suicide bombers, which became relatively commonplace in Iraq when al-Zarqawi was running the insurgency. The TTP say that this is now part of their strategy; it is facilitated by the fact that a *burqa* effectively covers the wearer from head to toe. The first occurred in December 2010 when a woman blew herself up at a food distribution point run by the World Food Programme in FATA, killing forty-seven and injuring over a hundred. In August 2011, a teenager detonated her suicide vest at a police checkpoint in Peshawar in August 2011.

The ISI and the *Jihadis*

Abbottabad, where Osama bin Laden was assassinated, was well known for two things: being the home of Pakistan's equivalent of Sandhurst and being a hotbed of radical Islamist groups. Pakistan's most violent and effective groups, Lashkar-e-Taiba (LeT) and Jaish-e-Mohammad (JeM), both had branches there. This apparently incongruous situation gives us a snapshot of the way Pakistan has long run its security affairs; creating and mentoring radical Islamist groups for use as proxies in pursuit of its own political agenda, be it facing off India or championing the Afghan Taliban. It is an expensive strategy—5,000 Pakistani military personnel and 35,000 citizens had been killed by militant Islamists by September 2011.[21]

It is inconceivable that Osama bin Laden could have been living in the Abbottabad compound without the knowledge and cooperation of Pakistan's Inter-Services Intelligence (ISI)—which answers to the Pakistani Army. Bin Laden's comrade, Jalaluddin Haqqani, whose ISI links are rarely disputed, had also relocated nearby.

As we have seen, bin Laden's compound was known locally as the Waziristan Haveli, which suggests that the provenance of its inhabitants was well known. Just a few months before his death, the leader of the Indonesian Al Qaeda branch, Umar Patek (who allegedly master-minded the Bali disco bombings), was arrested in Abbottabad, a long way from home, which must surely have caused security entities to ask questions.[22]

Information gleaned from the mobile phone of Ibrahim Saeed Ahmed—the 'courier' who unwittingly led the CIA to the Waziristan Haveli—show several calls to commanders of Harkat-ul-Mujaheddin (HuM), an Islamist organisation with long-standing roots in Abbottabad and Waziristan. HuM is closely linked to the Haqqani Network, with whom it has cooperated on joint operations in Afghanistan.[23] This connection would have enabled bin Laden to stay in touch with other Al Qaeda and Taliban leaders in Waziristan and make financial transactions.

By tracing calls made from the HuM contacts' numbers, US intelligence officials discovered that they, in turn, had been in touch with the ISI.[24] The ISI does not deny that it knew the compound housed an important Al Qaeda figure and even claims it alerted the Americans to it in 2009.[25]

Over the past thirty years, the ISI has played a major role in the establishment, survival and growth of various Islamist movements, including the Taliban. To understand how such a situation has arisen, we need to look at the origins of the ISI, which was founded within a year of the Partition (of Pakistan from India) in 1948. Naming the organisation the Inter-Services Intelligence belies its true make-up, since it is almost entirely dominated by the Pakistan Army, and the ISI director-general is always an army lieutenant-general.

The ISI is widely seen as exerting a disproportionate amount of power, leading some commentators to describe it as a state within a state. Islamic militancy thrives in Pakistan which, like neighbouring India, is a state predicated on religious antagonism. The military dictators who have ruled Pakistan for the majority of its existence were quick to see how Islamic militancy could be turned to their own advantage by ensuring a continued enmity against a powerful India, diluting nationalistic and separatist tendencies in the Sunni Pashtun and Baloch regions, and generally acting as a smokescreen for the absence of democracy.

The ISI has long been linked to the American CIA: many of its top brass trained in the United States, and it adopts similar methods, including setting up or adopting guerrilla groups which oppose hostile regimes. 'My enemy's enemy is my friend' is the guiding principle. Relations between the two agencies have not always run smoothly, however, as we have seen above.

During the Afghan war in the 1980s the ISI, under the military dictator Zia ul-Haq, supported, trained and armed the *mujahideen* and acted as a conduit for US and Saudi aid to the fighters. When the Taliban came to power in 1996, Pakistan, under Benazir Bhutto, was one of only three states to recognise their government's legitimacy, together with Saudi Arabia and the UAE.

After the attacks of 9/11, former Pakistan president Pervez Musharraf pledged his allegiance to the US in its war on terror. Yet prior to seizing power in 1999, when he was director-general of military operations at army headquarters, Musharraf had personally overseen ISI assistance to the Taliban. He had also, as Army Chief of Staff, dispatched hundreds of *jihadis* into Kashmir. No wonder the ISI was dubbed 'Invisible Soldiers Inc.' by its critics.

The problem for the US and Pakistan's President Asif Ali Zardari is that the ties and loyalties built between ISI agents and Islamist militants in the past still endure. It has often been noted that Pakistanis are Muslims first and Pakistanis second.

In July 2008 a delegation from the Pakistani coalition government was called to Washington. Prime Minister Gilani and Zardari (then leader of the Pakistan Peoples Party, PPP) were taken to task about the ISI and presented with a long list detailing the organisation's continued links with Islamist groups. The US insisted that ISI agents, under its then head, Lieutenant-General Nadeem Taj, were tipping off militants ahead of attacks on their strongholds. American doubts were clearly not dispelled. In May 2010 Secretary of State Hillary Clinton declared unequivocally on CBS that at least an element within the Pakistani government knew exactly where bin Laden, Mullah Omar and other Al Qaeda leaders were. When the Obama administration decided to raid the Abbottabad compound in May 2011, they did not risk informing the Pakistani authorities.

The problem probably does not lie with Zardari, nor necessarily with the upper echelons of the army and the ISI. In 2008, in response to US pressure, he attempted to take the ISI out of military control, and announced that it would be made part of the Ministry of the Interior. However, the army reacted so furiously that the idea was dropped by Prime Minister Gilani within twenty-four hours, perhaps for fear of a military coup.

In September 2008 (with Zardari now in place as president), army chief General Ashfaq Kayani installed a new ISI director-general, Pashtun Lieutenant-General Ahmed Shuja Pasha. Pasha is said to have close links with the CIA and to hold anti-Taliban views. His previous job as head of operations involved targeting Al Qaeda and the Taliban in the tribal districts.

Even if loyalty to the government line can be assured at the ISI's top level, it is not the case among the middle and lower ranks, many of whom have Islamist sympathies and a deep dislike of US interference in the region. Zardari's policy of facilitating US attacks and drone strikes on *jihadi* targets inside Pakistan has not been popular with the military.

An ongoing plot to unseat Zardari was first noted in a 2009 leaked cable from the US Embassy. The cable noted that Zardari and other politicians were seeking immunity from prosecution on corruption charges via a parliamentary bill, the National Reconciliation Ordinance (NRO), and that the ISI had been approaching politicians in a bid to persuade them to vote against it. This, the writer of the cable understood, 'signaled the start of a long-rumored campaign by the Pakistani Army to oust President Zardari'. By April 2012 Pasha and Kayani were overtly accusing both President Zardari and Prime Minister Gilani of 'conspiracy'. The judiciary joined forces with the generals in an intensified campaign and in June 2012 the Supreme Court convicted Gilani of contempt, linked to his refusal to re-open corruption charges against Zardari, and removed him from his post.

The Pakistan Army has a poor record in the tribal areas. Whenever it enters Waziristan it suffers high levels of casualties and many lower rank soldiers and middle rank officers are loath to fight their fellow Muslims. Despite government pledges to crack down on militant groups in the tribal areas it has only acted with considerable reluctance and even at the height of anti-terrorist activity in 2010–11 was still leaving most of the fighting to the US.

The ISI's sphere of influence extends beyond its national borders: as well as training groups in Kashmir, the ISI has also encouraged the establishment of *jihadi* groups within India's minority Muslim community such as the Student Islamic Movement of India (SIM) and a branch of LeT. Much of the region's chaos can be blamed on the ISI's meddling and manipulation, but it is too late to put the genie back in the bottle.

The Network Widens

As we have seen above, Pakistan has become a hub for *jihadi* groups and individuals from Asia and all over the world. In April 2001, just five months before 9/11, the authorities allowed at least half a million disparate *jihadis* and Islamists to gather near Peshawar for a three-day conference. Taped speeches by Mullah Omar and Osama bin Laden were broadcast over loudspeakers and won the most enthusiastic ovations.[26]

Pakistan is home to hundreds of *jihadi* groups, many of them sympathetic to the global *jihadi* ideology of Al Qaeda. The largest and most dangerous are Lashkar-e-Taiba (LeT) and Jaish-e-Mohammad (JeM). Lashkar-e-Taiba was actually founded in Afghanistan's Kunar province (in 1990) by its present leader, Hafiz Mohammed Saeed, a religious scholar. A local analyst confirmed in 2006 that the ISI was LeT's 'main source of finance'.[27] Like Al Qaeda ideologues, Saeed's ultimate ambition is to impose a global caliphate.

Although the majority of LeT's attacks have taken place within the Indian subcontinent, Saeed has often declared that the group's main enemies are India, Israel and the US and the group made good their threats with the horrific massacres in Mumbai on 26 November 2008 in which at least 200 people lost their lives. The group was also behind the seven blasts on Mumbai's suburban rail network on 11 July 2006 which took 211 lives, maimed 400 and seriously injured 768 more.

LeT is very active in the Kashmir conflict and is the only Pakistani Islamist group with a significant presence and support base in India (which has 151 million Muslims). It was also accused of an attack on the Indian Parliament on 13 December 2001 which killed twelve.

Further afield, arrests in Iraq in 2004 indicated a link between LeT and the insurgency there. Several Pakistanis arrested in Baghdad were known LeT operatives. The LeT membership is not exclusively Pakistani: fighters from Afghanistan, Sudan, Bahrain, Central Asia, Turkey and Libya have all been identified in their ranks. American David Headley was implicated in the Mumbai attacks and a foiled attempt to launch a similar assault in December 2010 at the offices of the Danish newspaper *Jyllands-Posten* which published the 'Mohammad cartoons'.[28]

LeT is also believed to have a branch in Germany and links with many global *jihadi* groups, via the Al Qaeda network, in the Middle East (especially Saudi Arabia) and beyond—all of whom send delegates to its annual convention and offer financial aid. LeT is a highly militarised organisation with 2,200 training camps and offices across Pakistan. The majority of these camps are shared with Al Qaeda and the Taliban. Recruits are given two to five months' training in handling AK rifles, rocket launchers, other light weapons and grenades.

The LeT pioneered the strategy of group suicide attacks whereby clusters of two to seven members storm and occupy a target building, killing as many people as possible before they themselves are killed or captured. This method has been mirrored by AQAM groups in Afghanistan, Iraq and Yemen.

Jaish-e-Mohammad (JeM) is a splinter group from Harkat ul-Mujaheddin (HuM) and was formed in 1994. Although it was outlawed by the Pakistani government in the wake of 9/11 it remains highly active, sometimes under other guises. The emir of JeM is Maulana (Mullah) Masood Azhar, who graduated from the *madrassa* Jamiya Uloom-e-Islami in Karachi. Many of the Afghan Taliban leadership graduated from the same institution and Azhar has maintained close links with them.

Azhar was arrested shortly after JeM's foundation in 1994. He was freed from prison when HuM operatives, including his brother Ibrahim Athar, hijacked Indian Airlines flight 814 from Kathmandu, landing it in Taliban Kandahar in December 1999; the hijackers demanded—and ultimately obtained—the release of Azhar in exchange for hostages.

The JeM was implicated, along with the LeT, in the December 2001 bomb attacks on the Indian Parliament and the November 2008 Mumbai massacres. It shares several aspects of LeT's modus operandi, including the use of small suicide brigades to storm and secure a target.

On 1 February 2002, the JeM murdered the kidnapped US journalist Daniel Pearl, who was investigating the links between Pakistani Islamist groups and Al Qaeda. They set a gruesome precedent by beheading him on film. In his March 2007 testimony in the US, senior Al Qaeda figure Khaled Sheikh Mohammed claimed that he had personally committed this atrocity.[29] On 7 May 2004, Abu Musab al-Zarqawi (seven months prior to officially becoming the leader of Al Qaeda in Iraq) mirrored his comrade's grisly deed by beheading US businessman Nick Berg on videotape.

Other groups based in Pakistan include Sipah-e-Sahaba Pakistan (SSP), a sectarian, Deobandi breakaway movement which was part of the Jamiat Ulema-e-Islam (JUI) until 1984 or 1985. Although it is now dominated by its political wing—which plays an active role in national politics—it was supported and funded by the ISI under Zia ul-Haq. Several of its brigades were sent to fight in Afghanistan with Osama bin Laden. One of its most notorious affiliates was Ramzi Yousef, who had met members of the group in joint Arab–Pakistan training camps in Afghanistan. Yousef is the nephew of Al Qaeda's Khaled Sheikh Mohammed; he has been given a lifelong prison sentence for the 1993 World Trade Center attack. Non-Pakistani Islamist groups based in the country, largely in FATA, include cells from the Islamic Movement of Uzbekistan, Islamic Jihad, the Libyan Islamic Fighters Group and the Eastern Turkistan Islamic Movement.

Conclusion: The Future for Pakistan's *Jihadi* Movement

The TTP has evolved from a nationalist entity with a Pakistan-centric agenda into a multinational one which is looking increasingly outwards. Its main concerns are still to do with expanding its own power base and alliances at home, its war with the regime and the US, and its support for and collaboration with the Afghan Taliban in its war with NATO. More recently it has also started to look outwards, exporting violence to other Muslim countries (in May 2012 the mayor of Timbuktu confirmed that Pakistani *jihadis* had arrived to train Islamist insurgents in northern Mali) and the West.

The TTP has embedded itself in various strongholds across the country; while its biggest power base remains the FATA and NWFP, the concentration of counter-terrorism activities in those areas has allowed the *jihadis* carte blanche in other areas such as Karachi and the Punjab.

It seems that the local population, particularly in the tribal areas, is largely sympathetic to the *jihadis*, which makes the task of rooting them out even harder. An Iraq-style 'Awakening' campaign is unlikely to succeed, given existing tribal loyalties and local culture.

In 2003 and 2007 the government encouraged some tribal elders to raise *lashkars* (a traditional *ad hoc* militia raised to fulfil one specific task) to evict TTP and AQAM groups from their areas. Even though they gathered thousands, they failed and were further discouraged from repeating the experience when the TTP began targeting them individually—by 2009, 300 elders had been assassinated.

The US, increasingly desperate to leave Afghanistan, sees Pakistan as key to its efforts. The US has secured the loyalties of the regime by massive injections of aid and contributions to mega projects such as the Satpara and Gomal Zam hydroelectric dams; these and further billions depend on a secret scorecard of US counter-terror objectives. However, while Presidents Zardari and Karzai may be willing to do America's bidding, both are deeply unpopular with their own people. Zardari risks being deposed by a military coup and Karzai's situation is equally precarious.

The ambiguous relationship between the Afghan Taliban, the TTP and the Pakistani state was thrown into sharp relief in the aftermath of the Mumbai massacre in 2008 when tensions between India and Pakistan reached critical levels. The Taliban groups announced that they, and their AQAM allies, would send brigades to fight alongside the Pakistan army in the event of an escalation. Local news media also reported cordial exchanges between the Pakistani Taliban and army and a temporary truce allowing the safe redeployment of 20,000 troops commissioned to fight the insurgency to the border with India instead.

Pakistanis speak of an entrenched mistrust of the Americans within the army and widespread scepticism regarding the 'war on terror'. From the Pakistani point of view, the US might leave them 'high and dry' with a hostile regime in Afghanistan and India an emerging superpower. It is not surprising that many in the army and ISI would prefer to see the Taliban reinstated and an Islamic state in Pakistan, creating an Islamist bloc across a huge area of Asia and reconfiguring the balance of power with India.

For these reasons, the West cannot fully count on Pakistan to support the 'war on terror'. If Zardari falls, a military regime might adopt a less obliging approach to the US and return to a more proactive role in regional politics via the ISI. Pakistan, with its semi-official support for and accommodation of the Taliban–AQAM nexus, its nuclear capability and deeply entrenched hatred of India, is potentially the most dangerous of all 'fields of *jihad*'.

6

Al Qaeda in the Islamic Maghreb: Algeria, Morocco, Tunisia and the Sahel

Kidnapping the two French spies and three other Europeans is a valid response to repeated aggression from France and the unrepentant foolishness of Sarkozy's policies.
AQIM statement, Al-Masad Media, December 2011

We are at war with Al Qaeda.
French Prime Minister François Fillon, July 2010[1]

The Maghreb, meaning 'west' in Arabic, consists of the North African countries to the west of the Nile: that is, Libya, Tunisia, Algeria, Morocco and the Western Sahara. Chapter 7 will be devoted to AQAM-related activity in Libya. The Maghreb is likely to be among Al Qaeda's most fertile territories over the next few years due, in part at least, to political turmoil throughout the region produced by the Arab Spring.

With the exception of Algeria, every Maghreb country has seen a political shake-up in favour of Islamist parties in 2011–12. In Tunisia—the region's most liberal country under dictator Zine el Abidinde ben Ali—the formerly banned Ennahda party gained the largest share of the vote in October 2011 elections with 41 percent. Ennahda members now hold the posts of prime minister, interior minister and foreign minister in the new coalition government. In Egypt, a complex electoral system produced an overwhelming majority for the Islamists, who gained 67 percent of the vote in January 2012—38 percent to the Muslim Brotherhood's

Freedom and Justice Party and only slightly less (29 percent) to the hard-line Salafist al-Nour. In Morocco, where King Mohammad VI conceded some of the protestors' demands rather than face a full-blown revolution, the moderate Islamist Justice and Development Party (PJD) won 107 out of 395 seats in the November 2011 elections, and the post of prime minister.

In Libya, AQAM-linked fighters—led by former Libyan Islamic Fighting Group emir Abdel Hakim Belhadj—played a major role in the rebellion that succeeded, after much blood and endurance, in toppling Muammar Gaddafi. Post-revolution, the country remains in turmoil and by early summer 2012, rival militias (including Belhadj's Tripoli Military Council) held sway in different parts of the country. There have been widespread protests by Islamists calling for the self-appointed, secular National Transitional Council (NTC) to be replaced by an Islamic state under Sharia. At the same time, the restive—and traditionally Islamist—eastern part of the country, Barqa, has declared its autonomy from Tripoli.

In Algeria the Islamists are divided on the issue of the protests. Influential Salafist leader Abdel Malek Ramdani, who lives in Saudi Arabia, issued a fatwa against rebellion: 'If the leader is Muslim you must obey and listen to him.' Sheikh Abdel Fateh Zeraoui, on the other hand—one of Algiers's most popular imams—openly called for reform and organised protests that were blocked by the Algerian secret police, the sinister Directorate of Intelligence and Security (DRS).

Al Qaeda 'central' clearly had high hopes for a revolution in Algeria in 2011 but this has yet to materialise. Ayman al-Zawahiri posted an October 2011 statement on the forums inciting the Algerians to rise up: 'As I congratulated our people in Libya on their victory over the tyrant, I call upon our people in Algeria to follow in their footsteps. Oh lions of Algeria, your brothers in Tunisia and Libya have sent two tyrants to the wasteland of history . . . so why are you silent before the corrupt oppressors who wish to turn Algeria into a service agency to safeguard the interests of America and France in the Maghreb and on Mediterranean coastline?' Another senior Al Qaeda figure, Abu Yahya al-Libi, added his voice in a November 2011 video urging the Algerians to 'Overthrow this rotten regime that stole your revolution, wasted your wealth, caused you poverty and opened your country to the infidel west to enjoy your resources.' Although there have been repeated efforts to mount protests in Algeria, the police and the DRS have—to date—had no trouble dispersing them.

Algerian Islamists in exile established a satellite television channel, Rachad TV, in November 2011. Broadcasting criticism of the government and coverage of the Arab Spring, it is available inside the country, carried by Atlantic Bird and NileSat. On the Rachad TV website visitors can enter areas devoted to topics such as 'how to free your country' and 'how to organise and participate in unrest'.

In January 2012, the moderate Islamist party, Movement for a Peaceful Society (MSP), pulled out of the Algerian coalition government, saying this was a year for 'competition not alliances', hoping to capitalise on the electoral successes of fellow Islamist parties in other Maghreb countries.

This was not to be, however. The MSP formed a three-party 'Green Alliance' with fellow moderate Islamist groups Ennahda and Islah. The alliance was allowed to stand for election in the May 2012 parliamentary ballot but was never likely to win the support of the country's more radical Muslims after years inside the 'apostate' government structure. The Alliance bucked the regional trend when it won little more than 10 percent of the vote.

Hardline Islamist parties, including the Islamic Salvation Front (FIS) whose 1991 electoral victory prompted a military coup, were banned and asked their followers to boycott the elections. The voter turnout was low—the government say 48 percent but this is bitterly disputed on the ground; a BBC reporter in the capital, Algiers, said that only ten people had voted at the polling station she was covering. Nevertheless, the government had invited 500 international observers to monitor the elections and no irregularities were reported. The existing regime and its allies, headed by President Bouteflika, retained power with a big majority.

Despite the election results, if the regime resists the impetus for reform, it risks a replay of events more than twenty years ago when protests against the secular regime weakened its grip on power and forced elections. When the FIS party were denied their legitimate right to govern it precipitated the emergence of ultra-hard-line Islamist terror group the GIA and all-out civil war in which as many as 200,000 lost their lives. Some Algerians say that this explains their compatriots' reticence to mount a full-scale revolution or even vote for the moderate Islamists.

Others suggest that voters fear a weakened security environment which would give the local Al Qaeda franchise even more operational room.

Al Qaeda in the Islamic Maghreb (AQIM)—an umbrella group dominated by members of the Algerian Salafist Group for Preaching and Combat (GSPC) and including elements from the Libyan Islamic Fighting Group (LIFG) as well as the Moroccan Islamic Combatant Group (MICG) and Tunisian *jihadis*—was formed in 2007. AQIM has benefited from the Arab Spring in two main ways: it has taken advantage of the security vacuum—particularly in the Sahara and Sahel—to expand its area of influence, and it was able to procure vast quantities of sophisticated weaponry from abandoned or unguarded stockpiles in Libya during the revolution.

AQIM is now active throughout Algeria and in parts of Mauritania, Mali, Chad and Niger. It has also laid down roots in Nigeria, where it has established close links with, and has helped train and arm, Nigeria's Boko Haram, which is currently wreaking havoc in the north of the country.[2] Another group calling itself 'Al Qaeda in the Lands beyond the Sahel' emerged in early 2012 in northern Nigeria; it is not clear if this an offshoot of Boko Haram, AQIM or neither. Certainly the act that first brought it public attention, the March 2012 murder of two Western hostages, is reminiscent of the AQIM modus operandi.

AQIM has been active in filling the aid gap caused by security vacuums in the Sahel region. A UN report in January 2012 described the group providing 'services and humanitarian assistance in remote areas where state presence is reduced or non-existent'. The report also pointed out that this boosts the group's popularity, enabling it to 'Recruit followers and form networks to gather information and arms'.[3]

Clearly AQIM also has connections in Libya—there are longstanding ties between individuals that date back to the Afghan *jihad*. In a November 2011 interview, AQIM's Mokhta Belmokhtar (aka Khaled Abu al-Abbas and al-Aouer—'the one-eyed') confirmed that the organisation had seized large quantities of arms from Gaddafi's unguarded stockpiles during the Libyan revolution.[4] Sources describe convoys of trucks sent by AQIM into the Libyan desert where they loaded up with sophisticated shoulder-launched surface-to-air missiles (known as MANPADS) which are capable of bringing down a civilian aircraft. *Jihadis* were also able to help themselves to anti-tank RPGs, Kalashnikov heavy machine guns, explosives and ammunition. These were then spirited away over the border and into a safe haven in northern Mali. One such convoy was intercepted in Niger, a UN report stated, carrying '645 kilograms of Semtex plastic explosive and 445 detonators ... meant for Al Qaeda in the Islamic Maghreb camps in northern Mali'.[5]

The UN report also pointed out that the weapons are not only of use to AQIM but could be sold or passed on to other AQAM or related groups. Indeed, leaked e-mails from Syrian President Bashar al-Assad's inbox in February 2012 warned of a shipment of arms from Libya arriving by sea to arm the *mujahideen* in their fight against his murderous regime.[6]

Western security agencies are greatly concerned about the increasing 'Africanisation' of Al Qaeda, and the Arab Spring has seen that process move forward. AQIM is increasingly connected to other AQAM groups. Apart from its African and European connections (of which more below), in November 2011, AQIM emir Laaouar confirmed that the group was reaching further afield, having sent a delegation to 'Al Qaeda leaders in Pakistan' to begin operational collaborations with them.[7] In May 2012, Timbuktu mayor Hallé Ousman told *Magharebia* that groups of Pakistani *jihadis* had entered northern Mali to help AQIM and rebel Islamist Tuaregs consolidate the Azawad 'emirate' (of which, more below).

In the south of the country and the Sahel, AQIM has mounted border raids and carried out several kidnappings—in July 2010 they executed a 78-year-old French hostage, Michel Germaneau, following a botched rescue attempt by French special forces. This resulted in the former French premier, Nicolas Sarkozy, declaring war on the organisation. In the north, AQIM escalated its violence during 2011, after a period of relative inactivity, with targeted attacks on security institutions including suicide attacks on police headquarters and a military academy in Cherchell in which up to twenty trainees lost their lives. A suicide bombing in Marrakesh in a café packed with tourists watching the football World Cup final, which killed fourteen, has also been attributed to AQIM, which had been threatening an attack in Morocco. The fact that the bombers used the explosive triacetone triperoxide (TATP)—a chemical mixture nicknamed 'Mother of Satan' and often used by Al Qaeda—suggests responsibility even though AQIM did not officially claim the attack.[8] With its location by the Mediterranean Sea, AQIM also presents an ongoing threat to Europe. Its predecessor, the GIA, terrorised Paris in 1995 when it bombed the Metro and other targets.

Democracy Denied: The Birth of the GIA

Algeria endured more than a century of humiliation and cruelty at the hands of its French colonisers. Algeria's period of colonisation was one of longest in Africa, starting in 1830 and not ending until 1962, after eight years of bloody civil war in which up to a million Algerians died. The guerrilla National Liberation Front (FLN) led the fight against the French, which took place mostly in the country's northern Atlas mountains; helped by the indigenous Berbers who knew the region well, the FLN had the advantage over the French in that vertiginous, often impenetrable wilderness.

The FLN assumed power in 1962, with Ahmed Ben Bella as president. Ben Bella's socialist regime is remembered as benevolent and fair (perhaps with rose-tinted spectacles) among the Algerian people, but he was overthrown in 1965 by Boumedienne, who ushered in decades of authoritarian rule by various leaders selected and supported by the military in a one-party system dominated by the FLN.

In 1989, following riots and demonstrations, the FLN adopted new legislation which allowed for the formation of political parties and free elections. The Islamic Salvation Front (FIS) was founded in the same year under the leadership of Abbassi Madani and Ali Belhajj; the latter espoused a radical agenda and his impassioned speeches, opposing foreign interference and the Soviet-style planned economy the state had hitherto adopted, won him much support among the disenfranchised youth and Islamists alike. Even though Al Qaeda at the time rejected the principle of democracy, it is interesting to note that in a November 2011 video Abu Yahya al-Libi refers to Belhajj as part of the 'vanguard *mujahideen*', rehabilitating him in the *jihadi* lexicon and implicitly approving his historic participation in the political process.

In 1990, the FIS won 55 percent of the vote in local elections, proving particularly popular in the towns and villages. In the first round of parliamentary elections, which took place in December 1991, the FIS won 188 out of 232 seats and looked set to achieve a landslide victory in the second round, a deeply humiliating turn of events for the FLN, which had taken just fifteen seats. The army stepped in, cancelling the elections and forcing President Chadli Bendjedid to resign. Madani and Belhajj were arrested and sentenced to twelve years in jail and a state of emergency was imposed which was not lifted until February 2011 when President Abdelaziz Bouteflika offered this crumb to protestors. France, the former colonial power and supposed champion of *Liberté, égalité et fraternité*, did nothing to prevent the regime's suppression of the Islamists and its suffocation of the country's nascent democracy.

A five-member Higher State Council, chaired by new President Mohamed Boudiaf, took over on 11 January 1992. Less than six months later Boudiaf was assassinated by one of his bodyguards who had links to Islamist groups and another new president, Ali Kafi, took his place.

The FIS was banned and up to 30,000 members were sent to prison camps in the Sahara desert. Several new Islamist groups sprang up, among them the Movement for an Islamic State (MEI) founded by Said Mekhloufi, a former FIS member, and the Islamic Armed Movement (MIA) founded by Abdelkader Chebouti. Between July 1992 and January 1993, a new, extremely militant, group emerged—the Algiers-based GIA headed by Mansour Meliani. The GIA leadership included many Afghan veterans with well-established links to Al Qaeda. Unlike the other groups, the GIA perceived a wider enemy from the outset, targeting foreigners, particularly 'Jews and Christians'.

Reports of horrific civilian massacres in Algeria begin around this time but, whilst it is certain that later atrocities were carried out by the GIA, some commentators attribute some of these early attacks to internal security forces intent on terrifying the population into opposing the Islamist factions. It is hard to find two Algerians who can agree on exactly what happened at this time.

As for the exact timing of Al Qaeda's active involvement in Algeria, Hamida Layachi, an Algerian expert in Islamist groups in the Maghreb, asserts that Afghan-Arab fighters affiliated with Al Qaeda were involved in the very first Islamist guerrilla attack in Algeria in which ten soldiers were murdered at a border post in Guemmar on 29 November 1991—a date which precedes the parliamentary elections said to have started the civil conflict. According to Layachi, an Al Qaeda emissary called Kari Said visited Algeria to contact Meliani in 1992—at the point when he was breaking away from the MIA—and remained a go-between between the Al Qaeda core leadership and the GIA until his death in 1996.[9]

I was aware of top-level contacts between Al Qaeda and the newly formed GIA from 1993 onwards and have no reason to doubt Layachi's information. In a long and wide-ranging letter submitted to my paper, *al-Quds al-Arabi*, in August 2005, Abu Musab al-Suri describes how he visited Osama bin Laden in October 1993. 'We had a lot of meetings where we discussed at length the question of *jihad* in Algeria,' al-Suri recalled. 'We had contact with *jihadi* leaders [there], we used to meet on a regular basis with these leaders and study the situations and because I had a Spanish passport my movement was easier.' Until recently I had assumed that these meetings took place in Europe but a source has now informed me that al-Suri not only visited Algeria on a number of occasions but actually became bin Laden's official envoy to the GIA. Al-Suri became the editor of the GIA's extremely radical newsletter, *Al-Ansar*, in 1995–6 while he was living in London. Shortly afterwards he migrated to Afghanistan and joined Al Qaeda. I was astonished to find him with Osama bin Laden in the caves of Tora Bora when I interviewed the Al Qaeda leader in November 1996.

Those Algerian Islamists who were not in the FIS and did not form part of the GIA cohort now united under an umbrella organisation, the Islamic Salvation Army (AIS). When Liamine Zéroual became president-elect in January 1994 he opened negotiations with FIS and the AIS. The GIA responded by declaring war on the 'collaborators' of the FIS and AIS and several members of these organisations shifted their allegiance to the GIA, which had become the most effective and biggest guerrilla group in Algeria.

While the AIS may have fallen foul of the burgeoning *jihadi* movement, Belhajj—the co-founder of the FIS—watched developments from behind bars with interest and enthusiasm. A letter from him was allegedly found in the pocket of the GIA leader Cherif Gouzmi when he was killed by security services in 1994; in the letter Belhajj stated that if he were free, he would be a GIA soldier.

In August 1994 the GIA declared a caliphate, with Cherif Gouzmi as caliph. Gouzmi was killed just one month later and replaced in October by Djamel Zitouni. In his letter to *al-Quds al-Arabi* (August 2005), al-Suri claimed that he 'advised the emir of the GIA at that time, in private correspondence, that he must hit France hard not only as revenge but to force it to acknowledge its support for the military regime in Algeria which it is trying to keep secret. This strategy will mobilise the *umma* to support the Algerian *jihad* as they supported the *jihad* in Afghanistan.' It is a measure of al-Suri's (and by association, Al Qaeda's) influence on the GIA that just one month later, on Christmas Eve 1994, operatives from the organisation hijacked a French plane in Algiers. They were killed by French troops when they landed in France but this abortive attempt was followed in the New Year by a GIA call for *jihad* against France. Al-Suri notes with satisfaction that he remained in constant touch with Zitouni who 'sent me a special Algerian sweet that he took from an Algerian Army warehouse and I distributed this to the brothers in England and Spain'.

Despite a GIA threat that they would kill anyone who voted, elections in November 1995 confirmed Liamine Zéroual's presidency. The number of Islamist guerrillas in the country had reached its peak at around 28,000 with a significant number being foreign 'volunteers' sent by Al Qaeda.[10]

The GIA became the first *jihadi* group to attack inside a Western country with a series of bombs in France throughout the summer and autumn of 1995. In July, St Michel Metro station in Paris was bombed, killing ten and injuring eighty-six; another bomb at the Arc de Triomphe wounded seventeen people in August and an unexploded device was found on the TGV tracks near Lyons. In November 1995 a Jewish school was among several other targets.

The GIA started attacking civilians with increasing regularity and ruthlessness; their popularity diminished in proportion. They also stated that they would be targeting people of other faiths and in April 1996 seven Trappist monks were murdered and mutilated at Tibhirine: their tragic story was the subject of the 2010 film *Of Gods and Men*.

In July 1996 Zitouni was killed and Antar Zouabri became the new emir. Zouabri adhered to an extreme *takfiri* ideology which held that anyone not adhering to GIA Salafist doctrine was an infidel and government collaborator. A spree of ever more horrific massacres ensued and more than 1,300 were killed during the month of Ramadan (December

1997). According to Abu Qatada and other sources, the GIA had been systematically infiltrated by secret agents from the DRS who saw these civilian massacres as the means by which the GIA would bring about its own demise. The DRS allegedly worked behind the scenes to encourage an increasingly psychopathic agenda, culminating in the era's worst ever massacre on 1 January 1998 when 412 people were killed in Reliziane province. In total an estimated 200,000 civilians were murdered in Algeria between 1992 and 1998.[11]

The massacres traumatised and alienated the citizen population of Algeria—a situation repeated later in Iraq where al-Zarqawi's group launched terrifying attacks on citizens which resulted in Sunni tribal leaders turning against Al Qaeda. Indeed, when al-Zarqawi was killed, US intelligence services recovered several letters, among them one from Attyia al-Jazari (the Algerian)—a member of Al Qaeda's central *shura*—urging him not to make the same mistake as the GIA: '[In] Algeria between 1994 and 1995 when [the GIA] was . . . on the verge of taking over the government . . . they destroyed themselves with their own hands with their lack of reason, delusions, ignoring the people, their alienation of them through oppression, deviance and severity, coupled with a lack of kindness, sympathy and friendliness'.[12]

The Salafist Group for Preaching and Combat

A regional commander in the GIA, Hassan Hattab (also known as Abu Hamza), was sickened by the increasingly indiscriminate violence perpetrated by the organisation and broke away, taking hundreds of other guerrillas with him. They established a new, though scarcely less ideologically extreme, organisation, the Salafist Group for Preaching and Combat (GSPC) towards the end of 1998.

Significantly, the Al Qaeda leadership had also distanced itself from the activities of the GIA. Algeria's *jihad* had briefly been a rallying cry for Islamists throughout the Muslim world but now it was a source of shame. Key figures who had previously offered their help and support, like Abu Qatada and al-Suri, believed that they had been duped by Algerian intelligence agents—both expressed extreme regret over this in interviews with me. Material aid was cut off and production of the newsletter,

Al-Ansar, ceased. On the ground, the GIA's foreign *mujahideen* turned against their erstwhile leaders and joined Hattab's organisation instead. Osama bin Laden sent envoys to Hattab, endorsing his move and offering to help the embryonic GSPC get established.

In April 1999 Abdelaziz Bouteflika was elected president of Algeria. He determined to put an end to the civil war that had raged in the country for seven years and put his proposals for new civil concord legislation to the country in a referendum. The plan was the result of long-standing negotiations with the FIS and its armed wing the AIS, and contained a commitment to destroy the GIA. The population endorsed his agenda—official figures claim a 98.6 percent majority. An amnesty was offered to the various guerrilla factions which thousands of members of the AIS and other armed groups accepted. Several Algerian and Saudi *ulema* issued fatwas stating that *jihad* in Algeria was now illegitimate in the light of the national reconciliation process. To all intents and purposes, the GSPC was now the only armed guerrilla group in Algeria and it was considerably weakened.

The GSPC aimed to revive the popular enthusiasm for political Islam formerly inspired by the FIS and all but extinguished by the GIA. In pursuit of this they turned from the *takfiri* ideology that legitimised the targeting of civilians, focusing instead on civil institutions, the military, police and tourists. The group's first major attack in May 2002 saw fifteen Algerian soldiers assassinated near Tizi Ouzou, the capital of the largely Berber Kabylian region.

The in-fighting that had come to characterise the Algerian Islamist groups soon began to surface in the GSPC. This may have been exacerbated by the structure the group adopted which saw the vast country divided into nine zones, each with its own emir, ostensibly answerable to the overall leader, Hattab. Zone 1, the most important one, borders Algiers and part of the Kabylian region to the east and is always the domain of the organisation's leader. The next most important zone is Zone 9, deep in the Sahara.

Hattab's sphere of influence narrowed as a north–south divide emerged. One of the GSPC's most ruthless commanders, the late Amar Saifi (aka Abderazzak al-Para—like Hattab, he had been a paratrooper in the Algerian Special Forces) had assembled a small army made up of Mauritanians, men from Mali and Niger, as well as Algerians. His group now moved to the Zone 9 region whose emir, the one-eyed Mokhta Belmokhtar, approved of his guerrilla tactics along the borders. Saifi's group engaged in skirmishes with neighbours, including full-scale battles with troops in northern Niger. In February 2003 Saifi's men kidnapped a group of thirty-two terrified European tourists (mostly Germans) in the Sahara desert. One woman died, apparently of heatstroke, but the remainder were released after the German government paid an estimated $5 million as a ransom—money that went to fund future GSPC operations. Saifi became Algeria's most wanted guerrilla until he was captured by the rebel Movement for Democracy and Justice in Chad (MDJC), who handed him over to the Algerian authorities in May 2004.

Meanwhile the erstwhile FIS leader Ali Belhajj was finally released from prison in 2003; in July 2005 he was rearrested after appearing on Al Jazeera television commending the activities of Abu Musab al-Zarqawi, the leader of Al Qaeda in Iraq. Al-Zarqawi's men had kidnapped two Algerian diplomats in Baghdad; asked if he would plead for the diplomats to be freed, Belhajj said it was not for him to 'dictate to my brother *mujahideen* what they should or should not do'. The diplomats were executed.

Belhajj was released again in 2006 as part of an amnesty designed to placate the *jihadis*. Shortly after his release, his 18-year-old son Abdelkahar joined the GSPC taking the nom de guerre Muawiyah. Muawiyah became legendary in *jihadi* circles, cited as 'the role model for the youth'.[13] He died at the end of July 2011 en route to Algiers with three others to carry out a suicide mission; stopped by security officers, he blew himself up rather than be taken captive. Ali Belhajj himself was arrested in January 2011 when he joined Arab Spring protestors in Algiers. He was charged with 'inciting armed rebellion' but was not imprisoned, presumably because of his high profile. Al-Libi refers to all of this when he sends 'my condolences and consolation to my brother, Ali Belhajj, the Sheikh who speaks the truth in the face of the tyrants—may Allah protect him—on the martyrdom of his son'.

In Zone 9, both Belmokhtar and Saifi would receive visits from Al Qaeda emissaries in 2002/3. Their approach was nearer to the Al Qaeda agenda than the domestic focus favoured by Hattab who began urging moderation and even suggested limited rapprochement with the government.

Hattab was deposed in September or October 2003 by fellow GSPC commanders who now judged him weak and lacking in focus and strategy. His removal was approved, if not instigated, by the Al Qaeda leadership, who were disappointed by his new-found moderation. Hattab was replaced by Abu Ibrahim Mustafa (aka Nabil Sahraoui) in September 2003 and the latter immediately issued a statement aligning the group with Al Qaeda, 'We strongly and fully support Osama bin Laden's *jihad* against the heretic America; we also support our brothers in Afghanistan, the Philippines and Chechnya,' he said.[14]

The closer association with Al Qaeda that Abu Ibrahim Mustafa sought was not yet forthcoming, however. Despite his rhetoric about global *jihad* his active agenda was as domestic and inward-looking as his predecessors'. Abu Ibrahim Mustafa was obviously aware of this and one of his favourite statements was that the GSPC would gladly join the fight against the US and its allies if it was not so busy fighting the Algerian government and its military apparatus. Abu Ibrahim Mustafa was killed in a gun battle on 20 June 2004.

The man who succeeded him, Abdelmalek Droukdal (aka Abu Musab Abdel Wadoud), is AQIM's current emir. Droukdal was born on 20 April 1970 in Meftah, a small town in the Blida region, about 40 km southeast of the capital, Algiers. The people of this area—which was the original seat of the GIA—are well known for their uncompromising attitudes and pugnacity. Droukdal came from a strict religious family and was studious, attending Blida University where he began a postgraduate course in engineering. When the civil war broke out in 1992 he decided to give up his studies. In an interview posted on the Internet he describes how 'I managed to make contact with Sheikh Said Makhloufi, one of the commanders of the Algerian *jihad*, and I was honoured to join the *mujahideen* brothers in December 1993.'[15]

Droukdal is reputed to be a practical, calm, strong-minded and tough individual whose ideological basis is a mixture of Arab nationalism and political Islam. He is said to have been greatly influenced by the theorising, rhetoric and cold-blooded approach of Al Qaeda leader, Ayman al-Zawahiri. Little is known about his personal life, although it is rumoured among Algerian *jihadis* that he was recently married in the Atlas Mountains where he is hiding.

Contrary to what has been written about him, Droukdal affirms in the interview cited above that he did not attend Al Qaeda training camps in Afghanistan or Sudan. His experience has been entirely local and he describes his rise through the GIA/GSPC ranks, giving the impression of well-structured, militaristic organisations: 'I was assigned to prepare explosives because of my college education ... in 1996 I was put in charge of all military workshops for the al-Ahwal soldiers of the second zone. Afterwards I commanded the al-Quds brigade ... in 2001 I was summoned by the GSPC and I became their representative in the second zone until 2003 ... following the death of Sheikh Abu Ibrahim Mustafa I became commander of the GSPC during the summer of 2004.'

From the outset it was clear that Droukdal espoused a radical ideology and when Hassan Hattab accepted a renewed offer of amnesty for all *jihadis* from the Algerian government in September 2005, Droukdal announced that the GSPC 'cut all ties' with him. In reality Bouteflika's amnesty in 2005 was a bit of an own goal—he did the GSPC's job for them by weeding out the least radical from their ranks, leaving a hard core as a base for future operations and recruitment and a more suitable partner for Al Qaeda, which watched these events with interest.

Al Qaeda in the Islamic Maghreb

Droukdal was actively seeking a formal merger with Al Qaeda. Clearly they shared ideological goals and the fight against the 'far enemy' had become more urgent in Algeria, as Droukdal explained in an interview with the *New York Times* in 2008: 'We found America building military bases in the south of our country and conducting military exercises, and plundering our oil and planning to get our gas. Also, opening a CIA branch in our capital city, and starting an unusual Christian conversion campaign among our youths.'[16] He wanted to steer the GSPC towards a more globalised operational strategy and reasoned that the merger with the perpetrators of 9/11 would boost his organisation's profile and recruitment potential. Also, he had learnt the lessons of in-fighting and disunity from earlier experiences of the Algerian Islamists and he now applied this to his international relationships: 'We care about staying in contact with our brothers in Afghanistan or Iraq or any other *jihad* side. Our project is one. Therefore, we have to help, advise, consult each other, and exchange the experiences and coordinate the efforts to face the world's crusade war against Islam.'[17]

Droukdal sent an emissary, Younis al-Mauritani (who was recently detained in Pakistan), to talk to the Al Qaeda leadership then based in Pakistan.[18] Al-Mauritani became the main interlocutor between the two groups. Droukdal had also developed strong links with al-Zarqawi in Iraq, to whom he wrote several letters congratulating him on his 'successes'. Al-Zarqawi responded enthusiastically, dispatching emissaries who conveyed a suggested operational template for Droukdal's organisation in a series of meetings.

According to the Algerian newspaper *al-Khabar*, quoting unnamed GSPC sources (12 September 2006), it was al-Zarqawi who first approved the idea of a formal merger between Al Qaeda and the reformed GSPC in 2005. When al-Zarqawi was killed after a reckless television appearance in an exterior location which provided abundant clues for the CIA to pinpoint his whereabouts, Droukdal issued a communiqué celebrating his 'martyrdom' and eulogising this 'Lion of Islam'. Al-Zarqawi is still revered among young *jihadis* and, in death, has achieved iconic status.

Many groups claim affiliation with Al Qaeda, and Al Qaeda provides various degrees of association: there is the congratulatory nod, the wholehearted support, the expression of commonality, an alliance and, for some groups, the full-scale merger. The latter can occur only when rigorous ideological criteria have been met. Of all the *jihadis* in the Maghreb, the GSPC were considered the most useful to Al Qaeda, being well versed in insurgency and battle-hardened after more than fifteen years of constant civil strife.

The first evidence that the GSPC was nearing its goal came in a series of Internet statements from the Al Qaeda leadership congratulating the group on their activities. To establish his group's credibility in terms of 'global *jihad*', Droukdal announced that GSPC fighters were active in other 'lands of *jihad*' such as Afghanistan, Chechnya, Lebanon, Somalia and Sudan. Chat-rooms were buzzing with discussions about this new emir and many *jihadis* seemed to be of the opinion that Droukdal would prove as significant a leader as al-Zarqawi whom he so revered.

The 4 June 2005 transborder attack on the Lemgheity Mauritanian military outpost by 150 armed GSPC fighters seems to have been a turning point in the group's long quest to join Al Qaeda formally.

Mauritania is perceived as an enemy state by *jihadis* because of its stance towards Israel—with whom it maintains formal diplomatic relations—and because it supported the US invasion of Iraq. Reports that the GSPC had been actively recruiting inside Mauritania were borne out by the presence of a significant number of nationals from that country in the group that carried out the attack which left fifteen dead and seventeen injured. It may not have been a coincidence that the attack occurred just days before a US army division arrived in the Sahel for military exercises.

Subsequent attacks led to Osama bin Laden himself saluting the 'Algerian *mujahideen*' in an Internet broadcast and the GSPC replied in kind by posting congratulations to al-Zarqawi when Al Qaeda in the Land of the Two Rivers captured the Algerian diplomats Ali Belarussi and Izzedin Belkadi. 'Apply the judgment of God to them,' the GSPC statement exhorted, and when the men were murdered a month later, Droukdal reaffirmed his support.

In 2005 the GSPC announced the formation of a subgroup called Al Qaeda in the Land of the Berbers whose main purpose was to recruit and prepare North African fighters for Iraq.[19] Whilst this branding was not sanctioned by Al Qaeda 'central', it was effective. The policy served a dual purpose—it boosted the group's internationalist credentials and drew more young men into their orbit since Iraq, at the time, was the preferred *jihad* destination. Sources say that very promising recruits, particularly those volunteering for suicide missions, were often kept behind to boost the ranks of the GSPC.

The group gave the volunteers for Iraq basic military training—including how to handle and clean a gun, target practice, fitness and mental resilience building—in temporary GSPC camps in the Atlas Mountains in the north of Algeria and the Sahara desert in the south.

The group developed a successful tactic for avoiding capture or attack, by adopting a nomadic, migratory lifestyle, establishing camps and mobile training facilities which were moved every few days. In autumn 2011 joint security operations by Mauritanian, Malian and Algerian troops in the Sahel failed to track down any of AQIM's units there.

The GSPC trainers were not familiar with some of the more advanced techniques employed by al-Zarqawi's men, who had benefited from their collaboration in the insurgency with ex-officers from Saddam Hussein's elite Republican Guard. These men had shown Al Qaeda in the Land of the Two Rivers trainers how to make highly sophisticated IEDs, for example. The new recruits were promised they would learn these techniques on arrival in Iraq. In 2011 there was an escalation of IED attacks in Algeria, which suggests this deadly expertise had been brought back home.

The merger between Al Qaeda and the GSPC was announced in a video by Dr Ayman al-Zawahiri on the fifth anniversary of 9/11 in 2006. 'We pray to God they will be a thorn in the side of the Americans and French and their crusader allies,' he said. On 8 October the Algerian newspaper *al-Khabar* printed a statement from Droukdal who said his group had joined what he described as 'the real Islamist organization under the leadership of our brother and supreme chief, Dr Ayman al-Zawahiri', leading to speculation that Osama bin Laden was dead. Again, al-Zawahiri emerged as the motor driving Al Qaeda's expansionist strategy as it enlarged its network of affiliations.

The GSPC's first direct attack on an American target came just three days later, two months to the day after al-Zawahiri's statement. On 11 December 2006 a coach carrying employees of US corporation Brown Root & Condor was bombed, killing two and injuring eight. Brown Root & Condor was a subsidiary of the Halliburton group, which made billions of dollars 'rebuilding' Iraq and was run at the time by Dick Cheney, who would become US vice president in the Bush administration.

On 26 January 2007, Droukdal announced that his group was now officially rebranded the 'Al Qaeda *jihad* organisation in the Islamic Maghreb', a name designed to echo the label Zarqawi originally gave his group, the 'Al Qaeda *jihad* organisation in the Land of the Two Rivers'. Now Droukdal clarified the situation regarding Osama bin Laden: 'We had wanted to take on this name from the first day we joined Al Qaeda but needed permission from Sheikh Osama, may God preserve him. This obstacle has now been removed.'

On 11 April 2007 the newly formed AQIM carried out its first large-scale attacks and these bore all the hallmarks of its new ally. Two coordinated suicide attacks in Algiers entirely destroyed the front of the prime minister's house and demolished a police station. Twenty-three people died and more than 160 were injured. The most deadly attacks in years in Algeria, they strongly resembled Al Qaeda in Iraq's modus operandi, pointing strongly to the possibility that either Algerian *mujahideen* had returned home to share operational expertise gained on the battlefield in Iraq or Al Qaeda in Iraq had sent trainers over to prepare Algerian *jihadis* for their suicide mission.

As if to emphasise the cohesion between the branches of Al Qaeda, an attack mirroring the Algiers operation was carried out in Iraq the very next day. A suicide bomber managed to get into the Iraqi Parliament in Baghdad, located in the heart of the heavily fortified Green Zone, and blew himself up in the cafeteria, killing eight and wounding twenty. On 11 July 2007 AQIM struck again, this time in Kabylia when a suicide bomber drove a truck loaded with explosives into the Lakhdaria military base, killing ten and wounding thirty-five.

These suicide bombings shook the Algerian authorities, who had little experience of this phenomenon. In early May 2007 Algerian police had discovered a training camp in a palm grove outside the desert oasis town, el-Oued. According to the Algerian newspaper *Liberté* police found five wills and testaments on computers seized at the camp written by young men who had been trained as suicide bombers for Iraq.[20] Local sources say that the profile of the GSPC was greatly boosted by its new, global scope and by being rebranded Al Qaeda.

According to sources, AQIM leaders are so well known that they cannot show their faces in the towns and cities; instead they use local people, including Tuaregs, to convey messages for them. When five French hostages were seized in Niger on 15 September 2010, local accounts assert that AQIM fighters were helped by Tuareg tribesmen; the Tuaregs are motivated by anger and frustration at the lack of employment possibilities available to them and their consequent poverty.

In Mali, an ongoing Tuareg insurrection led by the National Movement for the Liberation of Azawad (NMLA) has as its aim the establishment of an autonomous state. Within the NMLA a hard-line Islamist faction, led by Iad ag-Gali, is demanding the implementation of Sharia throughout the whole of Mali and ag-Gali's Harakat Ansar al-din has conducted attacks in cooperation with AQIM.[21] In April 2012 the Tuaregs and AQIM took advantage of a military coup which destabilised Mali, seizing several key towns in the north which they proclaimed an Azawad state. Footage on YouTube showed convoys of vehicles entering the occupied towns waving Al Qaeda flags and, apparently, being welcomed by the inhabitants.

AQIM has learnt from al-Zarqawi's mistakes in Iraq and maintained good relations not only with the Tuareg but also with the Berber tribes in the Atlas Mountains to the north. There is a large Berber contingent in the northern divisions of AQIM; the Berbers are well known for their fighting skills and were largely responsible for the FLN's 1962 victory in their war for independence from the French.

After a period of relative calm, 2011 saw a resurgence of violence in Droukdal's northern constituency. Between April and June there were seventeen attacks targeting police, gendarmes and military targets, using IEDs, ambushes and armed assault. July and August saw twenty-three attacks, thirteen of which used IEDs and four of which were carried out by suicide bombers. The spate of attacks culminated in a double suicide bombing at Algeria's most prestigious military academy, the Academy Militaire Interarmes at Cherchell, in which eighteen were killed. The AQIM statement claiming responsibility linked the attack to the Arab Spring, blaming the Algerian government's 'support for Colonel Gadaffi'.[22] Shortly afterwards, Droukdal described the assassinations as 'a gift for Eid'.

The Islamic Emirate of the Sahara

The Sahel is vast and inhospitable, a band across Africa stretching five and a half thousand kilometres from the Atlantic to the Red Sea, with little rainfall and sparse vegetation. It is the point where the deserts to the north gradually transform into the more southerly savannah. The Sahara desert and the entire Sahel region have become an Al Qaeda hub and in 2010, AQIM announced the establishment of the Islamic Emirate of the Sahara here. It is home to several rival emirs including Abdel Kader Mokhta Belmokhtar, now leader of his own *al-Mulathamun* (masked ones) Battalion. Belmokhtar is in his forties and lost an eye fighting in the Afghan *jihad*. He has been active in the Sahel for more than sixteen years, and has been sentenced to death twice in absentia for killing border guards and customs officials in the course of his smuggling activities.

His group is particularly active in northern Mali and Mauritania. He consolidated his relationship with the local Tuaregs by marrying the daughter of the Barabicha tribe's chief in the late 1990s. In 2012,

AQIM-associated fighters would join forces with Tuareg Islamists to establish an Azawad autonomous region in northern Mali. Belmokhtar actually handed over control of Zone 9 to Yahya Djouadi in 2007, preferring to operate independently but under the AQIM umbrella.

The most ruthless and brutal AQIM group in the Sahara, the Tariq ibn Zayid or al-Fedayeen, is headed by Abdel Hamid Zayid (aka Mohammed Ghadir) who was born in the southern desert town of Touggourt. Unlike most Al Qaeda leaders, he is uneducated. He was originally a member of the FIS but joined the *jihadis* in the 1990s and became a member of the GSPC. The French hostage Pierre Camatte, who was held by him for three months until February 2010, described Abdel Hamid Zayid to *Jeune Afrique* as 'small, blighted with rickets, around fifty and sporting a goatee beard'.[23] His group carried out several kidnappings, along with Amar Saifi (better known as 'al-Para'), and murdered the British hostage Edwin Dyer in June 2009 as well as the Frenchman Michel Germaneau, who was executed in July 2010, and two of the five French employees of nuclear giant Areva who were kidnapped in September 2010 in Niger (the remaining three were released in February 2011).

Yahya Abu al Hammam is Abdel Hamid Zayid's lieutenant and, like him, ill-educated and ruthless. He is the leader of the 'Al Farqhaun battalion, which is based west of Timbuktu in Mali and participates equally in the kidnappings and executions. He may have been killed in September 2010 but the Algerian authorities often 'kill off' *jihadis* who then resurface.

In 2010 a 'home video' by a Tariq ibn Zayid fighter was found after a shoot-out between mercenary Tuareg and tribal militias hired by the Algerian and Malian governments. The film was broadcast by Al Jazeera, and provides a fascinating glimpse into the lives led by Adbel Hamid Zayid's men. It confirms that they are entirely self-sufficient, constantly on the move, sleeping in caves, making their own clothes—there is footage of a young man under a palm tree running up a garment on a manual sewing machine—and mending their own vehicles. They wash and get water from the region's few streams and oases and seemingly subsist on a diet of foraged roots and large indigenous reptiles.

In November 2011, AQIM's Zone 9 commander, Djouadi, was removed from his post following serious in-fighting between the southern emirs. He was replaced by Nabil Makhloufi, aka Abu al-Qama—a significant appointment because al-Qama was formerly a member of both the GSPC and the Libyan Islamic Fighting Group,[24] which suggests renewed collaboration between Libya-based *jihadis* and AQIM in the wake of the Libyan revolution. Indeed, in a November 2011 interview with a Mauritanian newspaper, Belmokhtar confirmed the role of Al Qaeda in the Libyan revolution, saying that 'the *jihadis* were the first to face Gaddafi's battalions' and adding that the weapons stockpiles AQIM had removed from Libya would be shared with Libya's 'Islamic Movement'.[25]

The emirate fighters operate in highly mobile groups travelling in convoys of vehicles. This makes life difficult for the security forces and many chases end with the *jihadis* disappearing over one or other porous borders or managing to lose their pursuers simply because they know the terrain so much better. The fight against Al Qaeda is further hampered by the high level of corruption; several sources have reported military officers selling arms to Islamist groups. Clumsy air strikes have often killed or maimed citizens rather than their intended targets, provoking anti-government sentiment which Al Qaeda is quick to exploit.

AQIM's area of southern influence now extends throughout most of the Sahel, from the Algerian Sahara to Mali, Niger, Nigeria, Libya, Mauritania and Chad. The emirate offshoot's main economic activity is kidnapping Western tourists—a lucrative business which analysts estimate netted them $70 million between 2006 and 2010.[26] The actual figure may be much higher—the ransom demanded for Michel Germaneau was €90 million, for example. Local governments also accuse them of collaborating with smugglers and bandits. Their activities have damaged local economies, which depend heavily on tourism, and the airline Point Afrique, which served most of the major pan-Sahel region cities, has stopped operating in the area.

AQIM's Islamic Emirate of the Sahara has garnered a significant number of recruits from Mauritania over the years; the country's Islamists were radicalised by government crackdowns in 2005 and the opening of an Israeli Embassy in the capital, Nouakchott. The embassy was closed in 2009 following threats to repeat a February 2008 bombing which killed twelve.

After the military coup of 2008 which brought the current president, General Muhammad Ould Abdel Aziz, to power, some Islamist parties became engaged in the political process but it was too late to prevent violence. The first suicide bombing ever to take place in Mauritania occurred in August 2009; the target was the French Embassy in Nouakchott. AQIM continues to attack inside Mauritania—in February 2011 an attempt to assassinate President Ould Abdel Aziz failed when the two trucks laden with explosives detonated prematurely and there were several subsequent attacks on military sites, most recently a base near Bassiknou in July 2011.

In addition to attacks in Mauritania, AQIM groups have been involved in several well-reported operations throughout the Sahel region since 2010: in September 2010 seven hostages from French multinational Areva were taken from Arlit in Niger and in June 2011 the town's military base was attacked; in January 2011 the French Embassy in Bamako, Mali, was raided and also in January 2011 two French hostages were seized in Niamay, Nigeria.

More recently, AQIM has become increasingly involved with Nigeria's deadly Boko Haram, which is discussed in more detail in Chapter 8. Niger's Foreign Minister, Mohamed Bazoum, told Reuters in January 2012: 'There is confirmed information that shows a link between Boko Haram and AQIM (Al Qaeda in the Islamic Maghreb), and it consists primarily of the training given to elements of Boko Haram.'[27] In early 2012 'Al Qaeda in the Lands Beyond the Sahel' emerged in northern Nigeria as we have seen above.

An AQIM splinter group of West African *jihadis* was formed in 2012. Jamaat Tawhid wa'l jihad fi Garbi Afriqqiya (Movement for Monotheism and Jihad in West Africa) is led by Hamada Ould Mohamed Kheiron (aka Abu Qumqum). The group broke away from AQIM because of the dominance of Arabs in the leadership; it has benefited from looted Libyan arms, aims to spread Sharia throughout West Africa and has declared 'war on France'. To date it has only carried out one operation—the kidnap of European aid workers from a Polisario refugee camp in western Algeria—but has been actively involved in the takeover of northern Mali by a Tuareg/Islamist alliance now operating under the moniker Ansar al-Din.

Morocco

Morocco's indigenous *jihadi* group, the Moroccan Islamic Combatant Group (GICM) which emerged in the late 1990s, is part of the AQIM umbrella. According to the Sinjar records (which listed fighters arriving to fight in Iraq and were captured by US troops on the Syrian border in 2006) Morocco produced the highest proportion of suicide bombers, with twenty-two of the twenty-four nationals arriving in Iraq volunteering for such a mission.

Morocco's indigenous terrorism problems stem from the regime's 1991 decision to send troops to join Coalition forces in their war against Saddam Hussein. Radical Islamist groups, led by veterans of the Afghan war, subsequently flourished and in 1993 a McDonalds fast food outlet in Casablanca and the Société Marocaine de Depot Bank in Oudja were attacked. In 1994 the Makro department store in Casablanca suffered a similar fate and two Spanish tourists were murdered at the Atlas Asni Hotel in Marrakesh. The Islamic political party Hizb al-Adala wal-Tanmiyya (Justice and Development Party) gained strength and by March 2000 was able to mobilise a million people to march against government plans to reform the *Mudawwana* (Islamic code for personal conduct).

Arrests throughout the 1990s testified to an uninterrupted level of guerrilla activity in Morocco. Evidence of an increasingly globalised network started emerging post-9/11 when security clampdowns revealed cells of operatives linked to a major Al Qaeda figure, Mullah Bilal. Bilal (aka Abdelrahim Mohammad Abdel Nashari), a founding member, was known in *jihadi* circles as the 'emir of the sea' prior to his arrest in November 2002. He is alleged to have masterminded the USS *Cole* attack on 12 October 2000[28] and to have been involved in the 6 October 2002 Zodiac speedboat suicide bombing of the French petrol tanker, the *Limburg*, off the coast of Yemen.[29] According to security services, Saudi nationals living in Morocco were observing the movements of NATO ships in the Straits of Gibraltar in preparation for an attack planned for May 2002 to be supervised by Bilal.[30]

The main *jihadi* organisation in Morocco is the Moroccan Islamic Combatant Group (GICM), which was established by Nafia Noureddine in 1991 when he was in Afghanistan. Peter Bergen has obtained transcripts of Noureddine's interrogation by Moroccan police in 2003 in which he describes how Osama bin Laden and al-Zawahiri agreed to help train and fund the group during a meeting he held with them in 2001.[31] Members of the GICM formed several cells abroad as well as remaining active at home. Moroccan authorities are alarmed by the infiltration of its security apparatus by Islamist activists—in January 2003, for example, an army sergeant, Yusuf Amani, was arrested for allegedly appropriating several Kalashnikovs from the Guercif barracks for a GICM cell in Meknes.[32]

The first major GICM attack inside Morocco came on 16 May 2003 when fourteen suicide bombers simultaneously targeted a Jewish community centre, a Spanish restaurant, a hotel, the Belgian consulate and the Jewish quarter of Casablanca, Morocco's largest city. Two bombers were arrested before they could blow themselves up but the others succeeded: forty-five people died and more than 100 were injured in the attacks which bore all the hallmarks of Al Qaeda and came just four days after similar attacks claimed by Al Qaeda in the Arabian Peninsula in Riyadh, Saudi Arabia. It has since emerged that these attacks were planned in conjunction with LIFG leaders living in Europe, and Abdel Rahman al-Faqih, who long acted as a go-between for LIFG and GICM, was convicted in absentia for his alleged involvement.

The Moroccan government responded with counter-terrorism legislation, liaising with the US, France and Spain and moving towards a more liberal and democratic system in a bid to placate the people—a policy which has been continued by Mohammad VI with his response to the 2011 Arab Spring protests. It seemed these measures were having some effect and a significant number of cells and networks were reportedly dismantled. However, during a raid in the summer of 2006, Moroccan police found documents discussing the merger of the GICM, the GSPC, the Libya Fighting Group and several smaller Tunisian groups.[33] It seems the blueprint for AQIM—which the GICM would join—was already being hatched.

More attacks inside Morocco followed. On 11 March 2007, 23-year-old Abdelfattah Raydi detonated his suicide belt in a cyber-café in Casablanca when the owner, having noticed how the youth was agitatedly scanning *jihadi* websites, locked the doors and called the police. Raydi had already been imprisoned following the May 2003 attacks in which he was implicated. Having identified four further members of

Raydi's cell, the police moved in to arrest them on 10 April. Seemingly following the same orders that had prompted Raydi's dramatic death, three blew themselves up rather than be captured, killing one police officer. The other youth was killed by police.

14 April 2007 saw a further attempted attack. This time the target was the symbolic triangle formed by the US consulate, the associated American Language Centre and the Belgian consulate in Casablanca. Having provoked suspicion by asking a security guard the way, brothers Omar and Mohammed Maha detonated their suicide belts after failing to gain entry to the US consulate, killing no one but themselves. These latest attacks were thwarted or bungled but they indicate a thriving culture among a radicalised youth which celebrates *jihad* and martyrdom. The use of suicide bombers also strongly suggests the involvement of Al Qaeda. The timing of the Casablanca events point to a further sinister possibility—that AQIM planned to announce its arrival on the 'terror' scene with dramatic simultaneous attacks in Algiers and Casablanca on 11 April 2007.

Morocco was not immune to the Arab Spring and there were several well-attended demonstrations across the country in February 2011 in solidarity with the protestors in Tunisia and Egypt. The regime responded in a relatively conciliatory manner with Morocco's King Mohammad VI offering reforms; a referendum on constitutional changes was planned for June 2011. On 28 April 2011 an AQIM *jihadi* cell responded with a horrific suicide bombing of a fashionable, Westernised Marrakesh café which killed sixteen and injured twenty.

The protests are still ongoing, if sporadic, with many feeling the reforms and constitutional changes did not go far enough. The moderate Islamist Justice and Development Party (PJD) won 107 out of 395 seats in November 2011 elections, and the king appointed his prime minister from the PJD in line with the new constitution. Neither the parliament nor the prime minister have much real power, however, and if the regime does not concede more of the protestors' demands and redress the country's democracy deficit, its disappointed and frustrated young people might turn, instead, to the more violent agenda of AQIM.

Tunisia

When the Islamic party, Harkat Nahida, performed unexpectedly well in the 1989 elections, Tunisian President Habib Bourgiba responded by banning the party, now renamed Ennahda (Renaissance), from participating in the country's electoral process. Ennahda's leader, Rachid Ghannouchi, was sentenced to death in absentia and fled to London where he lived until his triumphant return during the revolution to oust ben Ali in January 2011. Despite the rough treatment he received at the hands of the ben Ali regime, during his exile Ghannouchi rejected all attempts to recruit him to more radical Islamist groups, including Al Qaeda, earning himself their enmity in the process.[34]

In October 2011 Ghannouchi's party triumphed in Tunisia's first free elections, taking ninety of 217 seats, and his fellow Ennahda veteran Hamadi Jebali was appointed prime minister in the country's interim government in November 2011.

Ben Ali's government effectively placed itself at odds with Islamists of all persuasions. It was a staunch ally of the US during the 2003 invasion of Iraq; it banned women from wearing the veil and endorsed a secular society—all of which created a great deal of resentment among young radicals. Tunisia had its first taste of Islamist-linked violence in 1995 when a group calling itself the Islamic Front in Tunisia (IFT) murdered four policemen and issued a warning that all foreigners should leave the country. It was subsequently claimed that this was the armed wing of Ennahda but this could equally well have been a move to discredit the party with moderate Islamists. IFT is also alleged to have been involved with the GIA in Algeria. The members of this group fled Tunisia and formed part of various other groups, particularly those based in Europe.

Tunisians are a significant presence in the Sinjar records, suggesting that even though there was no organisation at home they were joining Al Qaeda in significant numbers after the outbreak of the Iraqi insurgency. By 2009, the Tunisian authorities had jailed around 1,000 people who were planning to leave the country and join the Iraqi *mujahideen.*[35] Tunisia's first experience of Al Qaeda–linked attacks came on 11 April 2002 when a suicide truck bomb exploded outside La Ghriba Synagogue on the island of Djerba, killing nineteen and wounding dozens of people. Initially the Tunisian authorities told journalists that the incident had been caused by a vehicle exploding as a result of a road accident but eight days later *al-Quds al-Arabi* received a fax from the Abu Hafs al-Masri Brigade, part of Al Qaeda, claiming responsibility. This attack on an island much frequented by visitors to Tunisia resulted in a dramatic loss of tourism revenue—the country's main foreign currency earner—and the country's economy sank to a ten-year low.

Outside the country, Tunisian nationals have been identified among many Al Qaeda–linked cells in Europe. In June 2007 a cell broken up in Milan, allegedly providing logistics for fighters to travel to Iraq, was comprised entirely of Tunisians. Tunisians have been involved in high-profile Al Qaeda international operations; for example, the assassins of Northern Alliance Commander Ahmed Shah Massoud, who posed as a news crew then blew themselves and their target up with a camera packed with explosives on 9 September 2001, were Tunisian.[36]

Sources say that Tunisians form a significant proportion of the AQIM *mujahideen*. It remains to be seen whether engagement with the political process will prove more attractive than violence for these young men now that Ennahda has succeeded in taking the reins of power.

7

Al Qaeda in the Islamic Maghreb: Libya

Oh people of Islam and jihad, Oh you hope of the Moslems, you have been chosen by Allah for a great responsibility, the responsibility of removing tyranny and establishing truth. Keep your trust in Allah and implement the Sharia of Allah in the Libya of Omar Al-Mukhtar.

Sheikh Abu Al-Hassan Rashid Al-Bulaydi,
AQIM head of Judicial Authority, November 2011
(posted on Libyan revolutionaries' official Facebook page)

As the revolution against Colonel Gaddafi neared its conclusion Al Qaeda and Islamic State of Iraq flags were flown in various towns across Libya, in particular around the Benghazi region. Having watched from the sidelines in Tunisia and Egypt, Al Qaeda–associated *jihadis* were game-changers in Libya.

Libya has a long historical association with Islamist ideology. Libyans feature prominently in the Al Qaeda roll call and the country also produced one of the Islamists' most inspiring twentieth-century icons, the leader of the insurgency against the Italian occupation of Libya from 1912 to 1931, Omar al-Mukhtar.

During the Libyan Arab Spring revolution, the rebels called themselves the 'grandsons of Omar al-Mukhtar'. He has also been adopted as a symbol of the post-revolutionary 'Free Libya' by the largely secularist National Transitional Council (NTC), who devote a whole page on their website to his story . . . having repackaged it so as to omit any reference to his extremist religious beliefs and the fact that he considered himself a *jihadi*.[1] The website Islamicthinkers.com, however, makes a point of comparing al-Mukhtar—the 'Lion of Cyrenaica'—to today's *jihadi* leaders in a biography that has attracted one and a quarter million hits.[2]

I will briefly summarise the biography of a man whose legendary status (and ability to inspire today's *jihadis*) rivals that of Osama bin Laden. Al-Mukhtar was born in 1862 near Tobruk in eastern Libya and, even as a child, was always known for being deeply religious. When he was 50 years old the Italians occupied Libya; despite his advanced years, al-Mukhtar swiftly assembled a *mujahideen* army, launching an insurgency which was to last the best part of twenty years. The Italians brutally suppressed any resistance and set up concentration camps in which at least 125,000 Libyans died. The *mujahideen* increased in numbers, drawn by the legend and charisma of al-Mukhtar. The Italians next attempted to buy him off, offering him an amnesty, wealth and power; al-Mukhtar refused, reiterating that he considered it his religious duty to fight this *jihad* and would never negotiate with the enemy. He was captured in September 1931, aged nearly 70, sentenced to death and hanged in front of hundreds of tribesmen in a bid to frighten them into submission. Omar al-Mukhtar was the subject of a 1981 Hollywood film (*The Lion of the Desert*) with Anthony Quinn in the leading role—perhaps because his nemesis was the Italian fascist regime, *jihad* against an occupying Western army is portrayed as heroism rather than terrorism in this instance.

The complexities of Libya's tribal system underlie the socio-political map of the country. There are at least 140 tribal networks, and hundreds of clans within them. It is possible to tell which clan or tribe a person comes from by their surname. Colonel Gaddafi, for example, hailed from the Gadaffa tribe, an Arabised Berber tribe from the Sirte region. If any reader would like to read a concise and basic account of Libya's tribal system, a link is available in the endnotes of this chapter.[3] In addition there are several ethnic groupings, the largest of which are the Arabs, the Berbers and the Tuareg.

Libya has always maintained its strong Islamic identity which is now meshed in with the revolutionary process. One of the main military leaders of the rebel army that eventually toppled Colonel Gaddafi was, as we have seen, Abdel Hakim Belhadj (not to be confused with Algerian FIS leader Ali Belhajj), former emir of Al Qaeda affiliate the Libyan Islamic Fighting Group (LIFG). Several sources have told me that there were many men from the LIFG and from Al Qaeda itself among the fighters who toppled Gaddafi; AQIM leader Belmokhtar confirmed this in a November 2011 interview.[4]

Libyan nationals and LIFG men are prominently represented within the Al Qaeda 'central' leadership and the two groups are linked by past ties and future ambition. Abu Yahya al-Libi, a senior LIFG ideologue, appeared in as much Al Qaeda propaganda material as Osama bin Laden and Ayman al-Zawahiri in 2010. According to the Sinjar records, Libya produced more *jihadis* (as a proportion of the total population) for the Iraqi insurgency than any other foreign country. It is reasonable to assume that the proportion of the Libyan cohort in Al Qaeda as a whole is similar.

According to sources, Belhadj was offered a role in the interim government—a claim endorsed by the *Daily Telegraph*[5]—but declined, amid rumours that he intended to play a role in a future, Islamic, state. In May 2012, he swapped his camouflage gear for sharp suits and announced that he was forming a political party which would run in future elections.

The post-revolutionary map of Libya remains undefined. The eastern part of the country, the former Cyrenaica, known as Barqa in Arabic, declared itself an autonomous federal state in March 2012. Despite assurances from the NTC chair Mustafa Abdel Jalil that the new Libya would be founded on Sharia law, the interim cabinet announced in November 2011 was composed entirely of liberal secularists.[6] Many of the NTC's most significant players (some behind the scenes) have dubious credentials: Jalil himself was Gaddafi's minister of justice where he presided over the systematic torture and imprisonment of dissidents; others are known to have connections with the CIA—Colonel Khalifa Haftar, for example, who returned to lead some of the rebel troops, was trained in Langley, Virginia; Prime Minister Abdel Rahim al-Keib also spent most of his adult life in the US.

Libya sits on the African continent's largest oil reserves of 46.6 billion barrels[7] and before the revolution 85 percent of its oil was exported to Europe.[8] With one eye on Libya's resources, NATO greatly feared an Islamist state in lieu of Gaddafi. Western leaders such as Tony Blair worked hard at rehabilitating the former leader and from 2004, Blair visited Gaddafi's tent in Tripoli on several occasions. By 2005 Blair had persuaded Gaddafi to give up his nuclear weapons programme and was able to use his apparent friendship with the dictator to the advantage of at least one multinational oil corporation, brokering an exploration contract for British Petroleum in 2007.[9] Having left office, Blair was a regular visitor to the Gaddafi clan, with Saif al-Islam boasting that he was a close friend of the family and an adviser to the $60 billion dollar Libyan Investment Authority fund.[10] The point is that the West preferred a tamed Gaddafi to a hostile, anti-US, Islamist regime, which explains why America was initially reluctant to endorse UN Security Council Resolution 1973, which instigated the no-fly zone and NATO intervention.

Certainly the West was hoping that the secularists would prevail in the post-revolutionary political struggle, having seriously underestimated the Islamist presence in the rebel army. These hopes were partly met when, in July 2012, the National Forces Alliance (NFA), a secular umbrella party, did unexpectedly well in the parliamentary elections. The NFA is led by Mahmoud Jibril, who was an economic planner for the Gaddafi regime and worked closely with Saif al-Islam Gaddafi.

It is unlikely, however, that the Islamists will abandon their political ambitions or that the many militias will lay down their arms and join a national army. Even as the votes were being counted, *The Times* concurred with my own sources that 'Libya is breaking down into tribes and city states, each with its own militia to enforce the law'.[11]

Several rival militias have emerged, dividing the country into areas of control and vying for the power they feel they have earned in recompense for their role in the revolution.[12] The NTC was unable to either disarm or control these militias, which include Haftar's militia; the Zintan Brigades, who captured Saif al-Islam and whose leader, Osama al-Juwali, was interim minister of defence; the Obeida Ibn Jarrah Brigade; the Misrata Brigade; and the Tripoli Military Council, originally headed by Abdel Hakim Belhadj. The militias have already been involved in several spats. In January 2012, the NTC accused Khalifa Haftar of attempting a military coup when his militia attacked Tripoli's Rixos Hotel, which was housing several prominent NTC members and, it was rumoured, millions of dollars released from Gaddafi's foreign bank accounts. A Haftar dynasty is already emerging with Khalifa Haftar's son, Belqasim, heading up a division within their militia. Grandson Saddam made the headlines in January 2012 when he and some armed accomplices stormed the Aman Bank in Tripoli.[13]

Whatever the composition of Libya's first democratically elected parliament, the new government will sideline the Islamists at their peril. They have already shown their teeth: at the end of July 2011, the Obeida Ibn Jarrah Brigade (the main Islamist militia in the uprising, named after one of the Prophet's companions) assassinated key rebel military leader General Abdel Fattah Younis, declaring that he was a traitor. Younis was Gaddafi's interior minister, until he defected to the rebels, and had presided over very brutal suppression of the LIFG and other Islamist groups in the mid-1990s.

If the electoral process fails to produce a universally acceptable government, civil war is inevitable, and it is not at all clear where the military establishment formerly loyal to Gaddafi would stand. Analysts have noted that online communications between Libyan Islamists and the AQIM leadership have been on the increase and one would assume that physical meetings are taking place to coordinate a regional strategy in order to exploit the deepening crisis.

Islamism in Libya

Nationalist and Islamist opposition groups had been active in Libya long before the revolution of 2011. As Arab nationalism waned at the beginning of the 1980s, there was an Islamist revival, inspired in part by Egypt's hard-liners who assassinated President Anwar Sadat, angry at his rapprochement with Israel. Ayman al-Zawahiri was among the men jailed for this crime.

Libyan nationalism meanwhile largely moved abroad. The secular National Front for the Salvation of Libya (NFSL) emerged in 1981, led by General Mohammad al-Magarieff, who had served as a diplomat for the Gaddafi regime. The NFSL, deeply opposed to Muammar Gaddafi who had seized power in 1969, was perceived as a potential Contra-style resistance group (serving Western interests) by the West and most of its founder members were in exile in the US or Europe. It is claimed that the Saudi Arabians contributed $7 million to the NFSL[14] and the

CIA helped it establish and train a 700-man militia called the Libyan National Army (LNA). The LNA was initially based in Chad, whence an attempt to assassinate Gaddafi was launched in May 1984. Fifteen gunmen surrounded his house and opened fire, but the Libyan leader escaped unscathed.

Although it did not manage a successful coup, and many of its collaborators within Libya were captured and executed in the course of the 1990s, the NFSL and the LNA continued in exile under US patronage. The LNA came under the leadership of Colonel Khalifa Haftar and moved to a base near CIA headquarters in Langley, Virginia. Haftar told *al-Hayat* newspaper on 18 December 1991 that he had 400 fighters who were receiving regular training and were waiting for the right time to return to Libya. Colonel Haftar had to wait the best part of twenty years for that day to come, re-emerging in Benghazi in spring 2011 as the field commander of the rebel forces. In August 2011 his authority would be disputed by the Islamist military leader, former LIFG emir Belhadj, and by the end of the year he was heading his own thuggish 'Haftar militia'. The NFSL held its last annual conference in July 2007 in the US, under the leadership of Ibrahim Abdulaziz Sahad who was also living in Virginia at that time.

The first notable armed Islamist groups in Libya emerged in the early 1980s. A key figure in the movement was Awatha al-Zuwawi and most founding members of the LIFG were in his entourage, including Abu Munther al-Saadi, who was to become the LIFG's 'spiritual leader'. Al-Zuwawi travelled to Afghanistan at the height of the *jihad* against the Soviet Army and spent some weeks there in 1986. The group engaged in sporadic skirmishes with government forces, mostly in the eastern part of the country and in particular Benghazi, Derna and Ajdabiya—this area, known as Cyrenaica or Barqa in Arabic, has long been the home of radical Islamists interconnected tribally as well as ideologically.

In 1989 Gaddafi ordered the first in a series of heavy-handed crackdowns, arresting and jailing between 5,000 and 7,000 young Islamists—including al-Zuwawi. Those who escaped the clutches of the security forces migrated abroad, many to Afghanistan where there was already a strong Libyan presence. It would be in Afghanistan that the LIFG began to take shape. Libyan *jihadis* often adopt the suffix al-Libi as part of their *nom de guerre*, making it more difficult to identify individuals but clarifying their provenance. The LIFG's first emir was Saif al-Libi; other members of the founding group who would later form the leadership included Khaled al-Sharif, Miftah al-Duwdi, Abdel Wahab al-Qayed—the older brother of Abu Yahya al-Libi—and Abdel Hakim Belhadj.

In Afghanistan, the Libyan contingent was largely based on the Pakistani side of the frontier in the Salman al-Farisi camp in Ghindaw.[15] The camp was shared by fighters who would later form part of Al Qaeda and the Taliban. Enduring relationships between *jihadi* groups and individuals were formed at this time.

LIFG recruits, like their Al Qaeda and Taliban counterparts, were given lectures by one of the most influential *jihadi* clerics of the time, the late Dr Abdullah Azzam. Later, Azzam's writings featured prominently on the LIFG website, as did audio and video recordings of Osama bin Laden and other global *jihadis*.

Although the Libyan *jihadis*' main goal concerned the overthrow of the 'near enemy', Colonel Muammar Gaddafi, they became familiar with the concept of a wider struggle against the US and the West—the 'far enemy'. They also learnt about the domestic challenges faced by their fellow African colleagues, forming close links with the Egyptian al-Gamaat al-Islamiya, Egyptian Islamic Jihad and the Algerian GIA.

After 1989 many of the Libyan *jihadis* remained in Afghanistan where they could make use of established training camps, encouraging Libyan recruits to join them and gain battle experience against the new enemy, Mohammad Najibullah and, later, the Northern Alliance.

The Libyans were able to take their time planning their campaign against the 'apostate' Gaddafi. They appointed regional emirs back in Libya and began establishing the necessary infrastructure for guerrilla war—safe houses, weapon caches, funding—and infiltrating the security services. As things became more uncomfortable for the Afghan-Arabs in the early 1990s, especially on the Pakistani side of the border, a trickle-back of fighters to Libya began in 1992. Many Libyans chose to accompany Osama bin Laden to Sudan, however, and here they would have become conversant with the global ideology he and Ayman al-Zawahiri were developing and their dream of an International Islamic Army.

Libyans have always featured strongly in the Al Qaeda cast list. Today's 'rising star' and Ayman al-Zawahiri's deputy is Abu Yahya al-Libi (Hasan Qayid). He has become one of the organisation's most ubiquitous spokesmen—in 2010 he featured in as many videos as Osama bin Laden and Ayman al-Zawahiri—and is considered to be an influential figure among the young, an effective communicator and recruiter. He spent the latter part of the 1990s with Al Qaeda in Afghanistan, where he ran an eponymous training camp (Shaheed Abu Yahya camp) and was arrested in Pakistan in 2002. He was handed over to US forces in Afghanistan and put in the Bagram 'detention facility'. His legend was assured when he and three other detainees picked the lock on their cell door and escaped into the night in July 2005. Now part of the Al Qaeda central *shura*, he has an unusual portfolio of additional roles: he is the leader of a Libyan group of Al Qaeda fighters in the Afghan–Pakistan border region (having replaced a fellow Libyan, Abu Laith al-Libi, who was killed last year); he is a top strategist and an Islamic scholar; he has useful links with the Sahel, having pursued his Islamic studies in Mauritania for two years; and he has closely monitored, and formed connections with, AQIM. In October 2011 he recorded a video encouraging an uprising against the Algerian government titled 'Algeria and the Battle of Patience'.[16]

Other well-known Libyans include Abu Anas al-Libi, who was among bin Laden's entourage in Sudan and helped plan the 1998 US Embassy bombings in Nairobi and Dar-es-Salaam; one of the early Al Qaeda pioneers of IT, his current whereabouts are uncertain. The late Abu Laith al-Libi fought in Afghanistan and returned to Libya in 1994 in the hope of starting an Islamic revolution, subsequently fleeing to Saudi Arabia—where he was implicated in the Khobar Towers bombings—and then back to Afghanistan where he has been one of the top commanders of AQAM battalions fighting with the Taliban. Abu Laith al-Libi was quick to learn the techniques for IED production, brought into the fray by men who had fought in the Iraqi insurgency. IEDs have been crucial to the military successes of the Iraqi insurgency and the Al Qaeda–Taliban nexus in Afghanistan. Abu Laith al-Libi was killed by a drone strike in 2008.

Abu Faraj al-Libi was the military commander of 'core' Al Qaeda until his arrest in 2005—he is now in Guantanamo; Abu Hafs al-Libi, who was killed in 2004, was al-Zarqawi's lieutenant in Iraq; Ibn Sheikh al-Libi (Ali Mohamed Abdelaziz al Fakhiri) commanded al-Khaldan, an Al Qaeda training camp in Afghanistan, until 2001—he was captured and first rendered to Egypt (where he was tortured into making a false confession regarding a link between Saddam Hussein and Al Qaeda) before being returned to Libya in 2006 where, according to Ayman al-Zawahiri, he was tortured to death in October 2009.

The Libyan Islamic Fighting Group and AQIM

When bin Laden relocated to Sudan in 1991, seventy of the 300 Afghan Arabs who accompanied him were Libyan. The LIFG leadership operated out of Sudan for several years, maintaining sleeper cells inside Libya. At the time, the *jihadi* movement was transfixed by events in Algeria. In an attempt to advance collaboration with the GIA, the LIFG and Al Qaeda dispatched a group of fifteen elite Afghan-Libyan fighters from Sudan in 1994 to help the '*jihad* effort' in Algeria, keep them in battle-ready condition and prepare to lead some Algerian fighters back to Libya for a reciprocal effort when their services would be required. These men did not return and the LIFG concluded that they had been murdered by their GIA 'comrades'. Rumours in London at the time had it that the Libyans had taken sides in an argument with a faction led by Mustafa Kartali against Djamel Zitouni, who had become enraged and ordered their execution. It is equally possible that the Algerian security forces, which had by then deeply infiltrated the GIA, assassinated them with a view to souring relations between the two *jihadi* groups and nipping the potentially powerful alliance in the bud.

The LIFG dispatched a second delegation of senior members to find out what had happened to the first. News came back that the GIA had captured two of these men—Abu Abdullah al-Libi and Abu Sakhar al-Libi. Worse, they had submitted them to horrific torture, including the removal of a metal rod that had been implanted in Abu Sakhar's hand to heal an injury incurred in Afghanistan and then killing him. Now the relationship between the two groups became impossible. Abu Abdullah managed to escape from Algeria without the GIA's knowledge and resurfaced in Europe.

When his intelligence services informed him of the Libyan Islamists' presence and activities in Sudan, a furious Gaddafi put immense pressure on Sudan's President al-Bashir to expel Libyan members of Al Qaeda and the LIFG. By all accounts, al-Bashir approached Osama bin Laden to effect the Libyan leader's wishes. Mindful of his own precarious situation in Sudan (the Saudis were similarly pressuring al-Bashir to hand over their compatriot to them) Osama bin Laden instructed the relevant departments in his organisation to furnish the Libyans with the means to go where they wished. Ironically, Gaddafi's timing brought fighters back to Libya to join the burgeoning effort to unseat him.

From June 1995, the LIFG, led by Abdel Hakim Belhadj (who had been wounded in Afghanistan), and other Islamist groups carried out a number of attacks against the Gaddafi regime, particularly in Benghazi and Derna. A large number of fighters returned to the country to join the effort to topple Gaddafi and establish an Islamic state but the regime's notorious secret police were effective in tracking down both hide-outs and personnel and the LIFG struggled.

The LIFG did not officially announce its existence until October 1995 after a summer of noteworthy attacks aimed at overthrowing the regime:

> The time has come for the Libyan Islamic Fighting Group to become a recognised movement, rather than a secret one, in light of the sensitive phase that the *jihad* project in Libya is currently engaged in. In addition, the Islamic Fighting Group hereby claims responsibility for the blessed *jihad* actions that have been taking place all over Libya since June. Confronting the evil dictators of this era, such as Qadhafi, has become one of the most important duties for Moslems.... We send a brotherly, friendly, and loving word of peace to all the *jihad* movements that have stood up in defence of Islam and those oppressed Moslems across the Islamic world.[17]

The LIFG kept up the pressure on the regime into 1996. The British government watched with interest—it was keen to exploit this opposition to Gaddafi who was, at the time, implacably opposed to the US and its allies and who was widely believed to have been behind the Lockerbie plane crash of 1988. According to British ex-spy David Shayler (whose testimony may not be the most reliable), MI6 supported and funded an LIFG assassination attempt on the Libyan leader's life in February 1996 which was thwarted by his security forces.

The Islamists could not prevail against the militarily superior and better equipped government forces and lost all their major battles. It is interesting to note, however, that the LIFG formulated a strategy at this time which closely mirrors what actually came to pass in 2011: they planned on seizing control of pockets of territory in the east and using them as a base from which to take control of the rest of Libya.

Following the 1996 attempt on his life, Gaddafi cracked down severely on the Islamists whom, he declared, 'deserved to die like dogs'. He demonstrated the brutality which characterised his response to the 2011 rebellion and used aerial bombardment and helicopters to attack Islamist strongholds in Benghazi, and laid siege to Derna. Many LIFG leaders fled the country—a significant number obtained political asylum in Britain, in particular London and Manchester—but there was one further attempt on Gaddafi's life in November 1996, when a fighter threw a hand grenade at him as he visited the central Libyan town of Brak. The grenade failed to go off.

By June 1996, Gaddafi had rounded up nearly 2,000 suspected Islamists and imprisoned them in the notorious Abu Salim jail in Tripoli: 1,200 would be killed in a single night in one of the Gaddafi clan's most notorious crimes against humanity, a brutal massacre that those leading the rebel armies against him in 2011 would not have forgotten. Human Rights Watch interviewed a survivor, Hussein al-Shafa'i, who now lives in New York. He gave a vivid description of events on that fateful night; he was able to witness everything from the kitchen where he was working as a cook.

> The incident began around 4:40 pm on June 28, when prisoners in Block 4 seized a guard named Omar who was bringing their food. Hundreds of prisoners from blocks 3, 5 and 6 escaped their cells. They were angry over restricted family visits and poor living conditions.... Half an hour later, two top security officials, Abdullah Sanussi, who is married to the sister of Gaddafi's wife, and Nasr al-Mabrouk, arrived in a dark green Audi with a contingent of security personnel... the prisoners asked Sanussi for clean clothes, outside recreation, better medical care, family visits, and the right to have their cases heard before a court, because many of the prisoners were in prison without trial. Sanussi said he would address the physical conditions, but the prisoners had to return to their cells.... Around 5 am on June 29, security forces moved some of the prisoners between the civilian and military sections of the prison. By 9 am they had forced hundreds of prisoners from blocks 1, 3, 4, 5 and 6 into different courtyards.... At 11

> am a grenade was thrown into one of the courtyards. I did not see who threw it but I am sure it was a grenade. I heard an explosion and right after a constant shooting started from heavy weapons and Kalashnikovs from the top of the roofs. The shooting continued from 11 am until 1:35 pm . . . I could see those who were shooting. They were a special unit and wearing khaki military hats. Six were using Kalashnikovs. . . . Around 2 pm the forces used pistols to finish off those who were not dead.[18]

Others have described the massacre as being 'like shooting fish in a bowl'. The atrocities at Abu Salim made Gaddafi a prime target for Al Qaeda and its affiliates and he remained so until his death in October 2011.

LIFG attacks continued through 1997 but in September of that year the regime sent 20,000–30,000 soldiers with tanks, RPGs and heavy artillery to stamp out LIFG strongholds. The Islamists found themselves alone, prompting LIFG spokesman Omar Rashed to comment, 'The Libyan people in general have not passed beyond the stage of sentiment to the stage of action . . . we are suffering from the absence of the people in confronting Gaddafi and his regime, despite their rejection of his rule and despite their enmity towards him.'[19] All that would change in the course of the 2011 revolution.

By the summer of 1998, Gaddafi's security forces had succeeded in snuffing out the embryonic uprising and the LIFG abandoned its efforts for the time being. Some of its members repaired to Istanbul where they opened an office, several sought asylum in Western countries but the majority went to Afghanistan where Al Qaeda had become well ensconced under the patronage of the Taliban.

In 1998, Ayman al-Zawahiri and Osama bin Laden launched the Global Islamic Front (for Jihad against the Jews and Crusaders). The innovation was largely al-Zawahiri's—the Egyptian reasoned that the failure to create effective alliances between the *jihadi* groups in Egypt, Algeria and Libya had impeded the hopes they all shared, both regionally and internationally. The LIFG did not officially join the nascent global movement at this time but supported it and cooperated with it. Apart from sharing operational infrastructure, training camps and personnel with the Taliban, Al Qaeda, EIJ and other groups, there was a propaganda effort to share ideological and strategic material. When the US launched retaliatory attacks on Al Qaeda camps in southern

Afghanistan in the wake of the African Embassy bombings in August 1998, for example, the LIFG issued a statement which read:

> America is not only the enemy of the Mujahid Shaykh Usama Bin Laden and the Islamic movements, but rather the enemy of the entire Islamic nation.... The Islamic Fighting Group calls upon Moslems to confront this American aggression in order to respond to this bellicose attack against the people of our Islamic nation.... Whereas the American Administration relies on its fleets, its warplanes, and its missiles, we rely on Allah alone.[20]

The LIFG had access to the training camp north of Kabul commanded by Abu Yahya al-Libi. This camp enabled the LIFG to maintain strong ties with the other *jihadi* organisations which sent their recruits for training there. The LIFG also sent their men to camps run by other groups. At Al Qaeda's infamous al-Khalden camp, the deputy commander was also a Libyan, Ibn Sheikh al-Libi, and a large number of Libyan recruits received training there.

In the aftermath of 9/11, a significant number of LIFG men stayed behind in Afghanistan to fight with bin Laden's men, eventually fleeing with the Al Qaeda group as they were forced into the border hinterland and Pakistan. Others left for Iran, and many were captured on the way, whilst some chose to return to Libya.

Abdel Hakim Belhadj would be arrested in Thailand in 2004 and interrogated by the CIA who then handed him over to Libya, where he was imprisoned in Abu Salim jail. In 2011, Belhadj began a legal case against Britain, claiming up to $1 million compensation for allowing his 'extraordinary rendition' via UK territory Diego Garcia and contributing in this way to the torture he and his pregnant wife endured in Tripoli.[21]

The LIFG remained largely inactive within Libya for several years, although on 30 May 2005, in response to the arrest of several LIFG fighters in the eastern city of Derna, my paper received a communiqué from an Al Qaeda cell within Libya, signed by 'field commander Abu al-Bara al-Libi', threatening to 'cut off the heads of the unbelieving apostates unless they release our prisoners'; it seems the group lacked resources to launch any significant attack at that time, however.

Instead, Libyan fighters were forming a major cohort within the insurgency in Iraq. In 2004 Libyan recruits featured prominently in the 'Martyrs

Brigade' which specialised in suicide car bombings. In October 2005, al-Zarqawi's media group issued a full-length propaganda film featuring the activities of a Libyan suicide bomber called Abu-Dharr al-Libi, in which he urged fellow *mujahideen* to continue with suicide bombing 'because they are the things that massacre and affect the Americans the most'.[22]

The level of participation in the Iraqi insurgency by *jihadis* from any country had only been a matter for speculation or, at best, word of mouth reportage, but in 2007 some documents were seized by US troops which provide an accurate and vivid picture of the origins and capabilities of new recruits arriving to fight in Iraq via the Syrian border. The so-called Sinjar records are, in effect, the personnel records of new arrivals in Iraq through just one entry point between August 2006 and August 2007 (with a gap in the spring unaccounted for).[23]

The records, which bear the logo of the Mujahideen Shura Council (later named the ISOI), demonstrate a surprising level of bureaucratic thoroughness. Each individual file displays a photograph of the recruit above a 'personal information' form which records the name, alias, address, phone number of next of kin, date of birth, the duty he expects to undertake within the ranks of Al Qaeda, the items of value he has entrusted to the organisation, who recruited him and who facilitated his journey to Iraq.

The records document almost 600 individuals: 112 were Libyans and of these the majority hailed from the east, mainly Derna (fifty-three men) and Benghazi (twenty men). Two hundred and thirty-seven fighters came from Saudi Arabia, making them the most numerous but, on a per capita of population basis, Libya provided more fighters by far than anywhere else. There were 18.55 Libyan fighters per million population, compared with 8.84 per million Saudis. Libya's Derna region had the dubious distinction of having the biggest concentration of terrorists in the world, with one fighter leaving for Iraq per 1,000 people. Another characteristic of the Libyan contingent was their willingness to undertake suicide missions—85 percent volunteered for 'martyrdom operations' compared with an average of 56 percent among the rest of the nationalities represented.

Militants inside Libya were not entirely inactive—a suicide bombing in Derna in July 2007 was claimed by 'Al Qaeda in eastern Libya'. This may well have been the prelude to a formal merger between the LIFG and Al Qaeda which was announced in a video message on 3 November 2007 by Ayman al-Zawahiri and long-term Al Qaeda associate and the LIFG leader who had replaced Belhadj, Abu Laith al-Libi. Once more we see the active role played by Ayman al-Zawahiri in fostering alliances and affiliations.

Interestingly, in the light of the important role the towns played in the 2011 revolution, Abu Laith mentions Benghazi and Derna in his part of the announcement: 'It is with the grace of God that we are hoisting the banner of *Jihad* against this apostate regime under the leadership of the Libyan Islamic Fighting Group, which sacrificed the elite of its sons and commanders in combating this regime whose blood was spilled on the mountains of Derna, the streets of Benghazi, the outskirts of Tripoli, the desert of Sabha, and the sands of the beach.'

In response to the ominous merger, the 'Gaddafi International Foundation for Charity Associations' launched a rehabilitation programme for Libya's many imprisoned Islamists. Led by Saif al-Islam Gaddafi and based on the Saudi model, the aim was to convince the regime's erstwhile enemies to renounce Al Qaeda and *jihad* and agree to participate in civil society.

In April 2008 the first group of around eighty rehabilitated prisoners was released, with a further 200—including Abdel Hakim Belhadj—set free in 2010. Whether these were genuinely repentant—or simply pragmatic men who, being offered a way out of jail after up to a decade behind bars, become good actors—remains to be seen. Belhadj, for the moment, is adamant that he rejects Al Qaeda, and is concentrating on a credible political profile; but all that might change if the Islamists are cheated out of their chance to participate in the democratic process.

Certainly his repentance and avowed loyalty to the Gaddafi regime meant little to Belhadj as soon as the rebellion erupted; he swiftly organised, and assumed command of, the Islamist brigades within the rebel army—many of whom were LIFG fighters. In the course of the Libyan rebellion he was the first to enter Gaddafi's Bab-Alaziziya compound in Tripoli and led the final advance on the capital.

Saif al-Islam believed he had a 'special relationship' with Belhadj and the two men had an extensive correspondence from 2007 to 2009. Leaked US Embassy cables reveal that a diplomat in Tripoli was shown several handwritten letters from Belhadj (referred to as al-Sadiq) to Saif al-Islam discussing the contents of the document the ex-LIFG leaders would release in exchange for an amnesty.[24] The result, a 417-page Arabic-language document, 'Revisionist Studies of the Concepts of *Jihad*, Verification, and Judgment of People', in which the authors claim that their former violence was rooted in ignorance and a misinterpretation of Islamic jurisprudence, was written in collaboration with Noman Benotman, another former LIFG *shura* member living in London.

Because of this imagined affinity with the Islamists, Saif al-Islam seemed confident during the revolution that he could join forces with the rebels and create an insurgency against the CIA-backed element in the NTC. As events turned out, his hopes were a mirage, as the recantation document may also prove to be.

Conclusion

America and Europe rely on fuel exports from Africa. Libya sits on the continent's largest oil reserves at 46.6 billion barrels.[25] Algeria has the fourth largest oil deposits in Africa at 12.2 billion barrels and also possesses the world's fifth largest natural gas reserves.[26] Not only that, an ambitious mega-project, a gas pipeline from Nigeria, through the Sahara desert and Algeria to the Mediterranean coast, is planned for 2015.[27] Nigeria has proven oil reserves of 37.2 billion barrels, and 40 percent of its oil exports go to the US.[28]

Al-Zawahiri's dream of an interconnected swathe of Islamic states across North Africa, then, is the West's worst nightmare. If the Islamists prevail through the ballot box, however, and the West accepts the results, the chances for diplomatic accommodation are more promising. Extremist regimes which ascend to power through revolution—such as the Taliban or Iran's Ayatollahs—are more prone to a hostile, anti-Western stance.

If the political process does not provide workable new government solutions the whole of North Africa could be destabilised, with the possibility of civil wars, and AQAM groups flourishing in the chaos. AQIM has already benefited from the anarchy in Libya by seizing large quantities of weapons and the group clearly believes that it can extend its reach into Libya where it already has long-standing connections and loyalties through a shared *jihadi* past. Out of seven statements released by AQIM in 2011 to do with the Arab Spring, four were exhortations or congratulations to their comrades in Libya. Nor do some of the Libyan revolutionaries display antipathy towards Al Qaeda. On the contrary, Al Qaeda flags have been flown in celebrations across the country and the official Facebook page of the revolution, 17 February Intifada, carried statements by AQIM figures such as Sheikh Hassan Rachid al-Bulaydi.

With the Sahel already infiltrated and Boko Haram active in Nigeria, the influence and reach of AQIM are spreading. Islamist-led governments in the Maghreb and Egypt would be less likely to facilitate US military installations and activities than their predecessors, making attacks targeting AQAM groups very difficult. The Americans have faced enduring problems in establishing a military infrastructure in Africa in any case.

In February 2008 President Bush announced the formation of US Africa Command, or AFRICOM, a new US military group 'to promote US national security objectives in Africa and its surrounding waters', noting that 'Africa now supplies the United States with roughly the same amount of crude oil as the Middle East.'[29]

Diplomatic efforts to procure a host country for the AFRICOM contingent of around 3,500 soldiers (the US is coy about disclosing the exact number) have been ongoing since 2006 but few countries are prepared to take the risk of accommodating such a controversial military adventure. Some countries feel it would be the first step towards a much greater deployment of US military personnel on the continent, while others fear the attendant risk of terror attacks on their own soil. AFRICOM headquarters remain in Stuttgart, Germany.[30]

America's only official military base in Africa is in Djibouti but it has relied on the cooperation of several other African countries to maintain a covert presence dotted about the continent as this paragraph from a 2010 congressional briefing document explains: 'DOD [Department of Defense] refers to these facilities as "lily pads", or Cooperative Security Locations (CSLs), and has access to locations in Algeria, Nigeria, Botswana, Gabon, Ghana, Kenya, Mali, Namibia, Sao Tome and Principe, Sierra Leone, Tunisia, Uganda, and Zambia.'[31] Some of these 'lily pads' may well be compromised as a result of the Arab Spring and the concomitant increase in AQAM influence, in particular those in Tunisia, Algeria and Nigeria.

Al Qaeda's influence in Africa has also expanded since 2008 and the perceived 'victory' of the insurgents in Iraq and that of the Taliban in Afghanistan can only serve to boost AQAM groups' credibility and reach. As Mohammad Darif, political science professor at Hassan II-Mohammedia University in Morocco, put it in 2007, 'Al Qaeda has the same strategy as the US; it wants to win in Iraq so that it can transform the whole region'.[32]

AQIM and the LIFG have their roots in more than twenty years' armed struggle against their respective regimes. When these fall, as they have in Tunisia and Libya, it is unlikely that the Islamists will cede their demands for Islamic states in favour of Western style democracies. The question is only to what extent the extremists are prepared to moderate their vision and participate in the political process rather than using violence to achieve their aims.

8

Ongoing and New Alliances

Do not think jihad is over; rather, jihad has just begun.
Abu Shekau, emir of Boko Haram, Nigeria, July 2010

The affiliates are playing a more menacing role today . . . the broader Al Qaeda threat has become more geographically and ethnically diversified.
Daniel Benjamin, US State Department Coordinator for Counterterrorism, September 2010

The AQAM network continues to expand. As well as the major 'branches' discussed in previous chapters, Al Qaeda retains close links with the Islamic State of Iraq, Southeast Asia's Jamaa al-Islamiya, the Islamic Movement of Uzbekistan, the North Caucasus *mujahideen* and Palestinian groups, among many others. In addition, new groups have emerged: some in the wake of the Arab Spring, such as Al Qaeda in the Sinai Peninsula, others as a result of AQIM's growing reach through Africa, such as Boko Haram in Nigeria.

Even small groups with a local agenda, such as the Chinese Uyghurs, can be exploited by the global network to weaken the political structures of the world's greatest powers. There are many more—some experts say as many as forty *jihadi* groups have some connection with Al Qaeda—but I will limit my observations to those mentioned above which, in my opinion, are the most significant at this point in time.

Iraq

The Obama administration pulled all US troops out of Iraq days before its self-imposed 31 December 2011 deadline. The Al Qaeda–led insurgents' umbrella, the Islamic State of Iraq (I use the acronym ISOI to avoid confusion with the Pakistani Inter-Services Intelligence, the ISI) declared victory over the world's greatest superpower; President Obama, however, insisted that the American troops were leaving 'heads held high' and 'job done'.

The government the US have left behind, headed by Nouri al-Maliki, is the eighth most corrupt in the world according to Transparency International. Furthermore, post-Saddam Iraq is closely allied to America's regional nemesis, Iran, several key members of the al-Maliki government having been exiled in Iran under the protection and tutelage of the Ayatollahs.

In addition, while troop deaths have fallen off, sectarian and ISOI violence has increased since mid-2011. The average number of civilians who lost their lives through suicide bombing or IEDs was 6.6 per day in 2011, but already 12 per day in 2012 at the time of writing. Sectarian violence continues, targeting Shi'i pilgrims and worshippers, and more recently the imams of Shi'i mosques. Recent attacks have become more strategic and political, targeting security forces, police and government officials.

Al-Maliki's security forces appear to be ineffective against the insurgents and are increasingly infiltrated by Al Qaeda and other double agents. This is clear from the increased incidence of operations involving several coordinated attacks on different targets. On 15 August 2011 an unprecedented series of forty-two coordinated suicide, IED and mortar attacks occurred throughout the country, leaving eighty-nine dead and 315 injured. The ISOI announced that these were in retaliation for the killing of Osama bin Laden, threatening 100 strikes.

The West was clearly unprepared for the ferocity of the insurgency which erupted in Iraq in 2003 just as US President George W. Bush announced victory over Saddam Hussein. Al Qaeda was quick to exploit the potential for *jihad* and foreign fighters flocked to the new battleground. The leadership was keen to fight Western troops on Muslim territory, in line with the long-term strategy developed by Osama bin Laden and others in the late 1990s.

When I wrote my first book on Al Qaeda, the group's Iraqi branch, Al Qaeda in the Land of the Two Rivers (also known as Al Qaeda in Mesopotamia) was beginning to lose its grip on the insurgency which it had successfully dominated for some time. By 2006, the indigenous insurgents felt their cause had been hijacked by extremists, led by the Jordanian Abu Musab al-Zarqawi, whose worldview they did not share. The 9 November 2005 triple suicide blasts in Amman, Jordan, ordered by al-Zarqawi, shifted the balance of opinion very much against him. Sixty people were killed—more than half of them Jordanian and Palestinian guests at a wedding. There seemed to be little political rationale behind the attacks and resentment of al-Zarqawi and his cohorts snowballed. The sectarian conflict he was fomenting against the Shi'i also brought him into open conflict with indigenous insurgents and fierce battles between Al Qaeda fighters and nationalist groups ensued.

Al-Zarqawi drew well-documented harsh criticism from senior Al Qaeda leaders. As early as 2005 Dr Ayman al-Zawahiri warned him, 'You and your brothers must strive to have around you circles of support, assistance, and cooperation, and through them, to advance until you become a consensus, entity, organization, or association that represents all the honourable people and the loyal people in Iraq.'[1] Al-Zarqawi failed to comply and was subsequently demoted by Osama bin Laden in April 2006.[2] By early June he had been tracked down and killed by the Americans.

In January 2006, in an attempt to rejoin the fold, al-Zarqawi had been instrumental in the formation of an umbrella group of five or six insurgent groups to be called the Mujahideen Shura Council (MSC). The leader was Abdullah Rashid al-Baghdadi. The name is significant because the impression was to be given that the new group was led by an Iraqi. In October 2006 the MSC changed its name to the Islamic State of Iraq, saying that the change heralded a new military campaign and the aim of transforming Iraq into an Islamic emirate. Again, a man with an Iraqi moniker was named emir—Abu Omar al-Baghdadi. Many commentators have questioned whether al-Baghdadi actually exists and it seems plausible that the Iraqi branch of Al Qaeda—in reality led by Abu Ayyub al-Masri (an Egyptian)—would choose to operate under the cover of a fictitious Iraqi emir. The ISOI appointed its own shadow government and imposed Sharia law in the areas under its control—these include parts of Baghdad, Anbar, Kirkuk and the ISOI 'capital', Baqubah.

In the autumn of 2006 the US began a new strategy aimed at harnessing growing discontent among certain Sunni tribes in Anbar province. Led by wealthy businessman and tribal leader, Sheikh Abdul Sattar Abu Risha, the so-called Awakening tribes began to cooperate with the US military against the ISOI and formed their own militia, the Sons of Iraq. Paid $300 a month by the US military, the movement spread to other areas of the country and by 2007 had as many as 100,000 armed members. In January 2007, George W. Bush committed an additional 21,500 troops to Iraq—the so-called Surge. Coupled with the Awakening campaign, the US troops and the Sons of Iraq made a lot of ground against Al Qaeda in 2007.

Meanwhile Al Qaeda was trying to create a 'surge' of its own. The Sinjar records, mentioned in Chapter 7, testify to the fact that, although Al Qaeda was arguing that the ISOI was a largely indigenous organisation, the leadership was mostly foreign and at least 595 foreign *jihadis* came to Iraq to join the fight to oust the invading forces. The records reveal the countries of origin of Al Qaeda's recruits, and may be suggestive of the wider make-up of international AQAM brigades, in Yemen, Pakistan and Somalia for example. Forty-one percent (244) of the recruits were from Saudi Arabia; 18.8 percent (112) were from Libya. Syria (49), Yemen (48) and Algeria (43) also produced significant numbers.

Despite the success of the new American strategy (formulated by General Petraeus) the ISOI remained extremely dangerous. On 14 August 2007, the group carried out the most deadly act of terrorism in the history of the insurgency in Iraq and the second most deadly in the world after 9/11. Four coordinated suicide bomb attacks in two Kurdish towns targeted the Yazidi minority and killed 796 people, wounding 1,562. The Yazidi follow a religion akin to Sufism, considered heretical by the hard-line ISOI Salafists. On 13 September 2007, the ISOI claimed responsibility for the car bomb that assassinated Awakening leader Sheikh Abdul Sattar Abu Risha.

Ordinary Iraqi people became angered by, and weary of, the ISOI's religious and judicial extremism. The rapacious hatred of the Shi'i espoused by al-Zarqawi and his horrific violence against them went against the grain with the people of Iraq where Sunni and Shi'i had previously lived in harmony. Rumours of draconian punishments spread through the country and created a breach in the insurgency that, compounded with the Awakening campaign and the Surge, further weakened Al Qaeda in Iraq. From spring 2008 there was a steady migration of fighters and key figures from Iraq, to other battles or, sometimes, home.

The new Iraqi government and the US administration were so confident that they had beaten the insurgency that on 27 November 2008 the Iraqi Parliament passed the Status of Forces Agreement (SOFA) by which US troops would withdraw from Iraq's cities by 30 June 2009 and from the entire country by 31 December 2011.

In late 2008 the US had handed over control of the Sons of Iraq to the Iraqi government, which committed a fatal error in its dealings with these by now highly trained fighters. Half of them were dismissed and the remainder were meant to be absorbed into various ministries or the security forces but were let down, probably for sectarian reasons. These disaffected Sunni fighters represent a potent threat to the regime in the event of sectarian civil war or an armed uprising. Many rejoined the insurgency while those 'Sons of Iraq' who did not repent of their 'collaboration' became targets for Al Qaeda revenge squads.[3]

In January 2009, as part of a 'normalisation' process, the US handed over supervision and control of Baghdad's Green Zone—where all the most sensitive governmental buildings are housed—to Iraqi security forces. When US troops withdrew from Iraqi cities in line with the SOFA, the Iraqi government removed blast walls and other defences around and within the Green Zone.

Meanwhile Al Qaeda and other ISOI insurgents had regrouped, and 19 August 2009 saw a series of devastating attacks across the capital which killed 122. Two massive truck bombs hit the ministries of foreign affairs and finance while two smaller bombs went off in the suburbs. Several mortars were fired inside the Green Zone, forcing Iraqi Prime Minister Nouri al-Maliki to cancel a speech he was to give in a nearby hotel.

Worse was to follow on 25 October 2009 when a minivan and a bus packed with explosives seriously damaged the ministry of justice and Baghdad Municipal Council's building. The bombs were made inside the Green Zone, leading to speculation that the operation must have involved the collusion of indigenous security personnel. This attack claimed 155 lives and was followed on 8 December by a series of five blasts across Baghdad which killed 127 people. All the 2009 attacks were claimed by ISOI.

In spring 2010 US and Iraqi troops made a renewed effort to eliminate the insurgency and believed they had killed up to 75 percent of Al Qaeda leaders in the country. The political vacuum which emerged after March 2010 elections gave the insurgency new room to manœuvre, however, and on 10 May 2010 the ISOI carried out a series of bomb and sniper attacks in several major cities.

By summer 2010, civil leaders were warning that Al Qaeda was resurgent in the country and the Awakening leaders were becoming disaffected in the absence of the power-sharing opportunities they had been led to expect. On 24 August 2010 the ISOI carried out a 'spectacular' with coordinated blasts in thirteen cities from Mosul to Basra, killing fifty and wounding 270, in a powerful reminder that they were not a spent force. The violence in Iraq continues; civilian deaths average 12 per day in 2012 to date, compared with 6.6 per day in 2011 and 7.3 in 2010. At the height of the insurgency civilian deaths reached a daily average of 22 (in 2007).[4]

The sectarian conflict fomented by Al Qaeda has bitten deep into the fabric of Iraqi society. Major cities such as Baghdad and Mosul are divided into enclaves dominated by Sunni and Shi'i militias. Al Qaeda went to Iraq in response to the American-led invasion of the country; US troops withdrew at the end of 2011, but in the absence of an effective central government and a workable security infrastructure, Iraq remains an attractive *jihadi* destination. In August 2011, the ISOI released a statement announcing the 'martyrdom' of emir Abu Omar al-Baghdadi and naming his replacement as another Iraqi, Abu Bakr al-Hussani al-Quraishi al-Baghdadi. The group reassured the *jihadi* community that the ISOI was still strong and determined, adding that a new enemy had now entered the group's sights: Iran.

In addition, the group has become embroiled in Syria. The first months of 2012 brought a series of increasingly deadly suicide bombs to Damascus and Syria's largest city, Aleppo. On 10 February 2012, Ayman al-Zawahiri made Al Qaeda's call to arms official with a video message entitled 'Onward Lions of Syria' in which he exhorted Muslims from neighbouring countries Iraq, Turkey, Jordan and Lebanon to 'join the Syrian *jihad* with life, money, opinion and information'. Iraqi intelligence confirmed a migration of fighters and weapons from Iraq to Syria, using the logistical infrastructure put in place in the mid-2000s to facilitate the flow in the other direction.

Palestinian *Jihadi* Groups

The Al Qaeda leadership has always cited the Palestine–Israel conflict, and the West's unconditional support for the Jewish state, as its central casus belli. It is surprising, then, that Al Qaeda has not managed to establish an enduring presence or alliance in Palestine. Ayman al-Zawahiri is likely to target Israel in a bid to boost Al Qaeda's credibility in the wake of bin Laden's assassination and to prove his own leadership abilities. The Palestinian question exercises most Arabs and attacking Israel would boost Al Qaeda's popularity and aid recruitment. In this context, Israel's neighbours, Syria and Lebanon, become of great strategic interest for the Al Qaeda leadership. The Arab Spring uprising in Syria both creates new opportunities (because of the security vacuum) and a distraction (many *jihadis* from Lebanon have migrated to Syria to join the uprising).

There have been several attempts to form an Al Qaeda affiliate inside Palestine. In November 2008, Jund Ansar Allah (Soldiers of Allah's Followers) was launched in Gaza's Rafah and Khan Younis, with a 'military base' in an abandoned Jewish settlement. The group clearly intended to be an Al Qaeda offshoot, and emulated the organisation's methods. Its website used a popular Al Qaeda template, and posted statements by Osama bin Laden, Ayman al-Zawahiri and Abu Musab al-Zarqawi.

Jund Ansar Allah's mission statement expressed the desire to unite the Islamic resistance within Palestine (including Hamas and Islamic Jihad) and to engage in Al Qaeda's wider global *jihadi* programme. Jund Ansar Allah's eventual goal, according to their web statements, is an Islamic Emirate throughout the Middle East. The group's membership expanded rapidly throughout Gaza and numbered several hundred within months, including a significant foreign *jihadi* element.[5]

Jund Ansar Allah's leader was Sheikh Abdel Latif Moussa, an ex-doctor turned cleric whose criticisms of Hamas for being 'too moderate', for its ceasefire with Israel and its failure to implement Sharia law, drew thousands to his radical Friday sermons in Rafah's Ibn Tamiyah mosque.

The group's most significant attack was very dramatic, but ultimately a failure: on 8 June 2009 ten Jund Ansar Allah fighters mounted on horseback, some wearing suicide vests, charged IDF soldiers at the Nahal Oz checkpoint on the border with Israel. The soldiers opened fire and killed five of them outright. The group is implicated in other attacks—for example, on a wedding party attended by Fatah strongman Mohammad Dahlan, and on a hairdressing salon and a music shop. The group also issued statements calling for people on the beaches to dress more modestly.

On 14 August 2009, Sheikh Moussa and about 100 armed and masked men, some carrying RPG launchers, took over the area immediately surrounding the Ibn Tamiyah mosque and announced the establishment of an Islamic Emirate in the Gaza strip. Hamas police responded uncompromisingly: they shut off the area, set up roadblocks and called on the mosque's occupants to surrender. When that did not happen a seven-hour gun battle ensued in which at least fifteen Jund Ansar Allah fighters and six Hamas police were killed. Sheikh Moussa had escaped to his home where he was again surrounded. This time he detonated his suicide vest, killing himself and a Hamas policeman. Jund Ansar Allah was effectively destroyed.

The reason why Al Qaeda has not been more 'successful' in this crucial territory is that the majority of Palestinian resistance groups are essentially nationalistic. Hamas is the most powerful Islamist organisation within the resistance. Founded in 1987 by Sheikh Ahmed Yassin (the blind, wheelchair-bound cleric who would be assassinated by Israel in 2004) and Mahmoud Zahar, Hamas was closely linked to the Muslim Brotherhood, which was growing in strength throughout the Middle East at that time. Hamas's political agenda has historically been the liberation of all Palestinian territories (pre-1948) and the establishment of an Islamic state on them. It has never mentioned any global aspirations or endorsed the Islamic World Front agenda.

Hamas has a military wing, the Issadin al-Qassam Brigades, whose members became the first Palestinian resistance movement to use suicide, or human, bombs in 1994. In January 2006 Hamas won a surprise victory in the Palestinian parliamentary elections, taking 74 of 132 available seats (Fatah won 45 seats). When the US cut off aid to the Palestinian territories in protest, a Hamas–Fatah unity government was formed but this failed to procure the much-needed aid and arguments over security in Gaza led to the disastrous internecine 'Battle of Gaza' which saw Hamas retain control in Gaza—which Israel and Egypt subsequently blockaded—but lose its seats in the West Bank–based Palestinian Authority which remains under Fatah domination.

With its focus so firmly on its immediate domestic concerns, any alliance between Hamas and globally orientated groups like Al Qaeda or its affiliates is extremely unlikely. Indeed, Hamas has of late become more moderate and willing to engage in diplomacy rather than violence. Nevertheless, Israel has encouraged claims of a link between Hamas and Al Qaeda, and a number of smaller Salafist groups (including Jaish al-Islam and Jaish al-Umma) in order to discredit Hamas. Fatah leader and Palestine Authority President, Mahmoud Abbas, has also played the Al Qaeda card. During the conflict with Hamas in 2008 he claimed that an Al Qaeda affiliate was active in Gaza (which it was, see below) and that it was allied to Hamas[6] (which it wasn't).

Whilst Palestine-based groups such as Jaish al-Islam (JaI, The Army of Islam) may sympathise with the hard-line Salafist-*jihadi* outlook of Al Qaeda, there is no evidence to suggest that it has any foreign Al Qaeda men among its leaders or ranks. Whilst it is true that the group kidnapped the BBC journalist Alan Johnston and Al Qaeda–linked cleric Abu Qatada volunteered to negotiate his release, it cannot be classed as a global *jihadi* group.

Lebanon's Palestinian refugee camps are a more fertile recruiting ground and base for Al Qaeda. Ain al-Hilwah near Sidon on the southern coast and Nahr al-Bared in northern Lebanon are home to several *jihadi* groups with links to Al Qaeda which were established during the call to arms for the Iraqi *jihad*. The two main groups in Ain al-Hilwah—the largest camp in Lebanon and home to 80,000 refugees—are Usbat al-Ansar and two splinter groups: Jund al-Sham (the Army of Greater Syria) and, more recently, a new Al Qaeda–affiliated group called the Ziad al-Jarrah Brigades, which includes foreign fighters from Saudi Arabia and elsewhere among its ranks. Ziad al-Jarrah was one of the 9/11 hijackers.

Usbat al-Ansar was established by the Palestinian Hisham Sharaydi in response to Israel's invasion of Lebanon in 1982. Sharaydi believed in pan-Islamic cooperation against Israel and worked closely with Shi'i group Hizbullah. When Sharaydi was assassinated in 1991, the link with Hizbullah weakened and the more militant Jund al-Sham formed in 2002—its name referring to the pre-colonial geographical entity, greater Syria, which was broken up to form Lebanon, Syria and Palestine. With the onset of the Iraq war in 2003, both groups adopted a more global perspective, seeing themselves as part of the global Islamist movement opposed to Western interventions in the Muslim world. The groups sent many fighters to join the Iraqi Sunni insurgency, some of whom returned with weapons seized in battle. The group's funding is believed to come from 'wealthy *jihadi* networks in the Middle East'.[7]

The Ziad al-Jarrah Brigades emerged around 2004 when a group within Usbat al-Ansar decided that it was unacceptable to ally themselves with Hizbullah. This was at the time when a certain element within Al Qaeda was inciting against the Shi'i and the sectarian violence of Abu Musab al-Zarqawi erupted in Iraq. The Ziad al-Jarrah Brigades also claim that Hizbullah prevents them from attacking Israel and have launched attacks on the Shi'i group as well as UNIFIL forces on the Israeli border and Lebanese military targets. The Ziad al-Jarrah Brigades appear to be increasingly active and, according to a recent news report, received a visit from high-profile Al Qaeda man Abd al-Majid Azzam, the grandson of Abdullah Azzam, in March 2012.[8]

The Lebanese Army guards the entrances to, but rarely enters, the camp. Lawless, Ain al-Hilwah's square kilometre is like an outdoor prison, a mini failed state and a hotbed of radicalism. Palestinian refugees are oppressed and humiliated by Lebanese laws which prevent them from participating in the professions, owning property or even leaving the camps without a permit.

In June 2007 the *jihadis* in the camp engaged the Lebanese Army in a full-scale battle, mirroring the violence which had erupted in Nahr al-Bared camp further north. Nahr al-Bared is home to Fatah al-Islam, a group which emerged from the Syrian-backed Fatah al-Intifada and which also has long-standing links with Al Qaeda. Shakir al-Abssi, who led the group until December 2008, was close to Al Qaeda in Iraq leader al-Zarqawi and when Abdul Rahman Awad, Abssi's successor, was killed by Lebanese security forces in an August 2010 shoot-out in the Bekaa valley, it emerged that he was on his way to Iraq. At his funeral, Awad's supporters draped his body in the flag of the Islamic State of Iraq. Nevertheless, Fatah al-Islam denies it has links with Al Qaeda even though its statements are posted on websites associated with Al Qaeda and Al Qaeda forums.

Fatah al-Islam has stated that its aim is to establish an Islamic Emirate in the north of Lebanon. In 2007 the Lebanese authorities were so worried by this breakaway region that they decided to attack the camp.

A full-scale battle with the Lebanese Army ensued which lasted three months from June to September and saw 400 killed, of whom 170 were Fatah al-Islam fighters. Thirty thousand refugees fled the camp in the worst internal violence in Lebanon since the civil war of 1975–90.[9] Many of the captured *jihadis* were foreigners who said they had migrated from the *jihad* in Iraq. Two Moroccans were among the dead fighters. Sources say that Al Qaeda sent a contingent of foreign *jihadis* to join the battle.

The group was not entirely destroyed: in 2007 it mounted an attack on the UN peacekeeping forces on the southern Lebanese border with Israel and began a bombing campaign around Tripoli, targeting the Lebanese police, which continued into 2008. There is considerable sympathy for Fatah al-Islam among certain elements of the Lebanese security apparatus. Fifteen soldiers were charged with plotting against their own army in December 2008 and in summer 2009 Taha al-Hajj Suleiman, Fatah al-Islam's spokesman, escaped from Roumieh prison with inside help. He was recaptured two days later and several prison officers were dismissed.

The group has been quiet since its leader Abdel Rahman Awad was killed in August 2010 but the *jihadi* impulse in the camps is likely to be revived in the light of the Arab Spring, particularly events in Syria. Al Qaeda fighters on their way from Iraq may well use Nahr al-Bared, which is on the main road to Syria, as something of a staging post and reawaken the Palestinian struggle there.

Al Qaeda in the Sinai Peninsula

The advent of Al Qaida in the Sinai Peninsula, facilitated by a security vacuum in the aftermath of the Egyptian revolution, is a dangerous new development for Israel and potentially world shipping since the Sinai neighbours the Suez Canal. The Sinai Peninsula was captured by the Israelis during the Six-Day War in 1967 but was returned to Egypt following the 1978 Camp David accords. It remained heavily policed and militarised with a large presence of both Egyptian and Israeli soldiers in four military zones. In addition there is a 2,000-strong Multinational Force and Observers (MFO) mission tasked with monitoring Egypt's compliance with its peace treaty. The area is of considerable strategic importance: zone A comprises the entire strip down the east coast of the

Suez Canal until it joins the Red Sea while zones C and D run along the borders with Gaza and Israel.

The population of Sinai contains a large number of indigenous Bedouin tribes (approximately 360,000 people) who are frequently in conflict with each other and the Egyptian security forces. There are around fifteen Bedouin tribes in the Sinai; the most powerful around the strategically sensitive border areas with Gaza and Israel are the Sawarka and Rumaylat tribes. Because of their involvement with smuggling through the tunnels between Rafah in Northern Sinai and Gaza, the Bedouin and Gaza's Islamists have developed a grassroots network. As a result there is a great deal of sympathy among some Bedouin tribes with Salafist ideology.

The Bedouin feel marginalised and discriminated against—ideal partners, then, for the *jihadis* who are moving into the area from either Gaza or beyond. They have few employment prospects and the police, military and diplomatic services are closed to them. The Bedouin tribes are also angered by their exclusion from the income accruing from tourism (which is mostly run from and for the benefit of Egyptians from Cairo) and the region's abundant natural resources. The Sinai contains large oilfields and is one of Egypt's top four oil-producing areas.[10]

In January 2011, as the revolution took hold in Cairo, Bedouin tribesmen took control of much of the Sinai, clashing with police and security services, who put up little resistance. Taking advantage of the security breakdown, the tribesmen stormed Sinai's prisons and freed prisoners, among them several men convicted of terrorist activities. These included Ali Abu Faris, a member of Tawid wal Jihad, which was founded in the Sinai in 2004 and is largely composed of tribesmen and Palestinian Salafists. They carried out the 2005 Sharm-el-Sheikh bombings targeting tourists in the Old Bazaar, the Moevenpick Hotel and the Ghazala Gardens hotel—in all, 88 people were killed and more than 200 wounded. Several Bedouin were also arrested in conjunction with these attacks.

In the wake of Hosni Mubarak's ousting in February 2011, the Sinai became increasingly lawless and was awash with weapons, mostly from Sudan. On 29 July 2011 tribesmen attacked the police station in northern Sinai's main town, al-Arish, killing five people. *Al-Ahram* reported on the increasing links between the tribesmen involved in such attacks and Al Qaeda, revealing that most of the fighters came from one village which had become a *jihadi* stronghold full of people 'who raise the black flags of Al Qaeda'. The paper also noted that of fifteen men arrested in connection with the attack, ten were Palestinians.[11]

The Sinai-based insurgents, whether tribesmen or *jihadis*, are well placed to wreak economic havoc on Israel and the Egyptian government. A major state-owned (Gasco) natural gas pipeline runs from al-Arish (in Egypt) to Ashkelon (in Israel) and it has been regularly attacked since the revolution. In July 2011 a massive hole was blown in the pipeline by rocket-propelled grenades, causing a fire which raged for days, burnt several local houses and caused around $700 million lost revenue for Egypt. In February 2012 the pipeline was completely shut down after another attack. Israel gets 40 percent of its gas supply from Egypt and the pipeline also serves Jordan, Lebanon and Syria.

Egyptian-born Al Qaeda leader Ayman al-Zawahiri talked about the pipeline attacks in his 'A Message of Hope and Glad Tidings to Our People in Egypt' series: 'I salute the heroes who blew up the gas pipeline extending to Israel,' he said in August 2011, 'And I ask Allah to reward them . . . for they have expressed the rage of the Muslim *umma* for this crime which has continued since the era of Hosni Mubarak.' The 'crime' to which Zawahiri refers is not just the supply of gas to his nemesis, Israel, but 'the supply of Egyptian natural gas to Israel at prices that are lower than the market price'.[12]

In August 2011, reports emerged of Al Qaeda–linked cells training in the northern Sinai.[13] An Egyptian security spokesman told CNN that several *jihadis* reported having seen Al Qaeda explosives expert, Ramzi Mahmoud al-Mowafi, in the area.[14] Al-Mowafi was apparently among the thousands who escaped from four Cairo prisons in coordinated jailbreaks during the first weeks of the revolution.[15] Al-Mowafi is said to have contacted members of existing *jihadi* groups already operating in the Sinai including Takfir wal Hijra—who took an active part in the uprising—and the largely Palestinian group Jaish al-Islam.

Also in August 2011, leaflets were distributed in the area around the Rafah crossing, and outside mosques, proclaiming the establishment of Al Qaeda in the Sinai Peninsula (AQSP), calling for an Islamic emirate of the Sinai, the rupture of Egyptian–Israeli relations and threatening imminent attacks.

The first attack with which the group is clearly associated came on 18

August 2011 and bore similarities to the 2008 attacks in Mumbai carried out by Al Qaeda–linked group LeT. In the first part of 2011, several Al Qaeda leaders, including Anwar al-Awlaki, had called for a repeat of this pattern of coordinated attacks by small groups of 'commandos'. On this occasion, four groups of three fighters carried out cross-border raids, shooting indiscriminately at Israeli targets and tourists. Eight civilians (some Israeli, some foreign tourists), five Egyptian troops and eight attackers were killed. In the aftermath, Israeli security forces entered Egyptian territory in pursuit of the surviving attackers, which led to massive demonstrations in Cairo, the occupation of the Israeli Embassy there and the hasty evacuation of its ambassador.

The security vacuum that has arisen between the fall of the Mubarak regime and the establishment of a new state apparatus has given Islamist groups the chance to offer alternative civil mechanisms based on Sharia law. As the Taliban discovered to their advantage in Afghanistan in the 1990s, any semblance of policing and justice are welcomed by a jittery populace where civil institutions have collapsed. In August 2011, Egyptian papers reported that an umbrella group called the Salafist Group of Northern Sinai had established Islamic courts and was introducing a security force of 6,000 men. 'We will work to serve justice between people even if we have to use force through youth members,' said one of the founders, Suleiman Abu Ayoub.[16]

In early 2012 another group called Ansar al-Jihad appeared, claiming responsibility for pipeline attacks. The change of name is most likely a rebranding exercise; the new group announced its allegiance to Ayman al-Zawahiri and endorsed his leadership of Al Qaeda with an online message in January 2012.

In March 2012, as Israeli planes attacked Gaza, killing at least twenty-five Palestinians, hundreds of heavily armed Bedouin tribesmen with rocket-propelled grenades surrounded the Multinational Forces Observation mission headquarters in northern Sinai and held its occupants, mostly American military, hostage.[17]

Although al-Zawahiri praised the pipeline bombings, neither Al Qaeda in the Sinai Peninsula nor Ansar al-Jihad has been officially recognised by Ayman al-Zawahiri or the leader of any other Al Qaeda group.

Boko Haram

The real name of this northern Nigeria-based terror group is Jama'atu Ahlis Sunna Lidd'awati wal-Jihad (People Committed to the Propagation of the Prophet's Message and Jihad), but it is more usually referred to as Boko Haram (meaning 'Western Education a Sin' in the local Hausa dialect), based on a statement by one of its founders.

Nigeria, Africa's top oil producer, is a federal republic comprising some thirty-six states, suggestive of the divisions and differences present in Africa's most populous country. Nigeria's 160 million inhabitants are roughly divided between the Christians in the south and the Muslims in the north. There are also three main ethnic groups, the Hausa, Igbo and Yoruba. The country was battered by civil war from 1967 to 1970, which resulted in widespread famine and disease that caused the deaths of more than 3 million people. Nigeria emerged from thirty-three years of military rule in 1999 and is now a democracy, albeit a fragile one; the current president, Goodluck Jonathan, was elected in February 2010. Despite its huge oil revenues, most of Nigeria's people live on less than $2 a day.[18]

Boko Haram is based in Maiduguri, Borno state, in northern Nigeria. Local commentators say that the group emerged from the embers of the so-called Nigerian Taliban which was founded in 2003 by operatives from Benin, Cameroon, Chad and Niger among others. The group was forced underground by a security clampdown and Boko Haram appeared in 2006 under the leadership of cleric Mohammad Yusuf.

Boko Haram seeks to overthrow the Nigerian government and restore the Sokoto Islamic Caliphate that existed in northern Niger, southern Cameroon and Nigeria before the British took over in 1903. The group hit the headlines in July 2009 when it engaged in a five-day battle with police in and around Maiduguri in the course of which more than 800 people were killed. Mohammad Yusuf boasted at the time that the group had been bolstered by fighters from Somalia and that many of his men had been trained 'by those who have made Mogadishu ungovernable'[19]—a clear reference to al-Shabaab (which announced its official merger with Al Qaeda in February 2012). Within days, Yusuf had been killed by the police.

Under the leadership of Abubakar Shekau, the group became increasingly militant, clearly identifying itself with the Taliban and Al Qaeda.

Shekau took to appearing in videos wearing a *keffiyeh* and flanked by Kalashnikov rifles, mimicking the late Osama bin Laden. Recruiting from Nigeria's impoverished, unemployed, disillusioned and often illiterate youth, Boko Haram grew quickly—most estimates suggest it has at least several thousand members—and by 2010 had embarked on a series of attacks on Christian and security targets.

Nigerian President Goodluck Jonathan, who is from the Christian south of the country, believes that the military, police force and even his government have been infiltrated by Boko Haram agents.[20] Contact with AQIM also began around 2010 and Boko Haram members were sent for training in explosives and guerrilla warfare in Al Qaeda camps in the Sahara desert and northern Mali.[21] The group began to attack beyond its own northern enclave, making incursions into southern Niger where it forced several schools to shut down. Niger increased its defence budget by 65 percent in response and Nigeria's internal security now uses up a quarter of its entire state budget.

In June 2011, the Nigerian newspaper *The Standard* reported that Boko Haram had put posters up around Maiduguri which 'Bore the name of Imam Abu Bakar Shekau, the group's leader and representative of the Al Qaeda network in Nigeria . . . the posters bear the symbol of an open Quran flanked on each side by Kalashnikov rifles, mirroring the logo of AQIM.'[22]

Following the killing of Osama bin Laden, Shekau posted a eulogy for the late Al Qaeda leader on *jihadi* websites, which included an explicit commitment to engage with AQAM's global *jihad* agenda, and in August 2011 it was followed by action when Boko Haram carried out a suicide bombing of UN headquarters in the Nigerian capital, Abuja. Twenty-five people lost their lives and the building was destroyed. Apart from the nature of the target and the chosen method, the explosives used were PETN and TATP, both commonly used by AQAM.

Attacks on the UN had heralded the imminent arrival of two earlier Al Qaeda alliances. Abu Musab al-Zarqawi's group in Iraq targeted the UN Assistance Mission near the Canal Hotel in Baghdad on 19 August 2003; al-Zarqawi was invited to formally pledge allegiance to bin Laden in 2004. UN headquarters in Algiers was bombed by the GSPC in September 2006 and the group merged with Al Qaeda in January 2007. A video showing the Boko Haram suicide bomber preparing for his mission is accompanied by a voice-over by Shekau in which he describes the UN as a 'forum for all global evil'.

In a telephone press conference in November 2011, Boko Haram's spokesman, Abu Qaqa claimed, 'We are one with Al Qaeda . . . they help us in our struggle.'[23] Clearly Shekau reasoned that an official link with Al Qaeda would boost Boko Haram's credibility, recruiting potential and its fundraising possibilities. In January 2012 seven Boko Haram members were caught crossing the Niger–Mali border with quantities of explosives and the contact details of AQIM leaders they were to meet.

Attempts at reconciliation between the government and Boko Haram have been doomed to failure. Former president, the Christian Olusegun Obasanjo, visited the late Mohammad Yusuf's brother-in-law, Babakura Fugu, and other Boko Haram figures to instigate peace talks in September 2011—two days later Fugu was shot dead as a 'traitor'.[24] A more moderate splinter group has recently emerged, however, the Yusufiya Islamic Movement (YIM), and it is possible that it will engage in negotiations with the government and ultimately participate in the political process. Meanwhile Boko Haram continues to send shockwaves through the region, having killed well over a thousand people, with 250 dead in just the first three weeks of 2012.[25]

Jamaa al-Islamiya

Jamaa al-Islamiya (JI), based in Indonesia, was the *jihadi* group behind the horrific Bali bombing of 2002 in which more than 200 young people were killed, at least half of them Australian. The carnage began when a suicide bomber blew himself up inside the Sari nightclub; when the terrified survivors emerged onto the street, a massive car bomb exploded, killing many more. Bali was hit again in 2005 when three suicide bombers attacked another tourist area killing at least nineteen people.

JI is believed to have carried out several other major attacks on Western targets including Jakarta's Marriott Hotel in 2003 and 2009, and the Australian Embassy in Jakarta in which eleven were killed and more than 160 wounded. Christian churches are regularly targeted by JI suicide bombers.

JI was founded in 1993 by exiles from the Suharto regime; leaders

Abu Bakar Bashir and Abdullah Sungkar returned to their homeland when the dictator was forced to resign (after thirty-two years in power) in 1998 following widespread protests and rioting in which up to 5,000 people died. Allied with other groups in Indonesia, Malaysia and the Philippines (including Abu Syaaf), the group made contact with, and gained the support of, Al Qaeda in the late 1990s. The *jihadis'* agenda is to establish an Islamic caliphate throughout the region. The Indonesian government has been effective in rooting out terrorism. The two main plotters behind the 2002 Bali atrocity, Amrozi Nurhaysin and Ali Ghufron, were captured and executed.

Umar Patek, who went on trial in February 2012, was arrested in Abbottabad in January 2011. He was apparently en route to Afghanistan where he wanted to fight with the Taliban. Patek allegedly built the massive bombs for all JI's major attacks; the 2002 Bali car bomb consisted of 700 kilos of explosives packed into four filing cabinets. Known as 'demolition man' because of his expertise with explosives, Patek has long-standing connections with the Taliban and Al Qaeda. He told investigators that he had received his training in Al Qaeda and Taliban camps in Pakistan and Afghanistan before returning to Indonesia after 9/11.[26]

Despite most of its original leaders having been either detained or killed, the group remains active. In September 2011 a suicide bomber attacked a church in Solo.[27] Claiming the attack afterwards a JI spokesman said, 'This will not be our last attack. Rest assured that we still have a lot of alternative models of attacks which of course will surprise you.'[28]

Eighty-five percent of Indonesia's 235 million people are Sunni Muslim—the world's biggest Muslim population in any one country. Post-Suharto, democratically elected coalition governments have all included Islamist parties; their share of the vote has fluctuated from 16 percent in 1999 to 22 percent in 2004 (in the wake of the Bali bombs and other JI attacks) and back down again to 17 percent in the 2009 legislative elections.[29] At the same time, local reports say that Islamic 'pietism' has greatly increased, suggesting that the connection between politics and individual faith has lessened in the ten years since the toppling of Suharto and the introduction of democracy.

The Islamic Movement of Uzbekistan

In February 2010, before the events of the Arab Spring refocused world attention on the Middle East, American Special Envoy Richard Holbrooke warned of a new *jihadi* problem emerging in the ex-Soviet Muslim states: Uzbekistan, Kazakstan, Kyrgyzstan, Tajikistan and Turkmenistan. Rich in minerals, oil and gas, the area is of interest to the US and emerging superpowers India and China. The region is more accessible in geographical terms to the latter of course, and Russia has a strong sense of entitlement to its ex-satellites.

NATO, however, is also concerned with logistics since its supply routes to troops in Afghanistan run through Uzbekistan. Holbrooke told Reuters that Al Qaeda had been actively attempting to foment *jihadi* activity in the area in a strategic bid to hamper NATO's campaign. 'I think the real threat in this region is less from the Taliban than from Al Qaeda, which trains international terrorists,' he said.[30]

Radical Islamists from Uzbekistan have a long history of involvement with both Al Qaeda and the Taliban and I will therefore focus on that country for the purposes of this chapter. Ex-USSR republic Uzbekistan's population is 96.3 percent Muslim. Uzbekistan's president, Islam Abdug'aniyevich Karimov, was first appointed in 1990 (a year before the demise of the Soviet Union) and has remained in power, having won a series of highly criticised elections. The state is officially secular and suspected militant Islamists are dealt with harshly—an estimated 7,000 are currently incarcerated.

Uzbek Islamic militancy dates back to the 1979–89 Afghan *jihad* against the USSR. In this instance Uzbek conscripts were sent to fight with the Soviet troops but were impressed by their opponents, the *mujahideen*, who demonstrated bravery and religious zeal. Having lived under state communism dominated by Moscow, the men discovered a new awareness of their ethnic culture and religion which they conveyed to others on their return.

Two such returnees, Tahir Yuldashov and Juma Namangani, formed a Salafist group called Adolat (Justice) in 1991. Adolat briefly imposed Sharia law in parts of the Fergana valley during the turmoil following the fall of the Soviet empire, but as Karimov reasserted his power the group was outlawed and its founders had to flee for their lives. Yuldashov and

Namangani spent several years in Tajikistan before moving to Peshawar in 1996 where they made contact with Osama bin Laden.

Uzbekistan has a short 150-km border with Afghanistan, making the latter an ideal safe haven for Uzbek Islamists. In 1998 Yuldashov and Namangani established the Islamic Union of Uzbekistan (IMU) in close association with the Taliban and Al Qaeda, whose global ideology the group shares. The IMU's domestic agenda is to create an Islamic emirate in Central Asia but it has remained largely outside Uzbekistan. It is alleged that the IMU also received funding and support from Pakistan's ISI.

The group had its own training camps in Afghanistan in the 1990s and fought with the Taliban against the Northern Alliance during the civil war. Yuldashov became a member of Al Qaeda's central *shura* and Osama bin Laden started to fund the group. When Taliban envoy Mahmoud Wattakil was sent to warn American diplomats of an imminent Al Qaeda strike prior to 9/11, he said that the source of his information was the IMU leader, which confirms that Yuldashov was in the Al Qaeda inner circle.[31] Namangani, meanwhile, became deputy minister of defence in the Taliban government.

Namangani and many other Uzbek fighters died in the November 2001 US air raids on Tora Bora. Those who survived were part of the 2003 *hijra* to Iraq, migrating back to Waziristan in 2006–7 where they currently run training camps and have their own enclave, composed of fighters from the ex-Soviet bloc, known as Bulgar Jamaat. According to captured *jihadis* there are at least 2,000 Uzbek fighters in the region.[32] Yuldashov was killed in a drone attack in South Waziristan in 2009. Under present emir Abu Osman Adil the group has expanded its presence into southeastern parts of Afghanistan under Taliban control such as Khost, Paktia and Paktika.

The IMU has a strong web presence; as well as its website at furqon .com, it has a media production wing, Jundullah, which has produced videos and audiotapes in several languages including Russian, German and English. Its propaganda material and online activities testify to a global ideology and detail the progress of *jihadis* in Afghanistan and Pakistan as well as further afield—in February 2012 Ulubek Kodirov pleaded guilty in Alabama, USA, to having plotted with the IMU, via the Internet, to kill President Barack Obama. Jundullah has produced several videos aimed at women and urging 'Muslim sisters to strive for martyrdom by all means at their disposal'; one, in the Russian language, shows two women wearing the *niqab* firing machine guns and handguns.[33]

The IMU has become increasingly enmeshed in the Al Qaeda–Taliban nexus. When German-born IMU military commander Bekkay Harrach (aka Abu Talha al-Almani) was killed in Afghanistan in January 2011, Jundullah announced that he had been leading a joint 'raid' conducted by the Taliban, the TTP, Al Qaeda and the IMU.[34]

The IMU has a significant German-born contingent. Two men who frequently appear on Jundullah videos are brothers Abu Adam al-Almani (aka Yassin Chouka) and Abu Ibrahim al-Almani (aka Mounir Chouka). In February 2011 the brothers produced a biographical video called 'Our Path to the IMU' which describes their *hijra* from Bonn to Afghanistan and provides some interesting insights into what happens when recruits arrive in the 'lands of *jihad*'. According to the Chouka brothers they were helped on their way by several different groups.

> Our journey lasted exactly one month and was very professionally organized. In the various countries, there were intermediate stations at which we were cared for, we got new travel documents, and, at a particular point in time, a mujahid who was working with the field service accompanied us to the ground of jihad. Shortly before our arrival in Afghanistan, at the last intermediate station, which was about a three-day trip away from the destination, they told us that this route was organized by the IMU . . . who made final preparations for us, gave us a computer and played us some videos about the movement.

At this point the youths were told that they could choose which group to join and 'we chose the IMU'.[35]

The Islamic Emirate of the Caucasus

'Our lands are occupied by Russian *kufr* (infidels) and the swinish way of life has been thrust upon us for too long': thus did Dokku Umarov announce the establishment of the Islamic Emirate of the Caucasus (ICE) on 22 November 2007.

Most people will remember the atrocious September 2004 attack on the school in Beslan in which 385 people, mostly children, were killed. Dokku Umarov condemned the massacre in a 2005 interview,[36] but it was masterminded by his close associate Shamil Basayev, the radical founder of the Riyad-us-Saliheen suicide squad which was revived by Umarov himself in 2009.

The ICE emerged from the independent republic of Ichkeria, which was established by Chechen separatists as the USSR fell apart in 1991. There were two distinct elements within the leadership: the secularist nationalists, led by President Aslan Mashkadov, who wanted a Western-style democracy, and the *jihadis*, fronted by Basayev, Umarov and Movladi Ugodov. This alignment will resonate with analysts observing the present post-revolutionary scenarios in North Africa. By 2006 the schism erupted into a full-scale confrontation; the Islamists claimed that nationalists were corrupt and had become Putin's puppet. They declared an Islamic Emirate of the Caucasus, with Dokku as emir.

Asked to precisely define the boundaries of the putative emirate Dokku replied, 'All lands in the Caucasus, where *mujahideen* who have given their allegiance to me wage *jihad*, I declare *wilayahs* of the Caucasus Emirate: *wilayah* Dagestan, *wilayah* Nokhchiycho, *wilayah* Ghalghaycho, *wilayah* Iriston, *wilayah* of the Nogay Steppe, the combined *wilayah* of Kabarda, Balkar and Karachay. I don't think that it is necessary to draw the borders of the Caucasus Emirate.'[37]

The links between Al Qaeda and the North Caucasus *mujahideen* can be traced back to the Bosnian *jihad* in 1992–5 which followed the break-up of the former Yugoslavia in 1991. The Chechens had an 'Islamic Battalion' consisting of Arab and other foreign fighters. These included Ibn al-Qutb, who was killed in 2002, and Yusuf Mohammad al Emirat aka Mohannad, who would later become the Islamic Emirate of the Caucasus's deputy military commander. He was killed by Russian security forces in April 2011.[38]

Also during the 1990s, the Al Qaeda front 'Benevolence International Fund' was used to channel money to Chechen fighters; Al Qaeda man Said al-Islam al-Masri worked in its Grozny office until 1998. When the Bosnian war ended in 1995, many Arab fighters went to Chechnya rather than return home, establishing families with local women. In particular, members of some Egyptian *jihad* groups went to Chechnya rather than seek political asylum in Europe.[39] At least three Guantanamo detainees captured in Afghanistan in 2001 were from the North Caucasus and *The Times*, reporting from Iraq in 2003, said that, 'The Americans . . . have also captured Chechens fighting with Fedayin units close to Baghdad.'[40]

Links between the groups are also clear from online material. The ICE website Kavkaz frequently carried material by Anwar al-Awlaki and is also used by the Taliban to post statements and reports of attacks. The Al Qaeda–linked site Ansar al-Mujaheddin announced a campaign to support ICE fighters in December 2010, noting the 'spread of *jihad* through Tartaristan and Bashkiristan' and urging a 'new generation' of scholars to come forward (echoing the frequently voiced complaint by older Arab *jihadis* that the non-Arab 'branches' and the younger generation in general are not up to scratch in terms of theological scholarship). A new group of Tartar and Bashkir *jihadis* was also announced on this site, called the Vilaiyat of Idel-Ural (VIU). The ICE network is considered an important avenue for moving into Eastern Europe and Europe itself.

The link between ICE and the wider AQAM–Taliban nexus is also suggested by the involvement of Awlaki and several Chechen *jihadis* in two thwarted attacks by Al Qaeda–affiliated sleeper cells in Europe in 2010 and 2011. The Ansar al-Mujaheddin website was used to raise funds and recruit for a group—Shariah4Belgium—which intended to target Christmas shoppers in Belgium in 2010. When this group was arrested it was found to contain three Chechens as well as men from Belgium, Holland, Germany, Spain, Morocco and Saudi Arabia. In April 2011, a cell was disrupted in the Czech Republic which included one Chechen, two Dagestanis, Moldovans and Bulgarians. Some of the men told investigators that they had attended training camps in Pakistan. Another link is through the IMU which, in March 2011, released a video message welcoming the ICE to 'global jihad' and noting 'in our *jamaat* there are many brothers who were trained or fought on the land of the Caucasus Emirate'.

The so-called bin Laden of Chechnya, Doger Sevdet (aka Abdullah Kurd) was an Al Qaeda commander who had been dispatched by bin Laden to the CE to recruit, train and coordinate foreign *jihadis* to fight in Chechnya. Sevdet was killed by Russian security services in the Vedensk region just four days after Osama bin Laden was killed in Pakistan; it is rumoured that he visited the Al Qaeda leader in Abbottabad in the months preceding his death.

In an interview posted on the group's website in August 2011, Dokku places his organisation firmly within the AQAM global alliance: 'We are an inseparable part of the Islamic *umma* . . . anyone who attacks Muslims are our enemies, our common enemies.' He also describes close contact with Al Qaeda, in particular through the man he would make his deputy in July 2011, emir Khamzat. He recalls meeting Khamzat on his way to fight in Iraq:

> Khamzat was accompanied by many *Ulema*, or Muslim scholars, and many Arabs. We had a strong discussion with Khamzat. Many of those present at the discussion are still alive today: some Gelayev's men and an Algerian Abu Amr without leg [sic]. I asked Khamzat, where he was going. He replied that he was going to Iraq: 'A true *jihad* is developing in Iraq, the emirate was proclaimed there'.

Dokku indicates that the young men in his group are even more radical than their predecessors: 'a new generation of Islamic youth forced us to proclaim an emirate . . . but I am proud of that decision.'[41]

While espousing the global *jihad*, the ICE harbours definite local ambitions, seeking to oust Russian influence from the region and expand the boundaries of the emirate. In recent years it has carried out several large-scale attacks against Russian targets. In December 2009 the group claimed responsibility for the derailment of the Nevsky express train in which twenty-seven people lost their lives. Suicide bombers attacked the Moscow Metro on 31 March 2010, costing forty-six lives, and on 7 February 2011, 21-year-old Magomed Yevloev detonated his suicide belt in the most crowded part of Domodedovo International Airport, Russia's busiest hub, killing thirty-seven. Both the latter atrocities were claimed by Umarov in video statements. Between 2008 and 2010, 1,214 people were killed by *jihadi* attacks in the Northern Caucasus and 2,162 were wounded.

The Uyghurs: Pushing the Limits Westwards and into China

The emergence of violent Islamist militancy within the borders of China is unlikely to pose any real threat to that monolithic state but does represent an expansion, however slight, of the regions affected by global *jihadism* and within the Al Qaeda framework. The potential to extend instability westwards via Central Asia has been recognised by Al Qaeda—and Western security agencies—for some time and the so-called five 'stans' of the ex-USSR have already been brought into the global *jihadi* framework by committed Al Qaeda proselytising. The Uyghurs are a Muslim minority group, numbering some 8 million, who live in Xinjiang province in northwest China. Xinjiang—which used to be known as East Turkistan—has its cultural roots in wider Turkistan and Central Asia. The Uyghurs speak a Turkic language and have their own, modified Arabic, script.

The province was annexed by China in the mid-1700s and given its current name which means 'new territories'. East Turkistan has twice re-emerged as a nation-state during the historical turbulence that preceded the establishment of the People's Republic of China—once between 1933 and 1934 and again between 1944 and 1949.

The drive for independence remains vigorous and is spearheaded by several Islamist groups, most notably the East Turkistan Islamic Movement (ETIM), led by Memetiming Memeti (aka Abdul Haq), and the Turkistan Islamic Party (TIP), led by Abdel Shakoor Damla. That these groups have turned to violence is almost certainly in response to Beijing's heavy-handed attempts to eradicate Islam from Uyghur society, despite the fact that Islam is an inextricable part of the cultural make-up of the people. Human Rights Watch reports that a local law, imposed by Beijing, states: 'Parents and legal guardians may not allow minors to participate in religious activities.'[42] China has also sent around 1.5 million Han Chinese to live in Xinjiang—the same tactic Beijing has employed to dilute Tibetan nationalism. The area is of great economic significance to the Chinese because it is rich in oil deposits and natural gas.

Unsurprisingly, Xinjiang has produced significant numbers of *jihadis* and of those a proportion have migrated from the national cause into global *jihadism*. Groups of Uyghurs are known to have trained and fought alongside the Taliban and Al Qaeda in Afghanistan and Pakistan—there were twenty-two among those captured by US troops in Afghanistan in the aftermath of 9/11 and several of them identified themselves as members of the ETIM. The connection between Al Qaeda and Uyghur Islamist groups the ETIM and TIP was consolidated during this time, and groups of Uyghurs were among those who went to fight in Iraq.

In 2007/8 as the US Surge and Awakening made its impact on Al Qaeda in the Land of the Two Rivers, a huge influx of fighters converged in FATA; among them, *jihadis* report, around 2,000 Uzbeks and a large group of Uyghurs. There are reports of Uyghurs forming part of sleeper cells internationally. In July 2010, for example, a cell that was disrupted planning an attack in Norway consisted of an Uyghur, an Uzbek and an Iraqi Kurd, all of whom had recently immigrated.

The Islamists also maintained their struggle at home. In November 2006 the ETIM posted a video on Islamist Internet sites declaring *jihad* against the Chinese state. China hosted the Olympic Games in 2008, which presented the Uyghur Islamist groups with the opportunity to gain some international media attention. In July and August 2008 the TIP carried out a series of attacks against Chinese targets and on 4 August two ETIM fighters drove a truck into a large group of border police in Kashi, Xinjiang, killing sixteen.

Rioting between Han Chinese and Uyghurs in July 2009 left 200 dead and Al Qaeda 'central' moved into the picture for the first time with Abu Yahya al-Libi releasing a statement condemning the 'massacre'. In October 2009, al-Libi backed the declaration of *jihad* against China, saying: 'China is working to destroy the Muslim identity and sever links between the people and their history.'

The TIP launched a fresh wave of attacks, killing dozens in the cities of Hotan and Kashgar in August 2011. TIP leader Abdel Shakoor Damla claimed responsibility for the attacks in a ten-minute video released onto Islamist forums. Damla's face was obscured in the video and it is believed the TIP leadership is now based in Pakistan, out of reach of Chinese security forces and close to the Al Qaeda and Taliban leadership. TIP cells have been actively involved in attacks in Pakistan and Afghanistan and are considered a very real threat by US intelligence. That Al Qaeda has acknowledged the legitimacy of the groups' *jihad* against China is a small, but potentially significant, widening of the global *jihadi* camp.

9

The Digital Battleground

Cyberspace is to be treated as a fifth 'operational domain for the armed forces—as important as land, air, sea and space'.
US Department of Defense, July 2011

Modern means of communication present great opportunities for production and information, and may Allah reward the knights of the Jihad Media with the best of all rewards.
Ayman al-Zawahiri, August 2011

Since I first wrote about 'Cyber *Jihad*' in *The Secret History of al-Qa'ida* (2006), there have been remarkable developments in this rapidly evolving field. I will not repeat the information contained in my previous book but many of the techniques I described then are still very much in use. Steganography, for example, which conceals information within other digital media, was in the news again in May 2012 when German forensic experts discovered *jihadi* training material hidden in pornographic films carried by a suspect arrested at Berlin airport as he returned from Pakistan.[1] The Internet is one of the most significant factors in the survival and evolution of Al Qaeda.

The Arab Spring highlighted the importance and efficiency of social networking for clandestine activity and logistics. *Jihadis* too routinely use Facebook, Twitter and text messaging for instant communication and sharing ideas. Never before has there been so much *jihadi* material in cyberspace spreading so far and so fast.

Every AQAM group has its own media wing which maintains high-quality websites and disseminates news, video and audio statements, footage of attacks, martyrdom videos, training material and, usually, at least one online magazine. Many have their own film production unit and press office.

Through the ingenious use of the dark web (of which more below) and mirror sites, *jihadis* are able to keep information online even when the authorities attempt to remove it. Third-party file hosting services enable *jihadis* to evade national intelligence services by enabling them to upload and retrieve material completely anonymously. Blogs and the contributions of individuals to *jihadi* forums help to maintain the mythology and draw of *jihad* for the susceptible potential recruit, whether to the battlefield or to 'lone wolf' terror.

Jihadi cyber warriors are constantly developing new ways to disrupt defence systems and the governmental and transport infrastructures which are nowadays so dependent on digital control rooms. The Internet provides for an expanding arsenal of instruments of war including hacking, viruses and Distributed Denial of Service (DDoS) attacks. Intelligence services develop ever more sophisticated cyber security techniques and the science of 'cyber forensics' evolves apace.

AQAM groups post videos on dedicated YouTube channels and links to these and a variety of other material can be found on any of several *jihadi* 'clearinghouses'. Most groups also have a translation department putting out material in several languages. With the zeal of academics, *jihadi* editors have taken to theorising about, analysing and critiquing the media, urging their own writers to strive for the highest standards of style and integrity. The late Anwar al-Awlaki oversaw the launch of several online 'glossy' magazines including the English-language *Inspire* and a magazine for women called *Shamikha*. The Taliban produce several magazines every month.

Cyber *Jihad* Continued

In July 2011 the US Department of Defense (DoD) released a 19-page strategy document, announcing that cyberspace is to be treated as a fifth 'operational domain for the armed forces—as important as land, air, sea and space'.[2] In February 2012, FBI Director Robert Mueller told the Senate Intelligence Committee that cyber-terrorism was about to become 'the number one threat' to national security.[3]

For AQAM too, the Internet is the new battleground: 'Hacking on the Internet is one of the key pathways to *jihad*,' says the narrator of Al Qaeda's 2011 video 'You are Responsible Only for Thyself'. 'We advise Muslims who possess expertise in this field to target the websites and information networks of big companies and government agencies in countries that attack Muslims, as well as those that are managed by media organisations opposed to Islam, *jihad* and the *mujahideen*.'[4]

There is an Arabic-language hacking site, XP10, on which thousands of visitors share tips and software daily. Anyone entering XP10 forums can discover how to 'hack mobiles . . . hack chat-rooms . . . create viruses' as well as procure a 'training course on piracy machines'. In a June 2011 essay about 'electronic *jihad*' Abu Maysara al-Gharib made the following suggestions for cyber-hostilities: 'Share military tradecraft and information about targets; spy on the enemy; steal from the enemy to raise funds for *jihad*; vandalise hostile websites; call for economic boycotts and raise funds; disseminate multi-media propaganda and tracts by prominent *jihadi* ideologues; attend non-*jihadi* online forums with a view to recruitment.'[5]

Cyber-*jihad* is attractive to AQAM for several reasons: it is cheap but has potentially devastating consequences; unlike physical, military confrontation, it is not asymmetric, relying largely on innovation; there are no physical barriers or checkpoints in cyberspace; attacks can be carried out from anywhere in the world and can affect a large number of targets and people. In addition, forward defence planning by governments and the military is extremely difficult given the rapid rate at which technologies are developing. Although so-called cyber-forensics are improving, the majority of Internet malefactors remain untraceable.

Nevertheless, in 2007 Younis Tsouli became the first person to be brought to trial in the UK for the new crime of 'incitement to commit acts of terrorism over the Internet'. As well as posting incendiary comments on *jihadi* forums under the moniker 'Irhabi007' (Irhabi being Arabic for 'terrorist') and creating forums for the Islamic State of Iraq, Moroccan-born Tsouli had been hacking completely unrelated websites and turning them into Al Qaeda bulletin boards. He and his co-conspirators Wasim Muqhal and Tariq al-Daour had also managed to hack the details of 37,000 credit cards and had carried out more than £2 million-worth of fraudulent transactions. Tsouli had translated hacking tutorials from sites such as MILWORM into Arabic and posted them as PDFs on *jihadi* forums and XP10. The PDFs teach PHP hacking, SQL, Linux/*NIX hacking and various kinds of database hacking. The case received even more media attention when the judge who was presiding over the hearing told the court: 'The trouble is . . . I don't really understand what a website is.'[6] This highlights a problem faced by many security services, which is that the Internet remains largely the domain of the young. As a consequence, youthful malefactors are frequently able to outwit those who would silence them online.

There have been numerous cyberattacks by *jihadi* groups. In September 2010 a cyber-*jihad* group called the Brigades of Tariq ibn Ziyad[7] managed to crash servers and networked computers at several large US corporations and organisations including Disney, NASA, Wells Fargo and Proctor & Gamble. The group sent out a malicious worm which became known as 'Here you Have' since this was the message they put in the subject line of the e-mail delivering the virus. The worm was able to disable antivirus software and establish a 'back door' by which the cyber-*jihadis* could remotely access any infected system. Cyber-forensic experts analysed the worm's 'digital DNA' and linked it to previous viruses released by a Libyan cyber-*jihadi* using the name Iraq-Resistance.[8]

A July 2011 conference in Singapore on 'The Geostrategic Implications of Cyberspace' heard that 'non-state actors' had hacked an American defence contractor's system from which 24,000 files had been copied, including information on aircraft avionics and satellites, network security protocols and surveillance.

In January 2012, a cyber-battle broke out between Israeli and Palestinian hacking groups after Kuwaiti Imam Tareq Mohammed al-Suwaidan tweeted 240,000 followers with a call for 'cyber *jihad* against the Zionist enemy'. A Palestinian hacking team calling themselves 'Nightmare' responded by taking down the Tel Aviv stock exchange, the first International Bank of Israel and El Al websites with DDoS attacks.[9]

Intelligence services also use cyberspace to spy to eavesdrop on terrorist groups. In December 2011 Al Qaeda's Global Islamic Forum released a warning regarding a virus: 'Some brothers—may Allah reward them—reviewed a fake copy of *Ansar al-Mujahideen* Software that included a

Trojan file. This file is a surveillance file that enables the hacker to view everything on your computer, including encrypted messages.'[10]

Groups such as Anonymous are far ahead of the game and often referred to in glowing terms on *jihadi* forums. Anonymous has hacked into national stock exchanges, military websites and even the DoD. The website cyberwarnews.info produces regular updates on all cyberattacks and governmental responses for those who wish to read more on the subject.

Obviously, Anonymous is not a *jihadi* organisation but its material and methodology are widely available, and its activities may suggest a template for the future of cyber-*jihad*. The group produces 'cyber-weapons' which can be downloaded on the Internet. During the Arab Spring, protestors armed themselves digitally with Anonymous's so-called Low Orbit Ion Cannon (LOIC) which produces massive DDoS attacks. The software infects the targeted computer networks with a virus which then enables the attackers to take control remotely. The affected computers are then instructed to send information in such overwhelming volumes that the server collapses. All legitimate traffic is blocked, resulting in huge financial losses for businesses. Anonymous has recently released another cyber-weapon called #RefRef which uses the targeted site's own processing power against itself, causing resource exhaustion.

In January 2012, in response to the US government's decision to take a strong stand against online piracy, Anonymous gathered a brigade of 5,600 coordinated hackers who targeted and crashed the computer systems of the US Department of Justice, the US Copyright Office and Universal Music.

Forensic work on Al Qaeda computers seized in Afghanistan and elsewhere confirm that *jihadi* hackers have been investigating digital networks controlling US energy facilities, water distribution, communication systems and financial institutions. Government departments and administration are entirely reliant on digital communications and storage—the DoD, for example, operates more than 15,000 networks and 7 million computers around the globe. These systems contain much of the US administration's military, intelligence and business operations, including the movement of personnel and material and the command and control of the full spectrum of military operations. A recent report to Congress by the DoD admitted that 'Our reliance on cyberspace stands in stark contrast to the inadequacy of our cybersecurity,' and added, 'We recognize that there may be malicious activities on DoD networks and systems that we have not yet detected.'[11]

The Dark Internet, Dark Net and TOR

As the Internet expands, the possibilities for finding hidden pockets within and outside the worldwide web increase exponentially. Naturally, these so-called dark areas are home to all sorts of illicit activities, including sharing *jihadi* material and communications. The most obscure area is known as 'the dark Internet', where obsolete addresses still exist even though they are no longer accessible by conventional means. These addresses can still be used as routers by skilled hackers, but being outside the Internet's web are completely anonymous. Networks of such addresses, known only to the participants, can be used to form a completely untraceable means of relaying information.

Dark Net (also referred to as Deep Net) is filesharing networks that use non-standard protocols and ports and, in addition, do not share IP addresses. Users can therefore communicate without fear of security interventions or ever being traced in the real world. Researchers exploring the Dark Net have been able to purchase guns and class 'A' drugs with ease and no traceability.[12]

Another well-travelled 'dark' zone is TOR (the Onion Router), originally developed for military use by the US Naval Research Lab, which operates a multi-layered, complex network of 'relays' which conceal the origins of a message or files, and as a 'safety net' encrypts all the IP addresses involved. The relays or bridges are run from participating 'friendly' computers round the globe. When the data arrive at the final destination, they appear to have come from the previous, anonymous source, rather than the genuine sender. For security services to identify the actual IP addresses of every 'layer' in order to trace the originator is presently impossible.

Social Networking

During the Arab Spring, opposition organisers were able to exploit online platforms such as Facebook and Twitter to galvanise support, organise demonstrations and give live warnings of impending attacks by police or security services. *Jihadis* too use these platforms to inform, communicate, proselytise and even recruit.

The 'Three Degrees of Influence' theory suggests that one's own emotions, attitudes or belief systems affect, in descending order, one's friend, one's friend's friend and one's friend's friend's friend. Social networking sites, then, are an ideal vehicle for persuasion and an effective recruitment tool since people are more likely to embrace the ideas or beliefs of people known to them. Unsurprisingly, *jihadis* exploit this potential to their own ends.

'We are active on Facebook and Twitter,' Taliban media chief Abdel Sattar al-Maiwandi told an interviewer, 'and we send news daily via cell phone text messages to many people . . . each of them sends it to his acquaintances inside and outside Afghanistan and so a chain of dissemination begins.'[13] Maiwandi explained that the Taliban also have an Internet radio station, 'Voice of Shari'ah', which is available all round the world on the various online platforms *jihadis* call 'pulpits'.

Facebook pages are widely used to circumvent security controls, censorship and restrictions, and can host information, photos, videos as well as links. In just one afternoon spent investigating the *jihadi* presence on Facebook in September 2011 we found Al Qaeda, Taliban, al-Shabaab and Lashkar-e-Taiba pages, all easily accessible and all with thousands of 'friends'. The mythology of *jihad* and the iconography of leaders, dead and living, are all enhanced and preserved on Facebook pages. There are hundreds of pages in Arabic, dedicated to Osama bin Laden, Anwar al-Awlaki, Abu Musab al-Zarqawi, Abdullah Azzam and other dead heroes of the *mujahideen*. As for the living, there are scores of different pages and groups under the moniker Ayman al-Zawahiri, in English and Arabic.

A trail which started with a suspicious-looking individual asking to be my 'friend' on Facebook led me to some alarming encounters. The further I followed links from one page to another, the more sinister the individuals: 'Born to Crush' lists his job as 'Employee of Allah (Mujahid)' and his page boasts a picture of him in Afghanistan or Kashmir with a Kalashnikov. What music does he like? 'Music is *Haram*.' People who inspire him? Osama bin Laden. Ambition? Martyrdom. The majority of his 'friends' are carrying weapons in their profile pictures.

Next I landed on Laskar Langit II's page. He had posted a profile picture of a masked man with a sub-machine gun. From there a link took me to Abu Waleed, a member of al-Shabaab. 'Defender Khan', who lives in Mumbai, says his hobby is target practice 'using Jews or Christians'—he has over 4,000 friends. Aadhi Wani lists 'Internet hacking' as an interest and has a picture of himself (presumably) in full combat gear wielding an automatic pistol. Closer to home, 'al-Mujahideen' lives in a named town in the north of England, where, he reveals, he is the boss of the 'Chunky Chicken' outlet.

The latter may well be dabbling at the edges of a world he has a vague interest in, but security experts say that this is where Facebook comes into its own. 'Dabblers' can quickly come into contact with real-life terrorists and become part of the *jihadi* social network where they are easily indoctrinated. Unsurprisingly, the security services in many countries turn the tables and use Facebook to entrap aspiring radicals by interacting using fake identities.

Facebook and Twitter are not particularly secure but October 2011 saw the emergence of a new service called Vibe which is anonymous, each short message being sent without username or identification. Users can decide whether to 'whisper' (to the immediate surrounding area) or 'shout' a message to the whole network. 'Whispering' is particularly useful to warn of police and security activity during protests or terror operations and may well replace Twitter as the communication platform of choice for those who do not want to be eavesdropped or identified.

Meanwhile AQAM groups continue to use Twitter, many with the Al Qaeda flag as an avatar. The al-Shabaab 'Press Office' Twitter account, @HSMPress, has well over 11,000 followers and makes audacious use of the platform—it recently conducted an entire interview with an Al Jazeera journalist in tweets. When American-born al-Shabaab commander Abu Mansour al-Amriki released a video (in March 2012) saying that he feared for his life after falling out with the group, al-Shabaab responded with three reassuring tweets. There is even a *jihadi* Twitter 'clearinghouse', @Ansaruddin1, which revealed the identity of the CIA chief in Kabul the day I was researching this subject; it also gave details of the new US presidential plane's communications system.

In the modern world, satellite television and digital video are arguably the most effective and influential media. Technology has moved on a long way from 1996 when Nadir Remli, an Algerian exile living in West London, offered 'the first ever footage of *mujahideen* in action' as a £6 mail order VHS video in the pages of *al-Tabsirah*.[14]

Through as-Sahab Media, its increasingly polished production unit, Al Qaeda makes sophisticated use of independent broadcast media to reach a global audience. As well as the regular subtitled statements from Al Qaeda leaders, the unit has embarked on more ambitious projects in recent years, including high-production-value documentaries. 'Knowledge is for Acting Upon' is a two-part marathon and features a quietly spoken bin Laden talking directly to camera. The film, in Arabic and English, describes the genesis of Al Qaeda, then the build-up to and aftermath of 9/11. This video, still accessible via Wikivideo at the time of writing, had had two and a half million hits.[15]

With the advent of YouTube, anyone can post video material and even set up his or her own television channel. *Jihadi* groups have been quick to exploit this opportunity. There is a channel devoted to the speeches of Anwar al-Awlaki, for example, called Shaheed Fisabilillah Channel. MujahidahInshaAllah4 carries material concerning the Taliban, while MAmriki deals with the situation in Yemen. The Slave of Allah Channel concerns itself with the rise of Islam in Europe and has nearly 86,000 viewers.

YouTube is also an effective platform for recruitment. In 2010 al-Shabaab released an extraordinary video featuring a rap song (sung without music—music is considered *haram*) and obviously aimed at Western youths. Over footage of robed warriors in training with machine guns, a softly spoken American-accented youth raps in rhyming couplets—including the unforgettable lines: 'Jihad against the armies of the Salib/I'm gonna become a Shahid [martyr]'.[16]

Islamist *causes célèbres* are extremely popular on YouTube. The story of the 'Girls of the Red Mosque' is depicted in several videos; one has had more than three million views.[17] The 'girls' in question were female students from the Islamabad Red Mosque's *madrassa* who battled the authorities for several months in 2007 in protest at plans to demolish the mosque. Images of several hundred *burqa*-clad women wielding six-foot wooden staves, threatening policemen and occupying government buildings, were beamed around the world. The affair ended in an eight-day siege of the mosque which was eventually stormed by heavily armed security forces; 154 people died in the violence.

Documentary videos on YouTube depict life as a *jihadi*, presumably with recruitment to the battlefield in mind. An *al-Ansar* video released in August 2011 shows a group of around twenty youths undergoing fire-arms and guerrilla warfare training in Waziristan.[18] The video is introduced with the following words: 'These young lions of Islam are acting upon Allah's command in the Quran: "And make ready against them all you can of power, including steeds of war (tanks, planes, missiles, artillery, etc.) [sic] to threaten the enemy of Allah and your enemy..." May Allah grant all able-bodied Muslims the opportunity to emulate these enthusiastic youngsters and also prepare themselves for Jihad in the cause of Allah.'

Throughout 2011, as-Sahab posted instalments of a long documentary, 'A Mujahid's Diary', which is still available on YouTube and which offers a glimpse of daily life as a *jihadi* in Waziristan. Here is a relaxed-looking individual fishing in a fast-flowing river. He takes his catch back to the training camp which is the size of a small village and makes no secret of its existence, the call to prayer echoing out across the valley from the camp's own minaret; the evening's entertainment consists of singing and firing a Kalashnikov into the air. We see the *mujahideen* wrapping the fish in leaves and salt to be cooked in charcoal. Next, prayers, a row of guns propped up outside over the shoes. In winter there is footage of heavily armed *mujahideen* trudging through six feet of snow in Afghanistan to set up an ambush. A NATO truck hits an IED to cries of 'Allah Akhbar'; in the aftermath, when the smoke has died down, we hear the sound of sobbing... it is an American soldier and his friend tries to comfort him. Next we see several dead faces, surrounded by mauve blossoms, smiling... the group's most recent 'martyrs' are buried in the earth.[19]

YouTube is also home to a relatively new phenomenon, the online *Nasheed* (plural *Anasheed*). These are voice-only songs about Islam, in praise of Allah and, increasingly, about *jihad*. The songs are accompanied by short films or still images. Musical instruments are considered *haram* (sinful) by Islamists; Ibn Tamiyyah—a scholar widely admired by *jihadis*—said that music is 'alcohol to one's soul'.[20] It seems that the unaccompanied voice is *halal* (allowed) and this has led to the evolution of extremely complex systems of accompaniment by one or several voices, either in harmony or in unison. Some of these vocal accompaniments are generated by computer programs which, apparently, is also *halal*.

Women singers are rare and there is much debate on Islamist forums about the matter. The male consensus seems to be as follows (from a forum): 'women are not allowed to sing if non-*mahrams* are present or are able to hear . . . therefore recording *nasheeds* (that will be distributed) is *haram* for all adult females, as men will be able to hear.'[21]

Anasheed have become a powerful subculture. Some accompany documentary footage, short films or even animations. The most popular *nasheed* on YouTube at the time of writing, with half a million views, was called 'Chechen Jihad *Nasheed*', sung to a backdrop of machine-gun fire.[22] Another accompanied black and white footage from old movies showing the Arab armies battling the Crusaders.[23] Some are more gruesome, glorifying martyrdom: 'Like the Strong Wind' is sung to a still backdrop of the shrapnel-riddled corpse of a young man.[24]

Social networking is not only used to disseminate information or to entertain. Anecdotal evidence suggests that many young suicide bombers in Afghanistan have been recruited via their mobile phones. Short videos glamorising a martyr's death in pursuit of expelling 'the Americans' with emotional *nasheed* soundtracks are sent via text messages and boys as young as 15 and 16 are responding to this call.

Material available on social networking sites has inspired several 'lone wolf' attacks in the West. In Britain, Roshanara Choudhry became radicalised after watching Anwar al-Awlaki sermons on YouTube and then tried to stab Stephen Timms MP, citing his support for the Iraq war as her motive. Nicky Reilly, a young man with learning difficulties, became obsessed with the idea of martyrdom after watching videos of 9/11 and suicide attacks on YouTube; he changed his name to Mohamed Abdulaziz Rashid Saeed-Alim and tried to detonate a nail bomb in the Exeter branch of the Giraffe restaurant chain.[25]

Many people express surprise that *jihadi* material is so freely available on YouTube but the platform does not offer any pre-screening censorship facility. Indeed, any form of censorship is almost impossible given that every minute, day and night, the California-based organisation (owned by Google) receives an average thirty-five hours of video from millions of contributors. It is only if somebody complains that a posting will be investigated and removed if it is illegal or considered inappropriate or objectionable.

Websites and their associated chat-rooms and forums continue to proliferate. I have noticed a definite increase in highly dangerous material presented with no effort made to disguise its true nature. On the Ansarullah website, for example, it is possible to download an entire explosives course given by the late Abu Khabbab al-Masri. The course was written up by 'students' and made into a well-presented PDF file.[26] There are numerous links on Facebook and web forums to third-party file hosting sites where this material can be downloaded. Only one Facebook page urges caution, and with good reason—a university student researching online terrorism was arrested and imprisoned for being in possession of a downloaded copy.[27] Another controversial download is the recent *Ansar al-Islam* file entitled 'inexhaustible weapons', which demonstrates how to make and adapt weapons.[28]

Evading Detection

The Internet is extremely difficult to police and *jihadis* have evolved elaborate techniques for evading detection. In 2011 a British Airways employee, Rajib Karim, was investigated by police following a tip-off from MI5. It transpired that Karim, based in Newcastle, had been exchanging e-mails with the late Anwar al-Awlaki in Yemen for more than two years, allegedly plotting a 'spectacular' attack involving aircraft. Cyber-forensic investigators unravelled the methods the two had used to create a digital fortress within which to communicate.

At the most basic level, all personal names and commonly used words were substituted. Al Qaeda has been using this technique ever since the 9/11 plotters famously sent the message that 'the wedding will be tomorrow' (that is. the attack will be tomorrow). Cyber-forensic investigators point out that, if they are not to attract the attention of intelligence interceptors, substituted words (or code words) need to have a similar frequency of use and not appear out of context or create semantic or grammatical oddities.

To elaborate: 'wedding' is the 2195th most commonly used word in English whereas 'attack' is the 792nd—this, potentially, might have drawn attention.[29] However, because the wedding could 'be tomorrow' it is not out of context and does not create any oddities. If the plotters had instead chosen the 793rd most commonly used word, which is 'herself', obviously this would have created both semantic and grammatical oddities.

Having established their coded vocabulary, Karim and al-Awlaki moved into the realms of increasingly sophisticated deception. First the messages were 'scrambled' by encryption software. With commercially available software the two parties share a 'key' which both scrambles and descrambles all communication between them. For greatly enhanced security, there are systems which make each message into an individually encrypted, custom-built, password-protected file.

Rather than sending or receiving the e-mails on personal computers, they were uploaded as files (in their strongest encrypted form) onto third-party public websites from which they could then be downloaded. As a further precaution Karim had used software called 'window washer' intended to delete all browsing history from his computer and the external hard drive. Investigators were only able to open the files when they discovered a file, disguised (using steganography) as a thumbnail picture viewer, on Karim's external hard drive with the formula needed to decipher messages.[30]

By 'hallmarking' its output with the as-Sahab logo, Al Qaeda 'central' ensures wide distribution of authenticated material. Rather than posting on a single website, it distributes its output through *jihadi* media organisations, clearinghouses and online discussion boards via links to third-party file-sharing sites. Other AQAM organisations follow this method, which effectively outruns intelligence and security services' attempts to block distribution.

Jihadis can verify the provenance of material according to the production outlet it is attributed to. Apart from as-Sahab, Al Qaeda 'central' operates the Global Islamic Media Front which also disseminates Mullah Omar's broadcasts and statements; Ansar al-Islam's media wing is al-Ansar Media Foundation; al-Kata'ib Media is al-Shabaab's production outfit—this Internet-savvy group have an online television station and a radio station too; Al-Malahim Media and Ansar al-Mujaheddin carry

AQAP material; KavKaz and IslamDin are the Caucasus Emirate's media outlets.

Once an item is uploaded onto the Internet it is endlessly multiplied, being reposted on a variety of sites, blogs, forums, Facebook pages and so on, and becomes very difficult to remove. Further longevity can be assured by creating any number of 'mirror' sites—the original site is replicated and hosted at alternative remote locations so that if one is shut down exactly the same site is widely available elsewhere. WikiLeaks and Anonymous have successfully used this method to evade hacking attempts on their sites by domestic intelligence services.

The *Jiihadi* Independent News and Publishing

Independent news and media production (mostly online) by AQAM groups has expanded rapidly in the past few years. The Haqqani Network leader, Sirajuddin Haqqani, explained their importance in a Q&A session with members of the Ansar al-Mujaheddin Arabic forum: 'Internet *Jihadi* networks' are the most effective means by which AQAM groups can 'break the media blockade imposed by the enemies of the faithful'.[31] Haqqani has a few gripes about his 'media *jihadis*', who seem to be unable to keep to deadlines . . . or the point. He expresses the wish that they would 'Publish their material in good time and in accordance with the issues of the day.'[32]

In a February 2011 interview, Taliban media chief Abdel Sattar al-Maiwandi described how his group recruits 'specialist media operatives' and opined that 'Wars cannot be won without the media'. The Taliban run their own efficient news feed in Arabic and English. 'The Western media misrepresent the facts,' Maiwandi claimed. 'If twenty of their soldiers are killed, they announce the death of only one . . . if one of their aircraft is shot down they hide the news if they can . . . failing that, they state that the plane crashed making an emergency landing.'[33]

Al Qaeda's foremost 'Media Sheikh', Attiyah Abdel Rahman, more commonly known as 'Sheikh Atiyallah', was killed in August 2011. His death generated nearly as many messages of condolences as that of Osama bin Laden, and over a period of several months. Atiyallah contributed to a video called 'You Are Held Responsible Only for Thyself—Part 2' in

June 2011. Here he too discusses the importance to the movement of the '*Jihad* media' and criticises the Western press for 'manipulation, fakery and misguidance'. Those who wish to find out the 'truth' are advised to go to 'the free cyberspace of the Internet'.

Atiyallah insists on professional standards as if he is lecturing a university journalism class: 'We always advise writers to verify, discuss and research all news items. . . . We advocate honesty and complete accuracy in transmitting news and information. . . . The journalist and media foundation should not be concerned about getting the story first or sensationalism . . . these motives arise from the disease of love of appearance and fame, from which we pray that Allah will protect us.'

The 'media sheikh' then issues instructions for a cohesive propaganda strategy: 'clarify the connection between the *mujahideen*'s wills, messages and statements, and our primary reasons for war, *Jihad* and fighting. State that we are oppressed and under attack, that we call for freedom, that we have a just cause . . . always put the case of occupied Palestine at the top of the list and America's never-ending support for Israel.'[34]

Most major AQAM groups translate their output into English. The Global Islamic Media Front has a translation department which produces additional subtitles to video messages in English, Arabic, Urdu, Farsi, Pashto, Malay/Indonesian, French, German, Italian, Spanish, Turkish, Swedish, Danish, Russian, Czech, Polish, Finnish, Dutch, Portuguese, Hungarian, Greek, Norwegian, Hebrew, Thai, Korean, Chinese and Japanese. The work of this department testifies to the variety of nationalities currently represented in the Al Qaeda cadres. They also provide downloadable transcripts in a variety of languages.

The editor of *Inspire* magazine, Samir Khan, who was born in the US and killed by a drone alongside Anwar al-Awlaki in late 2011, wrote an article explaining why he considered it important to release Al Qaeda material in English: 'In the West; in East, West and South Africa; in South and Southeast Asia and elsewhere are millions of Muslims whose first or second language is English. It is our intention to present the important issues facing the *umma* today to the wide and dispersed English speaking Muslim readership.' Samir Khan was one of a growing number of *jihadis* who have been brought up in the West. In another article in the first issue of *Inspire* he penned an article 'Why I Am Proud to Be a Traitor' in which the 'typical American kid' describes his conversion to Islam and his journey from Queens, New York City, to Yemen.

The brainchild of Anwar al-Awlaki and Samir Khan, *Inspire* magazine is published online. There have been ten issues to date, starting in summer 2010. They are well produced and contain such deliberately headline-grabbing material that the shocked Western media did much of the work for Al Qaeda in promoting and distributing the first two issues. Awlaki had earlier made global headlines when he claimed that '*Jihad* is now as American as Apple Pie', following the arrest of Texan housewife Coleen laRose, who had reinvented herself as Jihad Jane and become involved in a conspiracy to launch terror attacks on the US homeland. Now he applied the same sinister humour to a piece in the launch edition of *Inspire* entitled 'How to Make a Bomb in the Kitchen of Your Mom'. The latter was widely covered by the world's press and, in a descent into farce, MI6 hacked the magazine some months after its publication and replaced the bomb recipe with one for cupcakes.[35] The original document remains widely available on mirror sites, nevertheless.

Inspire was so 'American' in tone—although certainly not content—that many questioned whether it was indeed genuine or a product of the CIA. Having ploughed my way through several issues containing much turgid theology and workable instructions for constructing various types of bombs, I cannot see any reason why it should not be a genuine Al Qaeda publication. In addition, in letter 0010 of the so-called Abbottabad letters to and from bin Laden, the Al Qaeda leader mentions the magazine: 'regarding what you mentioned about Inspiration [sic] magazine', he writes to his correspondent, 'please send my pointers to the brothers in Yemen'.

The Taliban also produce an online magazine in English with the strange, presumably humorous, title 'In-Fight Magazine'. Issue 33 in September 2011 contained several photographs of, and a celebratory article about, the downing of a Black Hawk helicopter carrying SEALs from the same battalion that killed bin Laden.

In spring 2011, Al Qaeda produced the first issue of a '*Jihadist* magazine for women' called *al-Shamikha*. The magazine was widely heralded before it was released in physical and online form. A video promoting the magazine was posted on Islamic forums and was available on YouTube until recently when it was removed 'because its content violated YouTube's terms of Service'.[36] Again, the magazine was reported, mostly with derision, in the Western media but with more seriousness by certain Arabic satellite channels.

Al-Shamikha's first issue came with a free booklet, 'My House is My Kingdom', which is a good indication of the kind of lifestyle advocated within its covers. The cover shows a woman in a *burqa* carrying a submachine gun. The first page advises us that the distributor and publisher is al-Fajr—one of Al Qaeda's media outlets.

The first edition of *Al-Shamikha* includes articles about bringing up sons to be *jihadis* and how to live a pious Islamic life. In the diary of a *mujahideen* widow the author describes how she wished to follow her husband into the battlefields of Afghanistan but he was killed before she could get there. She relates how her little boys are already keen to join the *jihad* and that she considers it her duty to prepare them.

Another writer, Um Whalid al-Makiya, outlines the 'Jihad Path' which begins with 'separating oneself from the pleasures of the world'. A student, Fawzia Azukhagh, writes a letter from a Moroccan jail where she has been imprisoned on suspicion of belonging to Al Qaeda (probably not a good move to publish a letter in their magazine). Um Rajheb al-Maktesiya pens a poem urging Muslims to unite to fight corruption, bringing the context of the Arab Spring to the forefront. A photograph shows a banner from the Egyptian uprising reading 'All Dictators Must Fall'.

A second edition of *Al-Shamikha* appeared in February 2012 with articles including 'An Introduction to the Basics of Digital Security', which offers tips on Internet privacy, commentaries on the Arab Spring, advice for anyone considering marrying a *jihadi* and some tips on 'housekeeping skills'. The issue twice reproduces a harrowing picture of a dead Palestinian child surrounded by his terrified classmates and emphasises the duty of mothers to prepare their sons for *jihad*.

The first issue of another Al Qaeda magazine also appeared in 2011. July brought us the *Journal for Information Security and Hacking* from 'Al Qaeda's Technical Department'. This is largely a practical guide to the latest news in the information technology world, reporting on the 'Electronic Campaign against the Russian President', a woman in her seventies who brought down her country's entire Internet service, reviews of the new Apple iPad, Windows 7 and the new Al Jazeera app. There is an interview with an Egyptian who hacked the Algerian newspaper *al-Shoruq* and an approving account of the activities of the hacking group Anonymous.

Although online publications are the norm, some *jihadi* groups have started to produce physical glossy magazines. In the past, print output was limited to crudely assembled newsletters but in April 2010 the Taliban produced 'glossy' editions of its bi-monthly magazines, *al-Samud*, *Morchel*, *Saraq* and *Shahamak*. Containing well-written information about their activities, attacks and martyrs, the magazines—in Pashto and Arabic—are distributed in Afghanistan and the Gulf. Commentators surmise that they must have been printed on modern presses in Pakistan.[37]

The level of professionalism of both online and physical glossies, in terms of design, language and presentation, sits uneasily with the content which is largely violent and, essentially, basic propaganda.

Conclusion: The Future of Digital Warfare

Cyber-security experts are in agreement that it is only a matter of time before AQAM manage to pull off a cyber 'spectacular'. Consider the impact of AQAM gaining control over a nuclear facility, an air traffic control system, an energy grid, defence and security networks, transit systems, emergency systems, refineries, dams and so on. The remote-controlled drone system which has decimated the AQAM leadership must surely be a target.

There is an 'arms race in cyberspace' and a 'global cyber arms trade' that includes 'malicious viruses, zero-day exploits and massive botnetso'.[38] World powers are already using cyber-warfare to devastating effect. In 2008–9 the first cyber 'superweapon' was created. Called 'Stuxnet', it was said to have been developed by the Israelis and was tested at their Dimona nuclear facility in the Negev desert before being deployed in late 2010, targeting Iran's Nantanz nuclear fuel enrichment plant. Stuxnet infiltrated the control system and ordered the centrifuge motors to spin so fast that they blew themselves apart. One-fifth of Iran's centrifuges were destroyed over the course of more than a year before cyber-forensic specialists working for Tehran managed to identify and defuse the 'cyber dirty bomb' in February 2012.

The blueprint code for Stuxnet is freely available on the Internet and can be adapted to attack any control system. German expert Ralph

Langner told the *CS Monitor* that Stuxnet can be reduced to just four lines of code and that 'There is no way to prevent the production and transfer of bits and bytes that can be transferred anywhere in the world by Internet. Arms control with satellite surveillance is impossible. . . . So I'm afraid cyber-arms control won't be possible.'[39] It is perfectly feasible that a terrorist group like AQAM could access, copy and deploy 'cyber-missiles' like Stuxnet.

Al Qaeda has many supporters in South Asia where much of the digital industry is now based; it is likely to be recruiting among the region's talented technical community. In addition it is possible to buy in the services of technicians to conduct sophisticated cyberattacks or hacking operations. In the Philippines, the FBI arrested four computer hackers in November 2011 who had been paid by 'an Islamic Terrorist organisation' to hack corporate telephone systems.[40] Another serious security weakness is the possibility of infiltration or a duplicitous insider—WikiLeaks, of course, originated with US Army Private Bradley Manning. Al Qaeda and the Taliban are masters of this form of deception.

America now has a 'Cyber Command' unit within its military apparatus, as do its rivals for global influence such as China and Iran. In June 2011, Chinese military experts declared that cyber-warfare is now a military priority, 'Just as nuclear warfare was the strategic war of the industrial era, so cyber warfare is the strategic war of the information era,' spokesmen told Reuters. 'It is a form of battle that is massively destructive and concerns the life and death of nations.'[41]

Conclusion: The Next Generation

This is a war which knows no international borders and no single battleground.
Adam Gahdan, Al Qaeda's US-born spokesman

We are creating more enemies than we are removing from the battlefield.
Robert Grenier, former Head of CIA counter-terrorism unit, June 2012

The death of Osama bin Laden coupled with the Arab Spring provoked a number of articles, and even books, proclaiming that Al Qaeda was obsolete and defeated. Those optimistic voices have fallen silent as the terror group and its allies return to the headlines, seemingly able to fight on several fronts at once and launch serial 'spectaculars' whilst posing a continual threat to the West.

Under al-Zawahiri, AQAM has been able to refocus its strategy in the light of new opportunities afforded both by the Arab revolutions and by America's military expansion into Yemen and Somalia. The ongoing Syrian uprising—which threatens to spread into Lebanon—and the chaos of imminent civil war offer AQAM an unprecedented chance to consolidate a presence at Israel's borders and to escalate the Sunni–Shi'i sectarian conflict it has been fomenting for many years. Nobody now doubts the presence of a sizeable number of *mujahideen*, a third element in the battle between the rebels and the Assad regime.

Saudi Arabia and the Gulf Countries have been funding and arming Syrian opposition fighters and it is not inconceivable that some of that funding ends up in AQAM hands. The Syrian conflict may come to resemble the Afghan–Soviet war of the 1980s where the *mujahideen* became, in effect, a proxy army for the West and its allies.

There is a real danger of sectarian polarisation, multiple civil conflicts and, ultimately, a regional war pitting a Shi'i bloc—led by the West's regional nemesis, Iran and comprising Iraq, the Shi'i populations of Bahrain, Saudi Arabia and Lebanon, plus Hizbullah—against a Sunni coalition headed by Saudi Arabia and backed by the West. In such a scenario, in a great historical paradox, the West would find itself fighting on the same side as AQAM.

The post-revolutionary landscape in North Africa has also benefited AQAM, enabling it to consolidate its grip in the Sahel, acquire sophisticated military hardware (from unguarded Libyan stockpiles) and expand southwards into Nigeria and Mali.

Part of al-Zawahiri's strategic vision for AQAM is to strangle oil supplies to the West. Post-revolutionary Libya is in chaos and al-Zawahiri personally dispatched top Al Qaeda commander Abdel Basit Azuz to the oil-rich country in May 2012. Azuz is operating at least one training camp with 300 men under his command and has instructions to spread a *jihadi* network across Libya, having sent envoys to meet other Islamist groups as far west as Brega.[1]

Meanwhile the presence of strong AQAM groups on both sides of the Gulf of Aden has alarmed the US, which now considers Yemen to be the most dangerous incubator of terror threats against the West. In May 2012 the West ramped up attacks on *jihadi* strongholds in both Somalia and Yemen shortly after US counter-terrorism adviser, John Brennan, visited new Yemeni President, Abd-Rabouh Mansour Hardi, in Sanaa. In addition to shelling (from EU and US warships) and drone raids, US Special Operation troops, which were withdrawn in 2011 during the uprising against the Saleh regime, have returned on the ground along with CIA agents. AQAP responded to the arrival of US military and CIA 'advisers' in Yemen with a 'spectacular' suicide bombing of an entire regiment of Yemeni soldiers, killing at least ninety-eight and maiming hundreds.[2]

By sending more troops and military apparatus into the Middle East, the US may be inadvertently playing into Al Qaeda's hands. The reader may recall that the first of five key stages in Al Qaeda's long-term strategy was to provoke the US to send soldiers to Muslim lands 'where it would be easier for the *mujahideen* to fight them'. In addition, the outrage provoked by drone attacks and the deaths of innocent civilians may aid recruitment.

The ongoing problem the 'war on terror' faces is that, despite possessing vastly superior arms and military technologies, the US has been unable to achieve a definitive victory against *jihadi* groups—not even in Afghanistan or Iraq where it has launched full-scale invasions and engaged in many years of battle.

The task of destroying AQAM has become more challenging as time has gone on. Temporary victories—in Iraq 2006–7, for example—have so far failed to endure and have even been reversed. It is difficult to target highly mobile groups of fighters sustained by an increasingly complex, international network of franchises, alliances, cooperation and loyalties. Several sources affirm that AQAM now comprises up to forty groups and further expansion is part of al-Zawahiri's strategy. In late 2011 US State Department Coordinator for Counter-Terrorism Daniel Benjamin said, 'The affiliates are playing a more menacing role today . . . the broader Al Qaeda threat has become more geographically and ethnically diversified.'[3]

Cooperation and collaboration between the different groups are increasingly sophisticated. In November 2011, for example, the leader of AQIM's southern branch, Mokhta Belmokhtar, claimed that he had sent envoys as far as Pakistan to instigate joint operations with Al Qaeda leaders there.[4] Pakistani *jihadis* subsequently arrived in Timbuktu (in spring 2012) to help the insurrection in northern Mali, as noted above.

While the loss of Osama bin Laden was emotionally devastating for his followers, it was not, ultimately, that damaging to the overall organisation. Al Qaeda has long taken care to delegate roles and power, and has developed a system of deputies so that if one leader is killed or captured it will have a minimal impact on the group's survival and its ability to continue with its agenda undeterred. 'Our *jihad* . . . cannot be stopped, disrupted, or delayed by the death or capture of one individual, no matter who he is or how elevated his status,' said Abu Yahya al-Libi in a June 2010 video posted on Islamist sites. Al-Libi is himself al-Zawahiri's deputy and a likely future leader of the organisation.

Under Ayman al-Zawahiri, AQAM is refocusing its priorities, making Israel and Saudi Arabia primary targets. Al Qaeda has long been criticised for its failure to engage with the Palestinian struggle;

now the Arab revolutions have enabled the formation of an Al Qaeda franchise in the Sinai while large groups of *jihadis* are mustering in Syria and Lebanon, right on Israel's borders. Al Qaeda has long blamed the Saudi royal family for furthering America's hegemonic ambitions in the Middle East when it allowed 100,000 US soldiers into the 'Land of the Two Holy Places' prior to the first Gulf War in 1990; the Kingdom is also, of course, a major source of Western oil supplies, which AQAM would like to disrupt.

The current escalation of attacks against AQAP provoked strategic responses from al-Zawahiri: in a May 2012 video tirade against the 'US stooge and puppet', Yemen's President Abd-Rabouh Mansour Hardi, he urged the Yemeni people to support the *mujahideen*; meanwhile, in order to improve its popularity with the tribespeople, both AQAP and its offshoot, Ansar al-Shari'a, have started public service programmes, restoring water supplies and electricity for examples; as the Iraqi 'Awakening' campaign demonstrated, if the tribes turn against a group it spells their downfall. In another May 2012 statement, al-Zawahiri incited the Saudis to begin their own Arab Spring–style uprising. If the battle in Yemen becomes unsustainable, fighters will migrate northwards and into Saudi Arabia—a move that would be facilitated by instability in the Kingdom.

The regional turmoil resulting from the Arab revolutions has the potential to work against Al Qaeda in the long run if a bespoke new form of uniquely Arab government is allowed to evolve unimpeded by outside interference. It is a mistake to assume that Western governmental solutions will satisfy the Arab revolutionaries, a new generation which is seeking real change with its own cultural and ideological imperatives.

Unfortunately the West seems unable to refrain from involvement with the region's efforts to reinvent itself. As Western economies teeter on the brink, Gulf countries control sovereign funds to the value of $3 trillion or more available for recycling in arms deals, investment and services—in May 2012, British company BAE signed a new $3 billion deal to provide Saudi Arabia with hawk jets.

The problem is that this 'Golden Pot' of money is surrounded by Al Qaeda–infected countries where security is shaken by protest and revolution. Adopting the strategy Tony Blair has described as 'controlled change', the West has failed to challenge the brutal suppression of demonstrations in Bahrain and Saudi Arabia's embryonic uprisings. Meanwhile post-revolutionary governments can be pressured into cooperating with the Western agenda by promises of aid, loans, investment, trade and arms deals. China, Russia and India are also vying for influence in the regional shake-up, with one eye on control of strategic locations and the other on natural resources such as oil, gas and, increasingly, water.

If new, post-revolutionary governments in countries such as Egypt and Libya frustrate or dilute the protestors' demands it will inevitably result in an angry backlash favouring the radicals. Along with the electoral successes of Islamist parties, there is a full-blown Islamist revival across the region, closely linked to the resurgence of pan-Arabism, the notion of the *umma* and the urge to consolidate a post-revolutionary identity. More than fifty Islamist satellite TV channels are currently available throughout the Middle East and North Africa and while these channels present their message as moderate, their influence is quite the opposite.

The more moderate Islamist political parties may seek to dispel the fears of the West and to appease the secular liberals at home by diluting the notion of Islamic statehood with Western-style democracy; it is my impression that the majority of ordinary people in the Arab world do not want a hybrid form of government, however, but a state which at the very least references Sharia. If the Islamist parties fail to deliver the changes thousands have died for, this too might prompt a groundswell towards greater extremism and militancy.

What's in a Name?

It is now known that Osama bin Laden was considering changing the name of Al Qaeda. Papers found at Abbottabad attest to an anxiety that, because the name lacks religious connotations, the Muslim nation might 'lose the feeling that we belong to them'; in addition, the US had been able to wage its war on AQAM groups 'without appearing to offend the world's Muslims'. Bin Laden proposed a list of possible alternatives including Ta'ifat al-tawhid wa-al-jihad (Monotheism and Jihad Group), Jama'at wahdat al-Muslimin (Muslim Unity Group), Hizb tawhid al-Umma al-Islamiyya (Islamic Nation Unification Party) and Jama'at tahrir al-aqsa (Al-Aqsa Liberation Group).

In the past, bin Laden and other senior leaders had also expressed the fear that, post-9/11 and the subsequent attacks in Madrid (in 2004) and London (in 2005), the Al Qaeda 'brand' had gathered increasingly negative connotations, associating it entirely with terrorism, and that these had been exacerbated by the extremist conduct of Abu Musab al-Zarqawi, and the attacks on civilians he engineered.

When al-Zarqawi was killed in 2006, 'Al Qaeda in the Land of the Two Rivers' was, effectively, rebranded 'the Islamic State of Iraq', and placed under an indigenous leadership.

Whilst Al Qaeda in the Islamic Maghreb (AQIM, founded in 2007) and Al Qaeda in the Arabian Peninsula (AQAP, founded in 2009) chose to openly associate themselves with Osama bin Laden's group by adopting its moniker, many affiliates prefer not to. Somali group al-Shabaab, for instance, have resisted being rebranded what they really are—Al Qaeda in the Horn of Africa—as have certain groups in Gaza.

At the end of 2011, AQAP too joined the trend away from using the Al Qaeda name, by forming an offshoot, Ansar al-Shari'a. This resulted in improved recruitment and relations with the general population in certain areas.

The new *mujahideen* group in Syria has chosen to call itself the al-Nusra Front, again in an effort to avoid identification with the potentially off-putting Al Qaeda brand and also because of the controversy that arose in Libya when Muammar and Saif Gaddafi both claimed (in an effort to spook both the nation and the West) that Al Qaeda had infiltrated the opposition.

Sources say that Ayman al-Zawahiri has suggested a larger rebranding and restructuring of Al Qaeda whereby the entire organisation would be known as the Abdullah Azzam Brigades and each 'branch' becomes a 'brigade' named after a famous *jihadi*—in Iraq for example there is an Abu Musab al-Zarqawi Brigade whilst in Lebanon the group is named after 9/11 hijacker Ziad al-Jarrah.

In future we should no longer seek an overt identification with Al Qaeda in assessing the organisation's current status, significance and size, but look instead for a common purpose and those deep-rooted links of ideology, intelligence, ambition, allegiance, weapons supplies, finance and modus operandi that connect up an increasingly widespread collection of Salafi-*jihadi* groups. One does not usually have to dig deep to find the unmistakable hallmarks of AQAM.

The Third Generation

The writings and statements of both Osama bin Laden and Ayman al-Zawahiri testify that they always expected their struggle to be multigenerational and the organisation now consists of three generations of fighters. The older generation might not, however, have expected that the offspring of their offspring would be even more extremist and ruthless than ever.

In 2009, a fierce online debate broke out when a key Salafi-*jihadi* ideologue, Jordanian cleric Abu Mohammad al-Maqdisi, questioned the killing of civilians in Iraq and al-Zarqawi's zealous prosecution of his understanding of Sharia. The youths accused al-Maqdisi, who was formerly considered a radical in the *jihadi* fold, of 'moderating' his views. Since then the younger generation has been referred to as 'neo-Zarqawists' because they espouse his extremism and revere his memory.

Guardian reporter Ghaith Abdul-Ahad explored this subject when he interviewed veteran *jihadi* Khaled Abdul Nabi, long-time bin Laden associate and one of the founders of the Abyan-Aden Islamic Army which later came under the AQAP umbrella. Nabi spoke of 'problems' with the younger generation in Yemen—'when *jihadi* leaders try to moderate their positions', he said, 'the young followers will often splinter and form more radical groups, so each generation is more radical than the next.' Al-Zawahiri's potential successors, who include Abu Yahya al-Libi and Nasir al-Wahaishi, belong to a younger generation.

The profile of third-generation recruits to AQAM is little changed from their predecessors in that they are generally well educated and from the middle classes. These young people are Internet-savvy and technologically adept; US security services point to an escalating risk of serious cyberattack. This generation has also adapted new IEDs and car bombs to evade detection and jamming devices provided by Western security and arms firms.

The older generation frequently complain about their young

comrades' lack of 'Islamic scholarship', which suggests that, for some at least, the motivation for their violent undertakings is more political and ideological than an interpretation of Islam. At the same time, a simplistic *jihadi* mythology has evolved over the years and this seems to resonate with the third generation in particular; it is often referred to in communications between young *jihadis* and features strongly in the *Anasheed* culture discussed in a previous chapter.

Focusing on divine intervention, visions of paradise and the beauty of a martyr's death, this mythology is a recurrent thread in propaganda and motivational material. Divine intervention often takes the form of a weather event, as in this December 2011 account by Taliban commander Hafiz Ghulamullah: 'The enemy aircraft came immediately after Salat al-Isha but many of the brothers had not yet reached their trenches. Then Allah sent clouds and it started to rain!' Angelic figures dressed in long white robes are frequently sighted in the battlefield, sometimes removing injured fighters to a place of safety, sometimes fighting alongside the *mujahideen*. Paradise brings with it the alluring promise of the *houris*; in an Internet sermon, a British Islamist described how a 'martyr' had a dream in which he met a beautiful young woman who told him he was 'the chosen one' and that she and her sisters would meet him tomorrow—he was killed in battle the next day. The horror and mess of death are obscured by the overwhelming scent of musk which these young men believe emanates from a 'martyr's' bloodied corpse. The latest addition to this mythology, as evidenced by a plethora of poetic videos eulogising 'the Sheikh' on *jihadi* YouTube channels, is a serenely smiling Osama bin Laden awaiting his soldiers in heaven.

It is impossible to estimate how many *jihadis* there are in numerous camps and bases around the world but it is sobering to reflect that, as long ago as 2005, Western leaders were claiming they had killed 5,000–6,000 Al Qaeda–related fighters and two-thirds of the leadership. Given that the elimination of fighters and leaders has continued apace, and yet the organisation continues to launch attacks around the globe, we may be seriously underestimating its size.

Recruitment is clearly ongoing and the reasons young men are attracted to *jihad* have not changed or diminished. First there are the West's invasions of, and territorial incursions into Muslim lands and America's increasingly reckless drone strikes; then there is the perception that Muslims are humiliated and mistreated; and, in addition, the ongoing persecution of the Palestinians remains an open wound in the Muslim consciousness.

Latterly, there has been a series of incidents involving American soldiers which have greatly fuelled Muslim anger and aided recruitment to extremist groups. These include: the March 2012 killing of sixteen innocent civilians, including babies and children, in a village near Kandahar by a 'rogue soldier'; footage of US soldiers urinating on the corpses of Afghan men; the gang rape and murder of 14-year-old Iraqi villager Abeer Qassim Al-Janab, whose entire family was also shot dead by US soldiers, one of whom afterwards remarked that he 'didn't think of them as human'.[5]

More recently, AQAM has been working on recruiting second- and third-generation Muslims living in the West. We should expect this cohort to expand as it has been 'successfully' deployed in several horrific attacks: the London bombings of 2005, for example, were carried out by second-generation, British-born children of immigrants; latterly, in March 2012, a French Muslim, Mohammed Mehra, the son of Algerian immigrants, carried out a series of shootings that terrorised Toulouse, killing seven. A document insidiously titled 'Lessons and Treasures from the Battle of Toulouse' by Sheikh abu-Saad al-Amili was posted on the Internet in April 2012. Amili incites further attacks by disaffected youths, 'hidden soldiers of a new type that the enemy has not met before and cannot find . . . in Western dress with blue eyes, speaking foreign tongues'.

Al Qaeda clearly wishes to build on the phenomenon of the Western convert and has allowed several such men to climb through the ranks, becoming prominent figures and, presumably, role models. German convert Bekkay Harrach, who took the moniker Al Hafidh Abu Talha al Almani, was killed in action in 2011, having become an Al Qaeda commander. Harrach appeared in several as-Sahab videos speaking German to threaten his native country and declare his commitment to Islam and Al Qaeda.[6]

American Adam Gadahn, who converted to Islam in a Californian mosque in 1995, aged just 17, counted a Zionist grandfather and a committed Christian mother among his relatives. Now known as Azzam al-Amriki, he appeared in more as-Sahab (Al Qaeda's main media production unit) videos in 2011 than any other Al Qaeda leader. As a key media adviser and spokesperson it was al-Amriki who was tasked with delivering Al Qaeda's response to President Barack Obama's Cairo speech in June 2009.

Abu Mansoor al-Amriki, who became an al-Shabaab commander in Somalia, is an American citizen from Alabama originally called Omar Hammami. Among the most influential US-born converts was Samir Khan, who edited *Inspire* and was killed along with al-Awlaki in September 2011. Khan was born of Pakistani parents in Riyadh but grew up in New York.

In 2010 German nationals Fritz Gelowicz, his wife Filiz and Daniel Schneider were jailed for being members of the so-called Sauerland Cell whose large-scale plot to bomb US military bases in Germany was foiled. The cell accumulated 700 kg of hydrogen peroxide, enough to produce bombs which would be more powerful than those used in Madrid in 2004. The judge described the Germans as 'deluded extremists without even the most rudimentary understanding of Islam'. Filiz was released in May 2012 apparently in exchange for the release, by AQIM, of a German hostage.[7]

Filiz Gelowicz is considered something of a heroine among the third generation who communicate via bulletin boards and she is part of a growing vanguard of female *jihadis*. Samantha Lewthwaite, the widow of 7/7 suicide bomber Jermaine Lindsay, resurfaced in Kenya in 2011 where she became known as Dada Mzungu ('white sister'). Lewthwaite was implicated in a plot to bomb Western targets in Mombasa with fellow British-born extremist, 29-year-old Jermaine Grant. In July 2012, a *jihadi* website reported that Lewthwaite had moved to Somalia and was in command of an all-female terror squad.[8]

The most celebrated among the female *jihadi*s are two Saudis. Heila al-Qusayyer, who was arrested in July 2010, is a middle-class mother who allegedly headed a sleeper cell of sixty fighters which included young women in its ranks. She also allegedly raised funds for AQAP, persuading fellow Saudis to part with cash and jewellery which were laundered via various Islamic charities. Omm Hajjar Al-Azdi Wafa, usually known as Wafa, is from a family of extremists and has been married three times to prominent Al Qaeda men: her first and second husbands—Saud al-Qhatani and Abdul Rahman al-Ghamdi—were killed. The third, Said al-Shihri, decided he wanted to marry whilst still in jail undergoing the deradicalisation programme and did so in 2008. Not long afterwards, al-Shihri suddenly disappeared without explanation along with his brother Yusuf, who had been with him on the programme.

Wafa was expecting the couple's child and it was assumed that al-Shihri had been abducted or killed. When he suddenly appeared on television in spring 2009, bearing a Kalashnikov and declaring himself to be the military commander of AQAP, Wafa decided to join him in Yemen. Wafa had only given birth to her little daughter, Shada, one month before and was living in her parents' house in Riyadh. Having created a pretext to leave the house unobserved, she took her two other children (Yusuf, 9, and Wasaaef, 4) and the baby, and left the country under cover of a heavy sandstorm in spring 2009. She somehow made her way to the mountains of Yemen, telephoning her family weeks later to reassure them. Wafa has made several videos and written articles urging Saudi women to encourage their men to join AQAP and 'come to Yemen'.

How Terror Groups End

Despite trillions of dollars spent on the 'war on terror', the killing of Osama bin Laden and many other leaders, and the relentless pounding of AQAM strongholds and camps by shells, bombs and drones, Al Qaeda remains deeply entrenched around the globe. AQAM is an unprecedented phenomenon: a terror organisation with the clout—and many of the resources—of a state actor. It has armies and weapons, it has the apparatus of government and its own judicial system, it has funding and fiscal policies. In territorial terms it has yet to dominate an entire country, but has emirates in many locations, as we have seen above, including the two-thirds of Afghanistan under Taliban control, much of southern and central Yemen and most of the Sahel.

What, then, would it take to bring this bloody chapter of history to its conclusion? A 2008 study by the RAND corporation[9] analysed how terrorist organisations end and found five main scenarios. I will briefly apply each of these possibilities to AQAM.

First, 'The group is militarily destroyed.' This, according to RAND, is a rare outcome; the 2009 Sri Lankan government's defeat of the separatist Tamil Tigers after twenty-five years of fighting is a notable exception.

Militarily, AQAM claims to have prevailed in asymmetric warfare in Iraq and Afghanistan. A conventional military defeat seems unlikely, especially given the wide geographical distribution of the constituent groups, their intelligence capabilities, their flexibility to move from one theatre to another and the deeply entrenched network of roots established over decades of struggle.

In the second scenario, 'The group collapses due to infighting and splinter groups.' This is a possible scenario given the history of Islamist groups and their reputation for in-fighting. It is known that 9/11 and the issue of sectarian attacks against the Shi'i have proved deeply divisive in the past. However, Ayman al-Zawahiri and the younger generation of leaders are well aware of this danger and will act to prevent it. There is no evidence that this is a widespread problem for AQAM at present. Communication difficulties as a result of deep hiding and other measures taken to evade increasingly sophisticated intelligence methods might eventually lead to divisions between the constituent groups—a problem the Haqqani Network addressed in January 2012 when it announced a new umbrella for several Pakistani groups that had fallen out under just such circumstances, having been targeted by US drones for many months. The RAND report found that this scenario was ultimately much less likely in terror groups with a religious agenda since they have 'a clear vision of their goals that could be handed down to successors after the first generation of radical leaders departed or were eliminated'.

Three, 'Intelligence agencies arrest or kill key members.' The assassination of key members is the most common way of eliminating a terrorist group and many hailed the killing of Osama bin Laden as the definitive blow to Al Qaeda. However, as we have seen above, the horizontal structure of the organisation—which continues to expand—and the precautionary delegation of tasks and power ensure that the death of one, or even several, key figures can, apparently, be borne by the network.

The last two possibilities are, in my opinion, the most feasible in the case of AQAM. In a fourth scenario, 'The group joins the political process.' It could be argued that Al Qaeda's brand of radical, political Islam filled a void left by the anti-imperialist struggles of the 1960s and 1970s and provided an alternative narrative for dissent. Then, iconic leaders such as Che Guevara first brought an intellectualised perspective to terrorism, showing how the effects of imperialism were not only local but global. Al Qaeda's political impact—both direct and indirect—should not be undervalued. Al Qaeda has become part of the political discourse of our times, not just regionally, but globally, something no other terrorist group has achieved.

However unlikely the idea of AQAM leaders engaging directly with their enemies might seem, we have only to remember that the IRA's political wing, Sinn Fein, did just that. Former Republican leaders and fighters now sit in the Northern Irish Parliament at Stormont—Martin McGuiness, for example, is currently the deputy first minister.

In one of bin Laden's letters found at Abbottabad, dated April 2011, there is an intriguing hint of diplomatic activity: 'you mentioned that British intelligence said that England would leave Afghanistan if Al Qaeda promised not to target their interests', he writes to senior commander Attiyah Abdel Rahman (who was killed by a drone in August 2011). 'Do not agree to anything,' bin Laden counsels, '. . . but without slamming the door.'

It is my belief that, ultimately, Al Qaeda will form a political wing, probably under a separate moniker. Meanwhile tentative dialogue might be opened via proxies and third parties. The Taliban is an obvious candidate—they have already indicated their willingness to engage in diplomacy with the international community, as the opening of an office in Qatar suggests.[10] Islamist politicians from the Arab Spring countries might also act as interlocutors.

Although the RAND report advises that, to date, no terrorist group with a religious agenda has ever ended for this reason, the final suggestion as to how only Al Qaeda might cease its violent activity offers the most chilling prospect—that the group 'achieves its goals'.

Notes

Introduction: After bin Laden

1. http://www.guardian.co.uk/world/2012/may/09/underwear-bomber-working-for-cia
2. Full transcript of President Obama's speech available at: http://content.usatoday.com/communities/theoval/post/2010/01/obama-terrorism-is-a-challenge-of-the-utmost-urgency/1
3. http://www.infoplease.com/ipa/A0933935.html
4. http://worldnews.msnbc.msn.com/_news/2012/05/07/11583173-cia-foiled-al-qaida-plot-to-destroy-us-bound-airliner?lite
5. http://www.guardian.co.uk/world/2010/dec/12/stockholm-bombing-policing-lone-jihadists
6. http://india.nydailynews.com/newsarticle/4fbe3cd71f630a705f000000/%20amnesty-international-osama-bin-laden-raid-was-illegal
7. http://www.rense.com/general31/helda.htm
8. http://www.time.com/time/world/article/0,8599,1988375,00.html
9. http://epaper.dawn.com/~epaper/DetailImage.php?StoryImage=29_03_2012_001_001
10. http://www.dawn.com/2011/05/23/anp-leaders-said-military-protected-haqqanis-other-militants.html
11. http://calgary.ctv.ca/servlet/an/local/CTVNews/20120523/pakistani-doctor-shakil-afridi-convicted-high-treason-120523/20120523/?hub=Calgary Home
12. Khalid Al-Hamadi, 'Al Qaeda's Readiness to Launch Attack Greater than 9/11', *al-Quds Al-Arabi* (8 Nov. 2008).
13. http://www.alarabiya.net/articles/2011/08/02/160445.html
14. Nasser al-Bahri, *Dans l'ombre de Ben Laden* (Paris: Michel Lafon, 2010), p. 275.
15. http://www.guardian.co.uk/world/2012/apr/29/bin-laden-al-qaida-taliban-contact
16. Al-Bahri, pp. 210–12.
17. www.time.com/time/world/article/0,8599,2073420,00.html
18. http://tribune.com.pk/story/167870/bombs-targets-army-recruits-in-charsadda70-dead
19. http://www.guardian.co.uk/world/2011/aug/08/us-helicopter-afghanistan-night-raid
20. Al-Bahri, p. 273.
21. Ayman al-Zawahiri, 'And the Noble Knight Dismounts', broadcast eulogy for bin Laden, June 2011.
22. Ayman al-Zawahiri, 'Eighth Message to the Egyptian People', December 2011 (my trans.).
23. Ibid.

24. Ayman al-Zawahiri, 'And the Noble Knight Dismounts'.
25. http://aljahad.com/vb/showthread.php?p=39045
26. http://www.atimes.com/atimes/South_Asia/KJ15Df03.html
27. 'The State of Islam will Remain Safe', *al-Furqan Media*, 7 August 2011.
28. Al-Bahri, p. 158.
29. Abbottabad letter 0010 (http://www.ctc.usma.edu/posts/letters-from-abbottabad-bin-ladin-sidelined)
30. Al-Bahri, p. 196.
31. Al-Bahri, p. 112.
32. Olivier Roy, 'Al Qaeda in the West as a Youth Movement: The Power of a Narrative', *Microcon Policy Working Paper 2*, November 2008.
33. www.guardian.co.uk/world/2011/dec/06/al-qaida-kabul-attack-shia-pilgrims?newsfeed=true
34. http://nation.foxnews.com/ft-hood-shooting/2011/12/07/obama-regime-calls-ft-hood-shooting-workplace-violence
35. http://www.globalsecurity.org/org/news/2007/070706-ied-evolution.htm
36. http://www.guardian.co.uk/world/2010/sep/29/terror-attack-plot-europe-foiled
37. http://saharareporters.com/news-page/mayhem-boko-haram-goes-killing-spree
38. Al-Zawahiri, 'Eighth Message to the Egyptian People'.
39. http://costsofwar.org/article/pakistani-civilians
40. http://papers.nber.org/papers/w16152#fromrss
41. http://icasualties.org
42. http://www.bbc.co.uk/news/world-south-asia-14149692
43. http://theunjustmedia.com/Islamic%20Perspectives/april12/battle.pdf

1. The Arab Spring and Al Qaeda

1. http://www.washingtontimes.com/news/2012/apr/24/just-3-major-presidential-candidates-remain
2. http://www.presstv.ir/detail/227658.html
3. Abbottabad letter 0010.
4. Interview with al-Zawahiri by As-Shahab media, April 2009 (http://www.youtube.com/watch?v=WamYKbSX4Z0).
5. Abbottabad letter 0010.
6. See e.g. http://www.thedailybeast.com/newsweek/2011/06/05/egypt-the-revolution-blows-up.html
7. Christopher Dickey, 'Intelligence Test', *Newsweek*, 12 June 2011.
8. Interview with Noam Chomsky by *AlterNet Radio Hour*, 24 April 2012.
9. Abbottabad letter 0010.
10. http://www.aclu.org/national-security/fact-sheet-extraordinary-rendition
11. In chronological order these are: Tunisia, Algeria, Lebanon, Jordan, Mauritania, Oman, Saudi Arabia, Egypt, Yemen, Iraq, Bahrain, Libya, Kuwait, Morocco and Syria.
12. http://www.aljazeera.com/news/middleeast/2011/02/2011212518548557192.html
13. http://www.isn.ethz.ch
14. 'Affordable Homes Become as Important as Democracy in Saudi Arabia', *Gulf States Newsletter*, 8 April 2011, p.11.
15. http://www.fpif.org/articles/saudi_arabia_rolling_back_the_arab_spring

16. Unpublished polls referenced, respectively, in Benjamin Schwarz, 'America's Struggle Against the Wahabbi/Neo-Salafi Movement', *Orbis*, 51/1 (2007), 124, and Henneer Furtig, 'Conflict and Co-operation in the Persian Gulf: The Interregional Order and US Policy', *Middle East Journal*, 61/4 (2007), 638.
17. http://www.defaiya.com/defaiyaonline/index.php?option=com_content&view=article&id=1940%3Asaudi-arabia-to-raise-us-arms-deal-to-90-bn&catid=86%3Asecurity&Itemid=83&lang=en
18. http://www.isn.ethz.ch
19. Abbottabad letter 0017.
20. http://www.cbsnews.com/stories/2011/04/17/politics/washingtonpost/main20054781.shtml
21. http://bikyamasr.com/62200/jordan-cites-rise-in-attempts-to-smuggle-arms-into-syria
22. http://www.wnd.com/2012/07/5000-global-jihadists-amass-on-syrian-border/print/
23. http://tehrantimes.com/middle-east/94393-syria-hails-arrival-of-russian-warships
24. http://www.lccsyria.org
25. http://feb17.info/news/libyan-fighters-join-free-syrian-army-forces
26. 'Arab Unity in the Shadows', Al Jazeera TV English, 26 March 2009.
27. At the height of the Iraq war it had 170,000 troops there and 500 military bases. There are hundreds of bases in Afghanistan, scores throughout the Gulf, and significant troop presence in many countries, particularly Lebanon and Somalia. It also has several naval bases throughout the region, with the Fifth Fleet based in Bahrain.
28. http://www.bbc.co.uk/news/world-europe-12265740
29. http://www.csmonitor.com/World/Backchannels/2011/0127/Joe-Biden-says-Egypt-s-Mubarak-no-dictator-he-shouldn-t-step-down
30. http://www.nytimes.com/2011/12/18/opinion/sunday/kristof-repressing-democracy-with-american-arms.html?_r=1&pagewanted=all
31. http://www.guardian.co.uk/world/2011/jun/08/tony-blair-arab-spring-warning-west
32. http://www.haaretz.com/weekend/week-s-end/libya-war-logs-1.401754
33. http://www.fco.gov.uk/en/news/latest-news/?id=715652982&view=News
34. Interview with al-Zawahiri by As-Shahab media, April 2009 (http://www.youtube.com/watch?v=WamYKbSX4Zo)
35. *Inspire* was the brainchild of Anwar al-Awlaki and fellow US citizen Samir Khan.
36. http://www.kavkaz.org.uk/eng/content/2011/05/17/14313.shtml
37. Mohammed al-Shafey, 'Libya: Jailed Islamic Group "Preparing" to Renounce Armed Violence', *al-Sharq al-Awsat*, 7 July 2008.
38. http://www.cnn.com/2011/12/29/world/meast/libya-jihadists/index.html?hpt=hp_t1
39. http://www.tawhed.net/r.php?i=1607111d
40. http://articles.cnn.com/2011-08-26/world/libya.militants.analysis_1_libyan-islamic-fighting-group-prison-population-moammar-gadhafi?_s=PM:WORLD
41. 'Dear brothers who fought in Iraq and Afghanistan,' the announcer on the local radio exhorts, 'Now is the time to defend your land!'
42. http://abcnews.go.com/Blotter/libya-video-shows-unguarded-surface-air-missiles/story?id=14827930#.TwnRONUQp2J
43. http://www.csmonitor.com/World/Middle-East/2011/0218/Yemen-awash-in-guns-wary-about-unrest
44. http://www.thenational.ae/news/world/middle-east/us-makes-a-drone-attack-a-day-in-yemen
45. http://www.ansar1.info/showthread.php?p=130214#post130214

46. Spring 2011 edition of *Inspire* magazine.
47. Referenced in interview with Noam Chomsky by *AlterNet Radio Hour*, 24 April 2012.
48. www.time.com/time/world/article/0,8599,2109204,00.html?xid=gonewsedit
49. http://www.bbc.co.uk/news/world-middle-east-18789992
50. 'Die hard in Derna' cable, WikiLeaks website.
51. http://www.nationalreview.com/corner/282353/benghazi-sea-al-qaeda-flags-john-rosenthal
52. http://www.newsrescue.com/2012/03/libya-breaking-apart-factions-declare-independent-state-call-for-federalism/#ixzz1ovgWRAEW
53. http://blogs.rnw.nl/medianetwork/new-uk-based-algerian-satellite-tv-channel-launches
54. Abbottabad letter 0010.

2. Al Qaeda in the Arabian Peninsula

1. Interview with Jeremy Scahill for Frontline TV, 'Understanding Yemen's Al-Qaeda Threat', 29 May 2012.
2. Abbottabad letter 0019.
3. http://www.un.org/News/Press/docs/2011/sc10357.doc.htm
4. http://www.guardian.co.uk/commentisfree/cifamerica/2012/may/29/frontline-al-qaida-yemen-live-chat
5. Abbottabad letter 0010.
6. Abbottabad letter 0016.
7. http://interaksyon.com/article/19948/yemen-crisis-to-hit-4-m-people-in-2012-un
8. http://www.asharq-e.com/news.asp?section=1&id=23542
9. http://www.washingtoninstitute.org/policy-analysis/view/al-qaeda-attack-on-abqaiq-the-vulnerability-of-saudi-oil
10. Nick Fielding, 'Saudis Paid Bin Laden £200m', *The Sunday Times*, 25 August 2002.
11. www.telegraph.co.uk/news/worldnews/wikileaks/8182847/Wikileaks-Saudis-chief-funders-of-al-Qaeda.html
12. The fatwa was published in *al-Sharq al-Awsat* (London), in *al-Watan* (Saudi Arabia), and in *al-Riyadh* (Saudi Arabia).
13. http://www.asharq-e.com/news.asp?section=3&id=21770
14. http://www.globalpost.com/dispatch/news/regions/middle-east/saudi-arabia/110403/saudi-arabia-al-qaeda-terrorism-arrests
15. http://www.thebureauinvestigates.com/2012/02/22/militants-and-civilians-killed-in-up-to-20-us-somalia-strikes-new-study-shows
16. www.reprieve.org.uk/publiceducation/guantanamostats
17. Abu Walid al Misri, quoted in 'Afghan Arabs', *al-Sharq al-Awsat*, December 2004.
18. Al-Bahri, *Dans l'ombre de Ben Laden*, p. 210.
19. Ibid., p. 211.
20. Ibid., p. 236.
21. As reported by Reuters, 2 March 2001.
22. http://nationalyemen.com/2011/06/07/yemen-gives-wounded-al-qaeda-a-chance-to-regroup
23. Haidar interviewed by Abdel Satter Hateta, 'Al-Qaeda Overcomes the Tribes in Yemen and has Three Sources of Funding', *al-Sharq al-Awsat*, 1 March 2010.

24. http://nationalyemen.com/2011/06/07/yemen-gives-wounded-al-qaeda-a-chance-to-regroup
25. Al-Bahri, p. 236.
26. Interview can be found on: abdulelah.maktoobblog.com
27. http://english.aljazeera.net/news/middleeast/2009/12/2009122935812371810.html
28. Audiotape posted online via by Al Malahem Foundation.
29. http://www.msnbc.msn.com/id/40705420/ns/world_news-mideastn_africa/#.TyLGOdUQp2I
30. http://www.yemenpost.net/Detail123456789.aspx?ID=3&SubID=1781&MainCat=4
31. Ibid.
32. http://www.time.com/time/world/article/0,8599,1953426-3,00.html
33. http://news.blogs.cnn.com/2010/07/16/treasury-designates-anwar-al-awlaki-key-leader-of-aqap
34. Dipesh Gadher and David Leppard, 'The Most Dangerous Man in the World', *The Times*, 13 May 2012.
35. http://www.archive.org/details/ShaikhAnwarAl-awlaki
36. Ibid.
37. Ghaith Abdul-Ahad, 'Shabwa: Blood Feuds and Hospitality in al Qa'ida's Yemen Outpost', *Guardian*, 23 August 2010.
38. http://fieldsupport.dliflc.edu/products/yemeni/au_co/Yemeni.pdf
39. 'The Pied Piper of Jihad', ABC TV report, 10 February 2011.
40. http://www.time.com/time/world/article/0,8599,2089683,00.html#ixzz1VgFiObJJ
41. Unattributed report, 'Somali Insurgents Threaten to Join the New Front', *The Times*, 4 January 2010.
42. Fawaz al-Hadari, 'Qaeda Gunmen Quit Yemen Town under Tribal Pressure', *AFP*, 25 January 2012.
43. Al Jazeera English TV, 19 Feb. 2012, http://www.youtube.com/watch?v=r5xgNLZ7BzY
44. http://nationalyemen.com/2011/05/29/al-qaeda-win-the-battle-and-take-over-abyen-city
45. http://www.yemenpost.net/Detail123456789.aspx?ID=3&SubID=1781&MainCat=4

3. Somalia's al-Shabaab

1. Peter Bergen (ed.), *The Osama bin Laden I Know* (New York: Simon & Schuster, 2006), p. 122.
2. http://www.shamikh1.info/vb/showthread.php?t=148330
3. http://www.deepgreencrystals.com/images/GlobalOilChokePoints.pdf
4. See www.fundforpeace.org for the indicators taken into account.
5. 08ASMARA155 Classified cable, 24 March 2008, ARS ON AL-SHABAAB, SOMALI RECONCILIATION.
6. http://somaliweyn.somaliweyn.org/index.php?Itemid=9&catid=3:english-news&id=274:puntland-is-deeply-concerned-about-somalilands-growing-ties-to-al-shabaab&option=com_content&view=article
7. Al-Bahri, *Dans l'ombre de Ben Laden*, p. 207.
8. Ibid., pp. 59–61.
9. Ibid., p. 209.
10. http://www.nefafoundation.org/miscellaneous/FeaturedDocs/awlakishebab1208.pdf

11. http://www.bbc.co.uk/news/10602791
12. http://www.sunatimes.com/view.php?id=564
13. www.ansar1.info/showthread.php?p=133475#post133475
14. http://www.shamikh1.info/vb/showthread.php?t=151480
15. www.cbsnews.com/8301-502684_162-4524075-502684.html
16. Tristan McConnell, 'Young Men Who Reject Britain to Join Jihad in a Distant Land', *The Times*, 28 Jan. 2012.
17. Ibid.
18. http://www.sunatimes.com/view.php?id=392
19. http://www.sunatimes.com/view.php?id=564
20. Ibid.
21. Ibid.
22. Oscar Levy, 'Svensk shejk hugger av tjuvens hand', Nyheter24.
23. http://ansarullah.ws/en/report-about-the-pledge-of-alliance-of-the-%E2%80%98 gaaljecel%E2%80%99-clan-to-harakat-al-shabab-al-mujahideen
24. www.nytimes.com/2010/07/29/world/africa/29somalia.html?_r=1
25. Naja Abdullahi, 'Toxic Waste behind Somali Piracy', Al Jazeera English, 11 Oct. 2008.
26. www.unep.org/tsunami/reports/TSUNAMI_SOMALIA_LAYOUT.pdf
27. http://english.alshahid.net/archives/19461
28. webarchive.nationalarchives.gov.uk/+/http:/www.dfid.gov.uk/pubs/files/illegal-fishing-mrag-report.pdf
29. http://www.icc-ccs.org/piracy-reporting-centre/piracynewsafigures
30. http://www.reuters.com/article/2009/12/01/us-somalia-piracy-investors-idUSTRE5B01Z920091201
31. http://www.marad.dot.gov/ships_shipping_landing_page/national_security/maritime_security_program/maritime_security_program.htm
32. http://uk.reuters.com/article/2011/02/22/uk-somalia-piracy-idUKTRE71L1GO20110222
33. A local journalist traced the following 2011 payments made to al-Shabaab's 'marine office' in Haradhere: 'On Feb. 25: $200,000 from the release of the Japanese-owned MV Izumi after pirates received a $4.5 million ransom. On March 8: $80,000 from the $2 million release of the St Vincent & Grenadines-flagged MV Rak Africana. On March 9: $100,000 after the Singapore-flagged MV York was freed for $4.5 million. On April 13: $600,000 from the release of the German ship Beluga Nomination after a $5.5 million ransom was paid. On April 15: A $66,000 share of the $3.6 million ransom handed over for the Panama-flagged MV Asphalt Venture. On May 14: $100,000 from the release of two Spanish crew of the Spanish-owned FV VEGA.' (http://www.hiiraan.com/news2/2011/july/piracy_ransom_cash_ends_up_with_somali_militants.aspx).
34. http://ansarullah.ws/en/report-about-the-pledge-of-alliance-of-the-%E2%80%98 gaaljecel%E2%80%99-clan-to-harakat-al-shabab-al-mujahideen

4. The Taliban–Al Qaeda Nexus: Afghanistan

1. http://www.nation.com.pk/pakistan-news-newspaper-daily-english-online/international/01-May-2011/Defeat-of-US-in-Afghanistan-will-be-swifter-than-the-defeat-of-the-collapsed-Soviet-Union-Jalaluddin-Haqqani

2. 'The White House', in Linschoten and Kuehn (eds), *Poetry of the Taliban* (London: Hurst, 2012), p. 160.
3. 'Costs of War', Brown University's Watson Institute for International Studies (http://www.costsofwar.org).
4. www.theunjustmedia.com
5. www.time.com/time/world/article/0,8599,2094186,00.html
6. http://www.dw-world.de/dw/article/0,,6696806,00.html
7. The Durand line was named after the foreign secretary of the colonial government of India, Sir Henry Mortimer Durand.
8. The first Anglo-Afghan War lasted from 1839 to 1842; the second took place in 1878; the third in 1921.
9. Winston S. Churchill, *The Story of the Malakand Field Force: An Episode of Frontier War* (London: Longmans, Green & Co, 1898), p. 6.
10. A. Z. Hilali, *US–Pakistan Relationship: Soviet Invasion of Afghanistan* (Burlington, VT: Ashgate Publishing, 2005), p. 121.
11. Ibid.
12. Amir Mir, introduction to Muhammad Amir Rana, *A–Z of Jehadi Organizations in Pakistan* (Lahore: Mashal Books, 2004).
13. http://tribune.com.pk/story/254368/no-haqqani-network-sanctuaries-in-pakistan-sirajuddin
14. http://www.bbc.co.uk/news/world-asia-16821218
15. Al-Bahri, *Dans l'ombre de ben Laden*, p. 108.
16. Ahmed Rashid, *Descent into Chaos* (London: Penguin Group, 2008), p. 99, 268.
17. Interview with the Director of Military Affairs in Paktika: Mawlawi Sangeen, *as-Sahab* (English trans. provided by Dar al Murabiteen Publications, n.d.).
18. http://tribune.com.pk/story/254368/no-haqqani-network-sanctuaries-in-pakistan-sirajuddin.
19. Al-Bahri, *Dans l'ombre de ben Laden*, p. 184.
20. Ibid., p. 175.
21. Ibid., p. 191.
22. Ibid., p. 77.
23. Ibid., p. 82.
24. Ibid., p. 104.
25. Ibid., p. 180.
26. Ibid., p. 181.
27. Ibid., p. 182.
28. Sue Chan, 'Al Qaeda: Training in Afghanistan', cbsnews.com, 11 February 2009.
29. 'Purported al Qaeda Message: Unite with Taliban', NN.com, 12 February 2007.
30. The NEFA Foundation, 'Selected Questions and Answers from Dr. Ayman al-Zawahiri—Part 2', 17 April 2008 (http://www.nefafoundation.org/miscellaneous/FeaturedDocs/nefazawahiri0508-2.pdf).
31. http://www.cnsnews.com/news/article/suicide-bombings-afghanistan-pakistan-have-soared-decade-911
32. Author's own calculation based on several sources.
33. http://english.aljazeera.net/news/asia/2008/12/2008127621332785 7.html
34. http://www.dawn.com/2011/07/12/brother-of-hamid-karzai-killed.html
35. http://news.bbc.co.uk/2/hi/south_asia/8583018.stm

36. http://www.webcitation.org/query?url=http://www.thenews.com.pk/top_story_detail.asp%3FId%3D27544&date=2010-03-04
37. http://tribune.com.pk/story/138759/taliban-create-cell-to-hunt-spies-assisting-us-drones
38. http://www.nytimes.com/2012/01/20/world/asia/afghan-soldiers-step-up-killings-of-allied-forces.html?_r=1&pagewanted=all
39. http://www.washingtonpost.com/world/europe/france-halts-training-after-afghan-soldier-kills-4-french-troops/2012/01/20/gIQA77sADQ_story.html
40. http://www.guardian.co.uk/world/2011/nov/14/afghan-taliban-loya-jirga-security-plan
41. David Martin, 'U.S. Money is Taliban's No. 2 Revenue Source', CBS News, 31 Aug. 2011.
42. http://s3.documentcloud.org/documents/296489/taliban-report.pdf
43. http://asiafoundation.org/news/2011/11/asia-foundation-releases-2011-survey-of-the-afghan-people
44. http://www.dailymail.co.uk/news/article-2076564/Taliban-enemy-says-Joe-Biden-US-negotiate-deal-end-Afghanistan-war.html

5. The Taliban–Al Qaeda Nexus: Pakistan

1. M. Amir, *A–Z of Jehadi Organizations in Pakistan*, p. 64
2. http://www.travelersdigest.com/terrorism_hot_spots_2.htm
3. http://newamerica.net/sites/newamerica.net/files/policydocs/Cruickshank_Militant_Pipeline.pdf
4. http://www.guardian.co.uk/world/video/2010/jul/15/times-square-bomb-afghanistan
5. http://www.usatoday.com/news/world/2011-06-21-pakistan-bin-laden-poll_n.htm
6. http://www.democracynow.org/2011/11/28/nato_kills_24_pakistani_troops_in
7. Amir, *A–Z of Jehadi Organizations.*
8. http://san-pips.com/index.php?action=san&id=main&cid=230
9. Ibid.
10. Ibid.
11. NWFP is 74,521 km² and home to 19 million; FATA is 27,200 km² with a population of 6 million.
12. http://www.presstv.ir/detail/227658.html
13. Ibid.
14. 'Pakistan Forces Flee as Taliban Takeover Military Strongholds in Swat, NWFP', *India Defence*, 6 Nov. 2007.
15. http://news.bbc.co.uk/1/hi/world/south_asia/8219223.stm
16. http://www.newspakistan.pk/2012/01/07/Taliban-once-again-show-their-true-colors
17. Kim Sengupta, 'British Muslims have Become a Mainstay of the Global Jihad', *Independent*, 29 Nov. 2008.
18. Kathy Gannon, 'Al-Qaeda Recruiting Scores of New Jihadis', *Philadelphia Inquirer*, 18 July 2008.
19. http://www.telegraph.co.uk/news/worldnews/asia/pakistan/6226935/Pakistan-discovers-village-of-white-German-al-Qaeda-insurgents.html
20. An Egyptian suicide bomber attacked the Egyptian Embassy in Islamabad in 1995 but this was exceptional at the time.

21. Interview with Wajid Shamsul Hasan, Pakistani High Commissioner to the UK, on the *Today* programme, BBC Radio 4, 24 September 2011.
22. http://www.thejakartaglobe.com/home/how-umar-pateks-road-came-to-an-end-in -pakistan/435584
23. AFP: 'Afghanistan Says Kabul Suicide Gang Smashed', 3 February 2009.
24. http://www.telegraph.co.uk/news/worldnews/al-qaeda/8595814/Seized-mobile -phone-suggests-Osama-bin-Laden-link-to-Pakistani-intelligence.html
25. http://timesofindia.indiatimes.com/world/pakistan/ISI-told-US-intelligence-about -compound-in-Abbottabad-Pak-foreign-secretary/opinions/8161792.cms
26. www.institute-for-afghanstudies.org/AFGHAN%20CONFLICT/TALIBAN/ deobandi_conf_2001.htm
27. http://www.satp.org/satporgtp/countries/india/states/jandk/terrorist_outfits/ lashkar_e_toiba.htm
28. http://www.nytimes.com/2010/12/30/world/europe/30denmark.html?ref=david cheadley
29. Associated Press, 'Al-Qaida No. 3 Says He Planned 9/11, Other Plots', 15 March 2007.

6. Al Qaeda in the Islamic Maghreb: Algeria, Morocco, Tunisia and the Sahel

1. http://www.france24.com/en/20100727-french-pm-fillon-war-al-qaeda-killing -hostage-germaneau-north-africa
2. www.magharebia.com/cocoon/awi/xhtml1/en_GB/features/awi/reportage/2012/ 01/27/reportage-01
3. http://www.modernghana.com/news/374342/1/un-report-says-nigeria-militants -strike-fear-acros.html
4. http://www.fdesouche.com/256585-mauritanie-un-chef-daqmi-dit-avoir-acquis-des -armes-libyennes
5. www.magharebia.com/cocoon/awi/xhtml1/en_GB/features/awi/reportage/ 2012/01/27/reportage-01
6. These were published in the *Guardian*, 15 March 2012.
7. http://www.eurasiareview.com/26112011-aqim-emir-laaouar-speaks-out
8. www.telegraph.co.uk/news/worldnews/africaandindianocean/morocco/8485666/ Al-Qaeda-explosive-used-in-Marrakesh-bomb-investigators-reveal-as-family-mourns -slain-Briton.html
9. Hamida Layachi, 'Le GSPC et Al-Qa'ida ont conclu une alliance', *Le Monde*, 12 April 2007.
10. www.cfr.org/publication/12717/ alqaeda_in_the_islamic_maghreb_aka_salafist_group_for_preaching_and_combat
11. Jonathan Schanzer, 'Algeria's GSPC and America's "War on Terror"', paper for the Washington Institute, 15 October 2002.
12. http://ctc.usma.edu/harmony/CTC-AtiyahLetter.pdf
13. Ansarullah English blog (http://www.guardian.co.uk/world/2012/mar/14/assad -emails-lift-lid-inner-circle).
14. www.upi-fiia.fi/document.php?DOC_ID=220
15. English translation available at www.globalterroralert.com/pdf/1205/gspc1205.pdf
16. www.nytimes.com/2008/07/01/world/africa/01transcript-droukdal.html?page wanted=3&_r=1&sq=droukdel&st=cse&scp=6

17. Ibid.
18. Interview with Khalid abu al-Abbas (Belmokhtar) in *Nouakchott News*, November 2011.
19. 'Al-Qaeda in Iraq Endorses their Cohorts in Algeria', Jamestown Foundation, *Terrorism Focus*, 2/2, 24 June 2005.
20. www.alertnet.org/thenews/newsdesk/L06679771.htm
21. Al Jazeera television, 27 January 2012.
22. http://www.ctc.usma.edu/posts/aqim-returns-in-force-in-northern-algeria
23. http://www.jeuneafrique.com/Article/ARTJAJA2567p040-044.xml1/enlevement-terrorisme-al-qaida-aqmimoi-pierre-camatte-otage-d-al-qaida-pendant-89-jours.html
24. www.magharebia.com/cocoon/awi/xhtml1/en_GB/features/awi/features/2012/01/26/feature-03
25. Interview with Khalid abu al-Abbas (Belmokhtar) in *Nouakchott News*, November 2011.
26. http://www.ndu.edu/press/lib/pdf/Africa-Security-Brief/ASB-11.pdf
27. http://af.reuters.com/article/topNews/idAFJOE80O00K20120125
28. www.jamestown.org/terrorism/news/article.php?issue_id=2873
29. www.cooperativeresearch.org/entity.jsp?entity=abd_al-rahim_al-nashiri
30. www.jamestown.org/terrorism/news/article.php?issue_id=2873
31. Peter Bergen, *The Osama bin Laden I Know* (New York: Simon & Schuster, 2006).
32. www.realinstitutoelcano.org/documentos/47.asp
33. *International Herald Tribune*, www.iht.com/articles/2007/02/20/news/tunisia.
34. Interview with the author, London, 2006.
35. http://news.bbc.co.uk/1/hi/world/africa/8137442.stm
36. 'Trial of 4 Tied to Afghan's Killers', *New York Times*, 30 March 2005.

7. Al Qaeda in the Islamic Maghreb: Libya

1. http://www.ntc.gov.ly
2. http://www.islamicthinkers.com/index/index.php?option=com_content&task=view&id=564&Itemid=26
3. http://www.temehu.com/Libyan-People.htm
4. Interview with Khalid abu al-Abbas (Belmokhtar) in *Nouakchott News*, November 2011.
5. http://www.telegraph.co.uk/news/worldnews/africaandindianocean/libya/8905151/Libyan-officials-will-seek-death-penalty-for-Saif-al-Islam-Gaddafi.html
6. http://www.guardian.co.uk/world/2011/nov/22/libyan-prime-minister-abdulrahman-el-keib
7. http://www.bp.com/sectionbodycopy.do?categoryId=7500&contentId=7068481
8. http://www.alarabiya.net/articles/2011/10/21/172953.html
9. www.telegraph.co.uk/news/worldnews/africaandindianocean/libya/8745905/Libya-granted-oil-concessions-to-BP-on-understanding-Lockerbie-bomber-Megrahi-would-return-home.html
10. http://www.dailymail.co.uk/news/article-1284132/Tony-Blair-special-adviser-dictator-Gaddafis-son.html?ito=feeds-newsxml#ixzz0q40YD70x
11. James Hider, 'Hate and Fear: the Legacy of Gaddafi', *The Times*, 12 July 2012.

12. http://af.reuters.com/article/libyaNews/idAFL5E8D1504201202O1
13. http://www.majalla.com/eng/2012/01/article55228886
14. Jack Anderson, *Washington Post*, 6 December 1985.
15. 'The Roots of the "Libyan Fighting Group" . . . the Story of the Failure of the "Jihad Movement" During the Eighties', 11 April 2006, http://www.al-boraq.com/showthread.php?t=7247.
16. http://azelin.files.wordpress.com/2011/10/abc5ab-yae1b8a5yc481-al-lc4abbc4ab-algeria-and-the-battle-of-patience-en.pdf
17. 'Communiqué #1: The Declaration of the Establishment of the Libyan Islamic Fighting Group', http://www.almuqatila.com/AMEER/bayanat/bayan1.htm, 18 October 1995.
18. http://www.hrw.org/en/news/2006/06/27/libya-june-1996-killings-abu-salim-prison
19. Interview with Omar Rashed, LIFG spokesman in *Al-Nida'ul-Islam*, 26 April–May 1999.
20. 'Communiqué 14: Regarding the American Attack against Sudan and Afghanistan', http://www.almuqatila.com/AMEER/bayanat/bayan14.htm, 25 August 1998.
21. http://www.dailymail.co.uk/news/article-2034114/Libyan-rebel-leader-Abdel-Hakim-Belhadj-line-1m-payout.html
22. 'The Battle of Omar Hadeed', http://www.omar-hadeed.net, 7 October 2005.
23. Ed Brian Fishman, 'Bombers, Bank Accounts and Bleedout, al-Qa'ida's Road In and Out of Iraq', Combating Terrorism at West Point, July 2008.
24. http://www.telegraph.co.uk/news/wikileaks-files/libya-wikileaks/8294700/LIBYAN-ISLAMIC-FIGHTING-GROUP-REVISES-JIHADIST-IDEOLOGY.html
25. www.bp.com/sectionbodycopy.do?categoryId=7500&contentId=7068481
26. Ibid.
27. http://sweetcrudereports.com/2011/07/05/nigeria-algeria-20b-gas-project-ready-by-2015-jonathan
28. www.bp.com/sectionbodycopy.do?categoryId=7500&contentId=7068481
29. http://www.fas.org/sgp/crs/natsec/RL34003.pdf
30. Simon Tisdall, 'Africa United in Rejecting US Request for Military HQ', *Guardian*, 26 June 2007.
31. Lauren Ploch, 'Africa Command: U.S. Strategic Interests and the Role of the U.S. Military in Africa', *Congressional Research Service Report for Congress* (3 April 2010).
32. Craig Whitlock, 'Terrorist Network Lures Young Moroccans to War in Far Off Iraq', *Washington Post*, 20 February 2007.

8. Ongoing and New Alliances

1. www.globalsecurity.org/security/library/report/2005/zawahiri-zarqawi-letter_9jul2005.htm
2. http://www.csmonitor.com/2006/0405/dailyUpdate.html
3. http://www.guardian.co.uk/world/2010/may/13/sons-of-iraq-withdrawal-rebels
4. http://www.iraqbodycount.org/database
5. http://news.bbc.co.uk/1/hi/8203239.stm
6. http://www.timesonline.co.uk/tol/news/world/middle_east/article3447261.ece
7. Ghaith Abdul Ahad, 'Escape is Impossible', *Guardian*, 12 June 2007.
8. http://english.al-akhbar.com/node/4800

9. http://www.bbc.co.uk/news/world-middle-east-10979788
10. http://www.energean.com/Operations-Area-License-Fields-Egypt?la=en
11. *Al-Ahram*, 1 August 2011.
12. Ayman al-Zawahiri, 'A Message of Hope and Glad Tidings to Our People in Egypt, Part 7', As-Sahab Foundation for Media Production, 8 August 2011.
13. http://www.haaretz.com/news/middle-east/terrorism-experts-al-qaida-tightens-grip-in-sinai-peninsula-1.384697
14. http://articles.cnn.com/2011-08-16/world/egypt.sinai_1_arish-el-arish-gas-pipeline?_s=PM:WORLD
15. http://www.guardian.co.uk/world/2011/jan/30/muslim-brotherhood-jail-escape-egypt
16. *Al-Misri al-Youm* (Cairo, 10 August 2011).
17. www.time.com/time/world/article/0,8599,2109204,00.html#ixzz1pH8G0E0F
18. http://www.bbc.co.uk/news/world-africa-13809501
19. http://www.nigeriastandardnewspaper.com/ED14nigeria.html
20. uk.reuters.com/article/2012/01/31/us-nigeria-bokoharam-idUKTRE80U0LR20120131
21. http://www.bbc.co.uk/news/world-africa-18592789
22. www.nigeriastandardnewspaper.com/ED14nigeria.html
23. http://uk.reuters.com/article/2012/01/31/uk-nigeria-bokoharam-idUKTRE80U0KB20120131
24. http://www.vanguardngr.com/2011/09/breaking-news-boko-haram-family-spokesman-babakura-during-objs-visit-shot-dead
25. http://uk.reuters.com/article/2012/01/31/uk-nigeria-bokoharam-idUKTRE80U0KB20120131
26. http://www.smh.com.au/opinion/political-news/bali-bomber-sentenced-to-20-years-20120622-20rej.html
27. http://www.thejakartapost.com/news/2011/09/30/police-add-6-more-suspects-solo-bombing.html
28. http://prisonerofjoy.blogspot.com/2011/09/blog-post.html
29. http://inside.org.au/indonesia%E2%80%99s-islamic-parties-in-decline
30. http://www.reuters.com/article/2010/02/20/us-usa-centralasia-idUSTRE61J13920100220
31. http://news.bbc.co.uk/2/hi/south_asia/2242594.stm
32. Interrogation of Bryant Vinas report, 10/11 March 2009.
33. http://www.jhuf.net/showthread.php?11014-Manual-sisters-video-Film
34. www.spiegel.de/international/germany/0,1518,740326,00.htm
35. http://www.longwarjournal.org/archives/2011/02/german_terrorists_pa.php
36. Andrei Babitsky, Russia: RFE/RL Interviews Chechen Field Commander Umarov, 28 July 2005.
37. http://www.kavkazcenter.com/eng/content/2007/11/22/9107.shtml
38. http://www.longwarjournal.org/archives/2011/04/russian_forces_kill.php
39. Evan Kohlman, *Al-Qaida's Jihad in Europe* (New York: Berg, 2004).
40. http://www.jamestown.org/programs/nca/single/?tx_ttnews[tt_news]=1773&tx_ttnews[backPid]=185&no_cache=1
41. Interview with emir Dokku Umarov, 30 Aug. 2011, http://www.kavkaz.org.uk/eng/content/2011/08/30/15062.shtml
42. http://www.hrw.org/news/2005/04/10/china-religious-repression-uighur-muslims

9. The Digital Battleground

1. http://phys.org/news/2012-05-al-qaeda-porn-treasure-trove.html
2. http://www.defense.gov/news/d20110714cyber.pdf
3. http://www.investigativeproject.org/3426/fbi-director-warns-of-rising-cyber-threat
4. http://thesis.haverford.edu/dspace/bitstream/handle/10066/7255/ASM20110603.2.pdf?sequence=1
5. http://www.shamikh1.info/vb/showthread.php?t=114951
6. Frances Gibb, 'Judge Halts Trial to Ask What's a Website?', *The Times*, 18 May 2007.
7. Tariq ibn Ziyad was the Berber military commander who led the Muslim conquests of Spain around AD 720.
8. http://defensetech.org/2010/09/13/8930/#ixzz1mXLvOavJ
9. http://www.investigativeproject.org/3389/kuwaiti-cleric-calls-for-hacker-jihad
10. http://www.aljahad.org/vb/showthread.php?p=41767
11. http://www.aviationweek.com/aw/generic/story_channel.jsp?channel=defense&id=news/awx/2011/07/14/awx_07_14_2011_p0-348127.xml
12. http://www.bbc.co.uk/news/business-16801382
13. http://www.scribd.com/doc/49062636/Interview-taliban-webmaster
14. Alison Pargiter, *The New Frontiers of Jihad* (London: IB Tauris, 2008).
15. Transcript at http://www.alqimmah.net/showthread.php?t=9828; video may still be available at http://www.wikiislam.com/wiki/Videos_on_Islam:Knowledge_is_For_Acting_Upon
16. http://www.youtube.com/watch?v=FxRR5HetZ8I
17. http://www.youtube.com/watch?v=n4f89Jg-TnY
18. http://ansarullah.ws/en/al-ansar-mailing-list-presents-ashbal-waziristan
19. http://www.shamikh1.info/vb/showthread.php?t=134859
20. http://muslimways.com/library/.../music/why-music-is-haram.html
21. http://www.sunniforum.com/forum/showthread.php?14667-Female-nasheed-singers
22. http://www.youtube.com/watch?v=A2BtVQXcAjg&feature=endscreen&NR=1;
23. http://www.youtube.com/watch?v=roxyP1_Pj5w&feature=related
24. http://www.youtube.com/watch?v=cs2mWTIZQQQ&feature=related
25. http://www.telegraph.co.uk/news/2071320/Nicky-Reilly-charged-over-Exeter-bombing.html
26. http://ansarullah.ws/en/gimf-the-explosives-course-by-sheikh-abu-khabbab-al-misri
27. http://www.dailymail.co.uk/news/article-2037708/Student-wrongfully-arrested-suspicion-terrorist-awarded-20-000-police.html
28. http://www.shamikh1.info/vb/showthread.php?p=1058705982#post1058705982
29. http://www.wordfrequency.info/5k_lemmas.asp?s=y
30. http://online.wsj.com/article/SB10001424052748704570104576124231820312632.html
31. http://www.tawhed.net/n.php
32. http://www.tawhed.net/n.php
33. http://www.scribd.com/doc/49062636/Interview-taliban-webmaster
34. http://thesis.haverford.edu/dspace/bitstream/handle/10066/7255/ASM20110603.2.pdf?sequence=1
35. http://www.telegraph.co.uk/news/uknews/terrorism-in-the-uk/8553366/MI6-attacks-al-Qaeda-in-Operation-Cupcake.html
36. http://www.youtube.com/watch?v=7ZkA3CiNDCc

37. http://www.independent.co.uk/opinion/commentators/fisk/robert-fisk-glossy-new-front-in-battle-for-hearts-and-minds-1934020.html
38. http://giswatch.org/en/freedom-association/towards-cyber-security-strategy-global-civil-society
39. http://www.csmonitor.com/USA/2011/0922/From-the-man-who-discovered-Stuxnet-dire-warnings-one-year-later
40. http://www.strategypage.com/htmw/htiw/20111201.aspx
41. http://www.reuters.com/article/2011/06/03/us-china-internet-google-idUSTRE7520OV20110603

Conclusion: The Next Generation

1. http://articles.cnn.com/2012-05-15/africa/world_africa_libya-militants_1_libyan-islamic-fighting-group-senior-al-islamist-militants?_s=PM:AFRICA
2. http://www.upi.com/Top_News/World-News/2012/05/21/Suicide-bombing-kills-nearly-100-in-Yemen/UPI-71731337601347/?rel=76841337705766
3. (CNN) http://security.blogs.cnn.com/2011/09/12/al-qaeda-2-0-what-the-next-10-years-will-bring
4. www.centralasiaonline.com/en_GB/articles/caii/features/main/2011/11/30/feature-02
5. http://www.dailymail.co.uk/news/article-1340207/I-didnt-think-Iraqis-humans-says-U-S-soldier-raped-14-year-old-girl-killing-her-family.html
6. www.youtube.com/watch?v=T6g3htoMEcM
7. http://www.bbc.co.uk/news/world-africa-17479002
8. http://www.telegraph.co.uk/news/worldnews/africaandindianocean/somalia/9384893/Samantha-Lewthwaite-recruiting-all-women-terror-squads.html
9. www.rand.org/content/dam/rand/pubs/monographs/2008/RAND_MG741-1.pdf
10. http://www.usatoday.com/news/world/story/2012-01-03/taliban

Select Bibliography

Aaron, David, *In Their Own Words: Voices of Jihad: Compilation and Commentary* (Washington, DC: RAND, 2008).

Al-Bahri, Nasser, *Dans l'ombre de ben Laden* (Paris: Michel Lafon, 2010).

Allen, Charles, *God's Terrorists: The Wahhabi Cult and the Hidden Roots of Modern Jihad* (London: Abacus, Little Brown, 2006).

Amir, Muhammad, *A–Z of Jehadi Organizations in Pakistan* (Lahore: Mashal Books, 2004).

Baxter, Kylie, *British Muslims and the Call to Global Jihad* (London: Monash Asia Institute, 2007).

Bergen, Peter, *The Osama bin Laden I Know* (New York: Free Press, 2006).

Bergesen, Albert J., *The Sayyid Qutb Reader* (London: Routledge, 2008).

Bin Alden, Carmen, *The Veiled Kingdom* (London: Virago, 2004).

Bin Laden, Najwa, bin Laden, Omar, and Sasson, Jean, *Growing Up bin Laden* (New York: St Martin's Press, 2009).

Black, Antony, *The West and Islam: Religion and Political Thought in World History* (Oxford: Oxford University Press, 2008).

Burke, Jason, *9/11 Wars* (London: Allen Lane, 2012).

Burke, Jason, *On the Road to Kandahar* (London: Allen Lane, 2006).

Burleigh, Michael, *Blood and Rage: A Cultural History of Terrorism* (London: Harper Collins, 2008).

Chomsky, Noam, *Imperial Ambitions: Conversations with Noam Chomsky on the Post-9/11 World* (London: Hamish Hamilton, 2005).

Churchill, Winston S., *The Story of the Malakand Field Force: An Episode of Frontier War* (London: Longmans, Green & Co, 1898).

Cockburn, Patrick, *The Occupation, War and Resistance in Iraq* (London: Verso, 2006).

Coll, Steve, *The Bin Ladens* (London: Allen Lane, 2008).

Davidson, Christopher (ed.), *Power and Politics in the Persian Gulf Monarchies* (London: Hurst, 2011).

Emerson, Steven, *The American House of Saud* (New York: Franklin Watts, 1985).

Filiu, Jean Pierre, *The Arab Revolution: Ten Lessons from the Democratic Uprisings* (London: Hurst, 2012).

Groen, J. and Kranenberg, A., *Women Warriors for Allah: An Islamist Network in the Netherlands* (Pennsylvania, PA: Penn Press, 2010).

Hashim, Ahmed, *Insurgency and Counter-Insurgency in Iraq* (London: Hurst, 2006).

Hilali, A.Z., *US–Pakistan Relationship: Soviet Invasion of Afghanistan* (London: Ashgate Publishing, 2005).

Kohlman, Evan, *Al-Qaida's Jihad in Europe* (New York: Berg, 2004).

Landau, Paul, *Pour Allah jusqu'à la mort* (Paris: Rocher, 2008).

Linschoten, A., F. Kuehn and F. Devji, eds., *Poetry of the Taliban* (London: Hurst, 2012).

Mearsheimer, J. and Walt, S., *The Israel Lobby and US Foreign Policy* (New York: Farrar, Straus & Giroux, 2007).

Musharraf, Pervez, *In the Line of Fire: A Memoir* (New York: Free Press, 2006).

Naba, René, *Aux origines de la Tragédie Arabe* (Paris: Sachari, Bahari, 2006).

Nasiri, Omar, *Inside the Global Jihad* (London: Hurst, 2006).

Neumann, Peter, *Joining Al-Qaeda* (London: Routledge, 2008).

Pargeter, Alison, *The New Frontiers of Jihad: Radical Islam in Europe* (London: IB Tauris, 2008).

Rashid, Ahmed, *Descent into Chaos* (London: Penguin Group, 2008).

Roy, Olivier, 'Al Qaeda in the West as a Youth Movement: The Power of a Narrative', *Microcon Policy Working Paper 2,* Nov. 2008.

Sageman, Marc, *Leaderless Jihad* (Philadelphia, PA: University of Philadelphia Press, 2008).

Schanzer, Jonathan, 'Algeria's GSPC and America's "War on Terror"', paper for the Washington Institute, 15 Oct. 2002.

Scheuer, Michael, *Osama bin Laden* (London: Oxford University Press, 2011).

Summers, A., and Swan, R., *The Eleventh Day: The Ultimate Account of 9/11* (London: Doubleday, 2011).

Taibbi, Matt, *The Great Derangement* (New York: Spiegel & Grau, New York, 2009).

Tawil, Camille, *Brother in Arms: The Story of al-Qa'ida and the Arab Jihadists* (London: Saqi Books, 2010).

Unger, Craig, *The Fall of the House of Bush* (London: Simon & Schuster, 2007).

Weir, Shelagh, *A Tribal Order: An Account of the Arab Tribes in the Vicinity of Aden* (Austin, TX: University of Texas Press, 2006).

Zaeff, Abdul Salam, *My Life with the Taliban* (London: Hurst, 2010).

Acknowledgments

First and foremost I would like to thank Susan de Muth for her meticulous research and help with editing this book.

Thanks too to all our sources, too many to mention, who have shared or corroborated information: individuals in several countries, professional reporters, security experts, Internet researchers, academics and bloggers—you know who you are.

To my family—Basima, Khaled, Nada and Kareem—thank you for your patience during the many hours this book has kept me away from you.

I am grateful, too, to Lynn Gaspard of Saqi books for her encouragement and good judgement, to Rima Cherri for her capable translations and to Pat Sundram at *al-Quds al-Arabi* for her all-round support and unflappability.

Index

Celebrating Independent Publishing

Thank you for reading this book published by The New Press. The New Press is a nonprofit, public interest publisher. New Press books and authors play a crucial role in sparking conversations about the key political and social issues of our day.

We hope you enjoyed this book and that you will stay in touch with The New Press. Here are a few ways to stay up to date with our books, events, and the issues we cover:

- Sign up at www.thenewpress.com/subscribe to receive updates on New Press authors and issues and to be notified about local events
- Like us on Facebook: www.facebook.com/newpressbooks
- Follow us on Twitter: www.twitter.com/thenewpress

Please consider buying New Press books for yourself; for friends and family; or to donate to schools, libraries, community centers, prison libraries, and other organizations involved with the issues our authors write about.

The New Press is a 501(c)(3) nonprofit organization. You can also support our work with a tax-deductible gift by visiting www.thenewpress.com/donate.